CROUCHING TIGER HIDDEN DRAGON

Wang Du Lu

Script Writer
So Man Sing

Translators
Wayne Moyung
Stephen Ip

Editors
Shawn Sanders
Angel Cheng

Production Artists
Hung-Ya Lin
Calvin Choi

US Cover Design
Hung-Ya Lin
Yuki Chung

Production Manager
Janice Chang

Art Director
Yuki Chung

Marketing
Nicole Curry

VP Operations
Thomas Kuo

English translation by
ComicsOne Corporation 2002

Publisher
ComicsOne Corp.
48531 Warm Springs Blvd., Suite 408
Fremont, CA 94539
www.ComicsOne.com

First Edition: January 2003
ISBN 1-58899-175-X

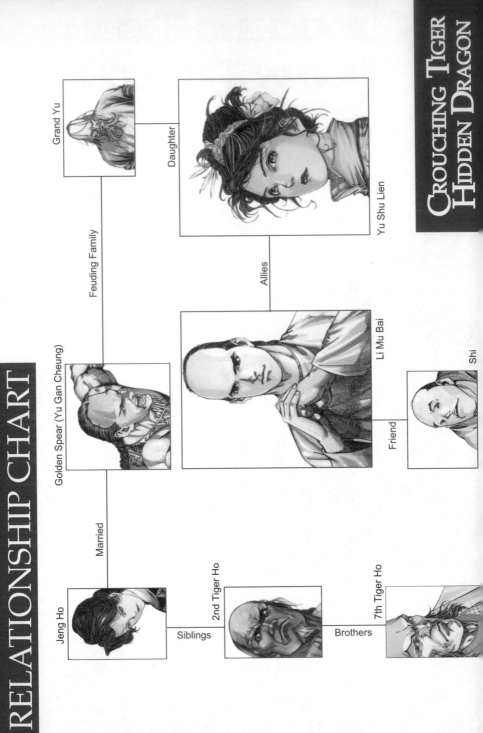

RELATIONSHIP CHART

CROUCHING TIGER HIDDEN DRAGON

Grand Yu

Daughter

Yu Shu Lien

Feuding Family

Allies

Golden Spear (Yu Gan Cheung)

Li Mu Bai

Shi

Friend

Married

Jeng Ho

2nd Tiger Ho

7th Tiger Ho

Siblings

Brothers

CROUCHING TIGER
HIDDEN DRAGON

Chapter 2————————————○

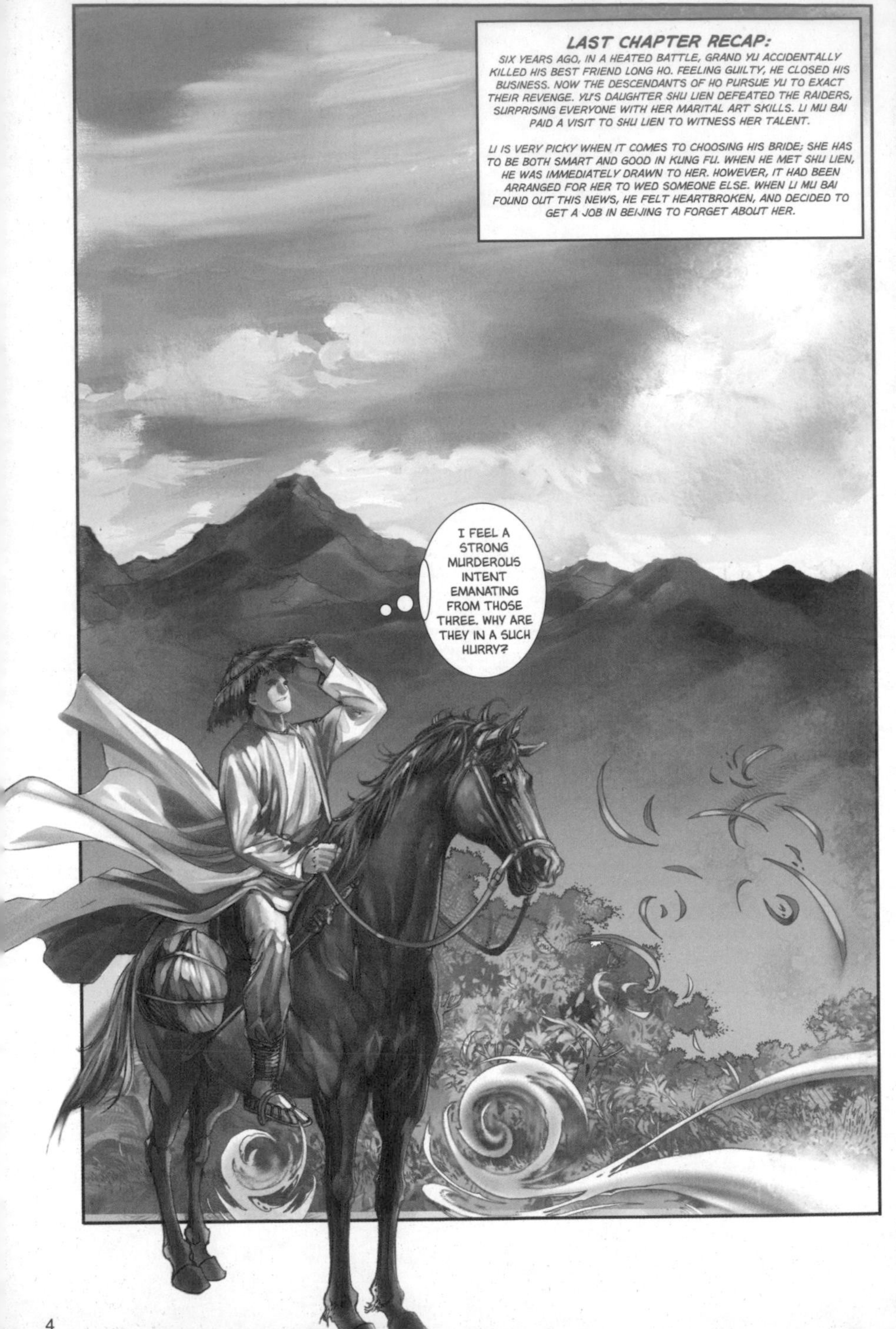
LAST CHAPTER RECAP:
SIX YEARS AGO, IN A HEATED BATTLE, GRAND YU ACCIDENTALLY KILLED HIS BEST FRIEND LONG HO. FEELING GUILTY, HE CLOSED HIS BUSINESS. NOW THE DESCENDANTS OF HO PURSUE YU TO EXACT THEIR REVENGE. YU'S DAUGHTER SHU LIEN DEFEATED THE RAIDERS, SURPRISING EVERYONE WITH HER MARITAL ART SKILLS. LI MU BAI PAID A VISIT TO SHU LIEN TO WITNESS HER TALENT.
LI IS VERY PICKY WHEN IT COMES TO CHOOSING HIS BRIDE; SHE HAS TO BE BOTH SMART AND GOOD IN KUNG FU. WHEN HE MET SHU LIEN, HE WAS IMMEDIATELY DRAWN TO HER. HOWEVER, IT HAD BEEN ARRANGED FOR HER TO WED SOMEONE ELSE. WHEN LI MU BAI FOUND OUT THIS NEWS, HE FELT HEARTBROKEN, AND DECIDED TO GET A JOB IN BEIJING TO FORGET ABOUT HER.
I FEEL A STRONG MURDEROUS INTENT EMANATING FROM THOSE THREE. WHY ARE THEY IN A SUCH HURRY?

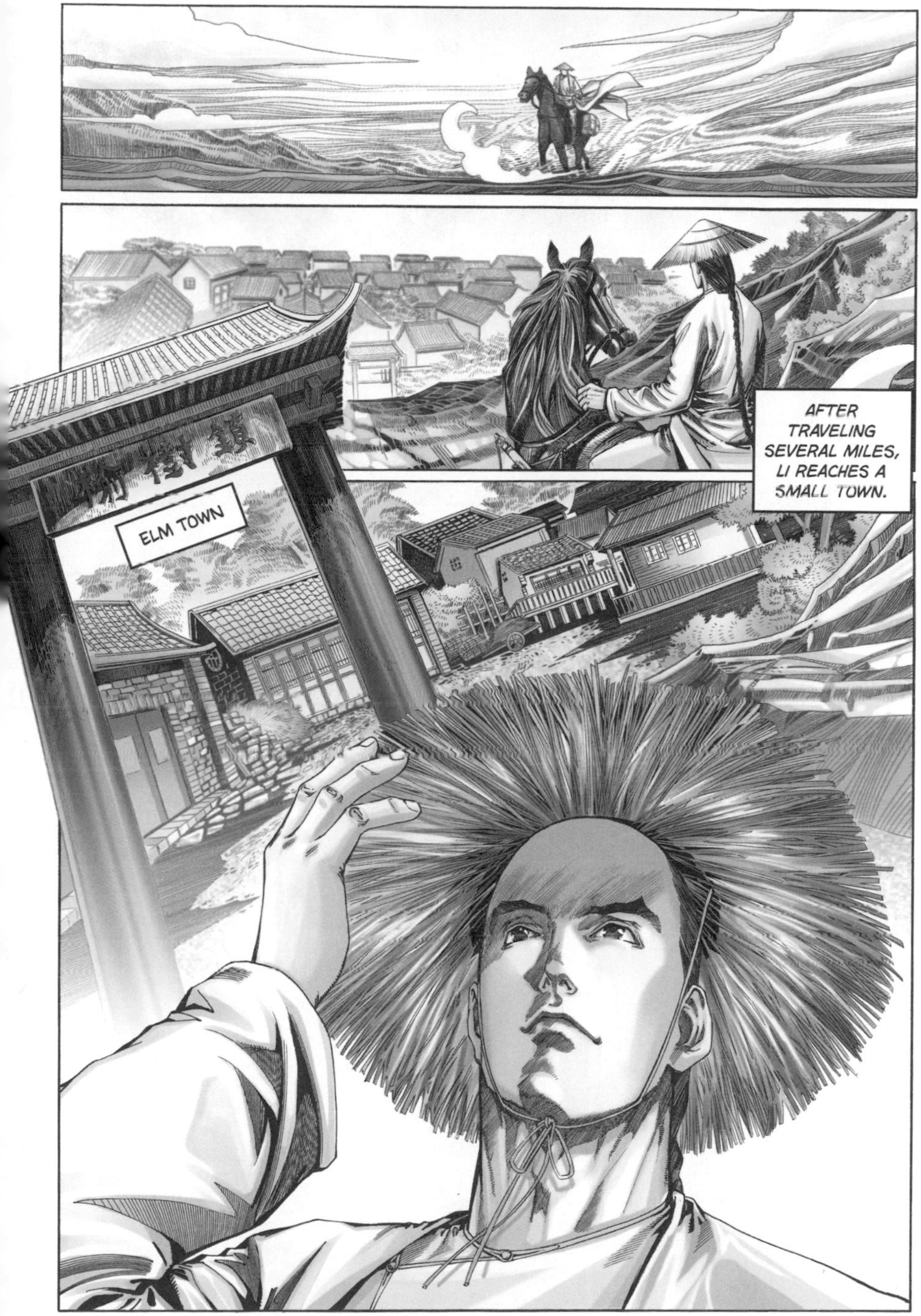

AFTER TRAVELING SEVERAL MILES, LI REACHES A SMALL TOWN.
榆樹鎮
ELM TOWN

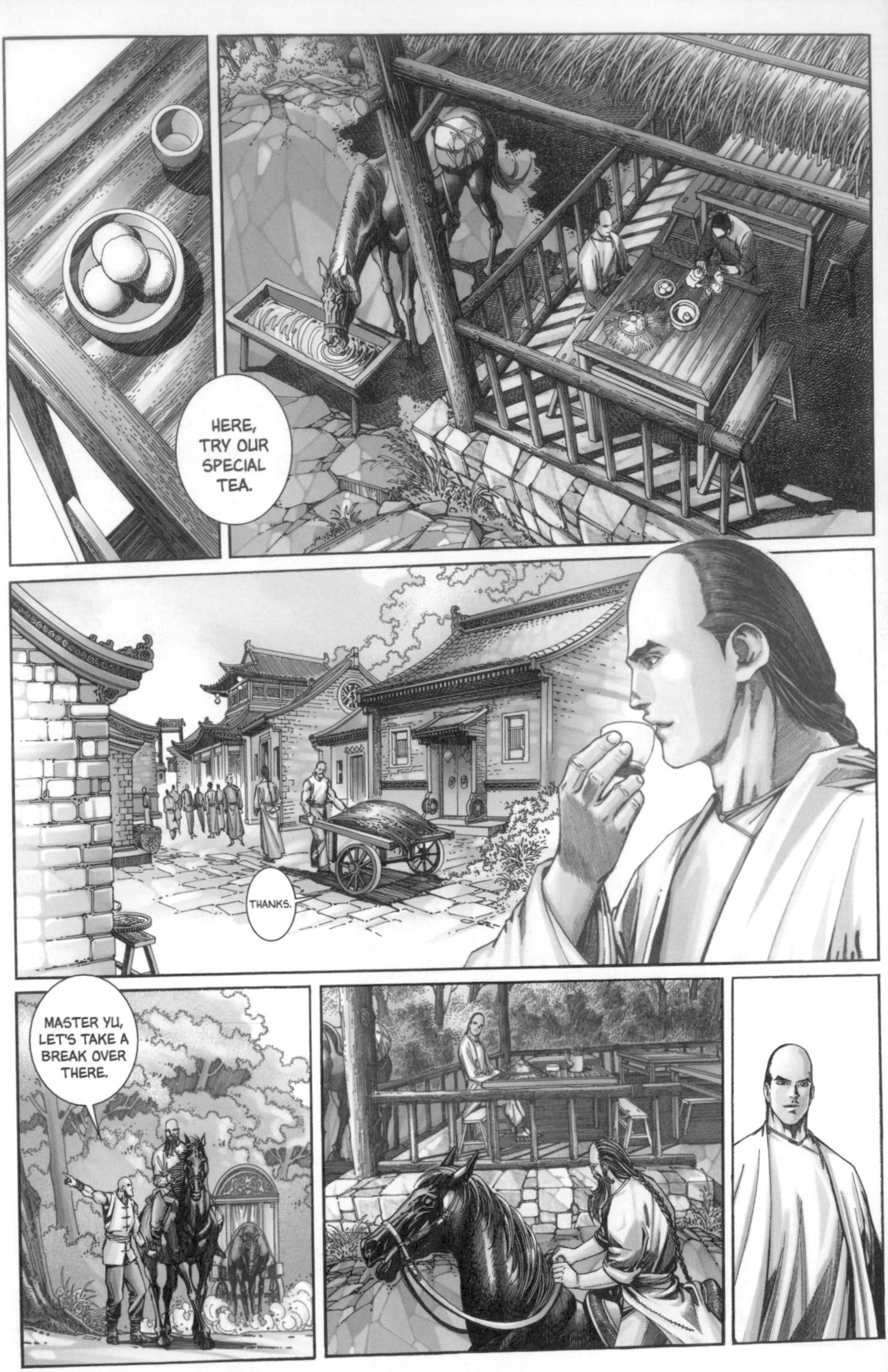
HERE, TRY OUR SPECIAL TEA.
THANKS.
MASTER YU, LET'S TAKE A BREAK OVER THERE.

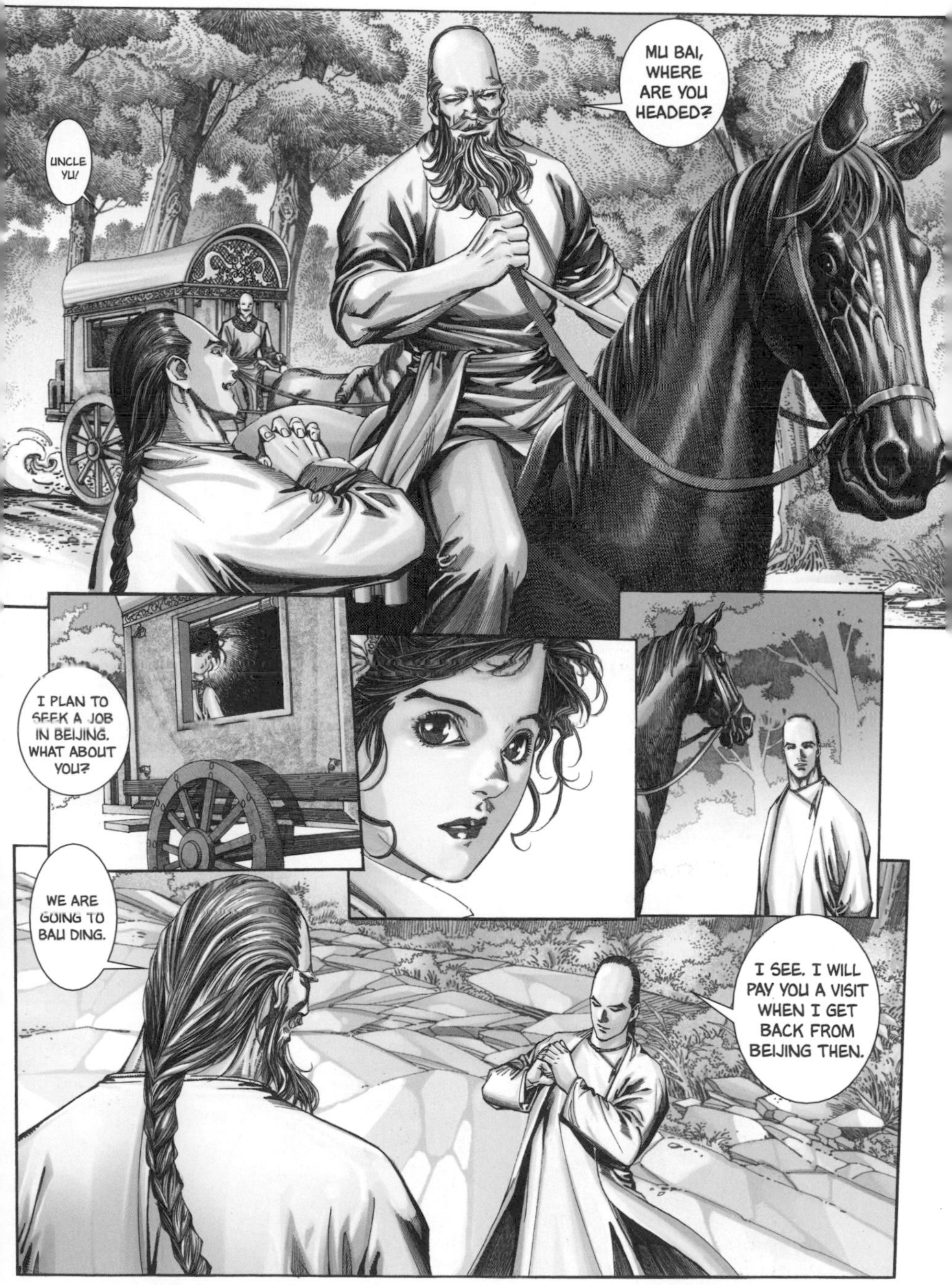
MU BAI, WHERE ARE YOU HEADED?
UNCLE YU!
I PLAN TO SEEK A JOB IN BEIJING. WHAT ABOUT YOU?
WE ARE GOING TO BAU DING.
I SEE. I WILL PAY YOU A VISIT WHEN I GET BACK FROM BEIJING THEN.

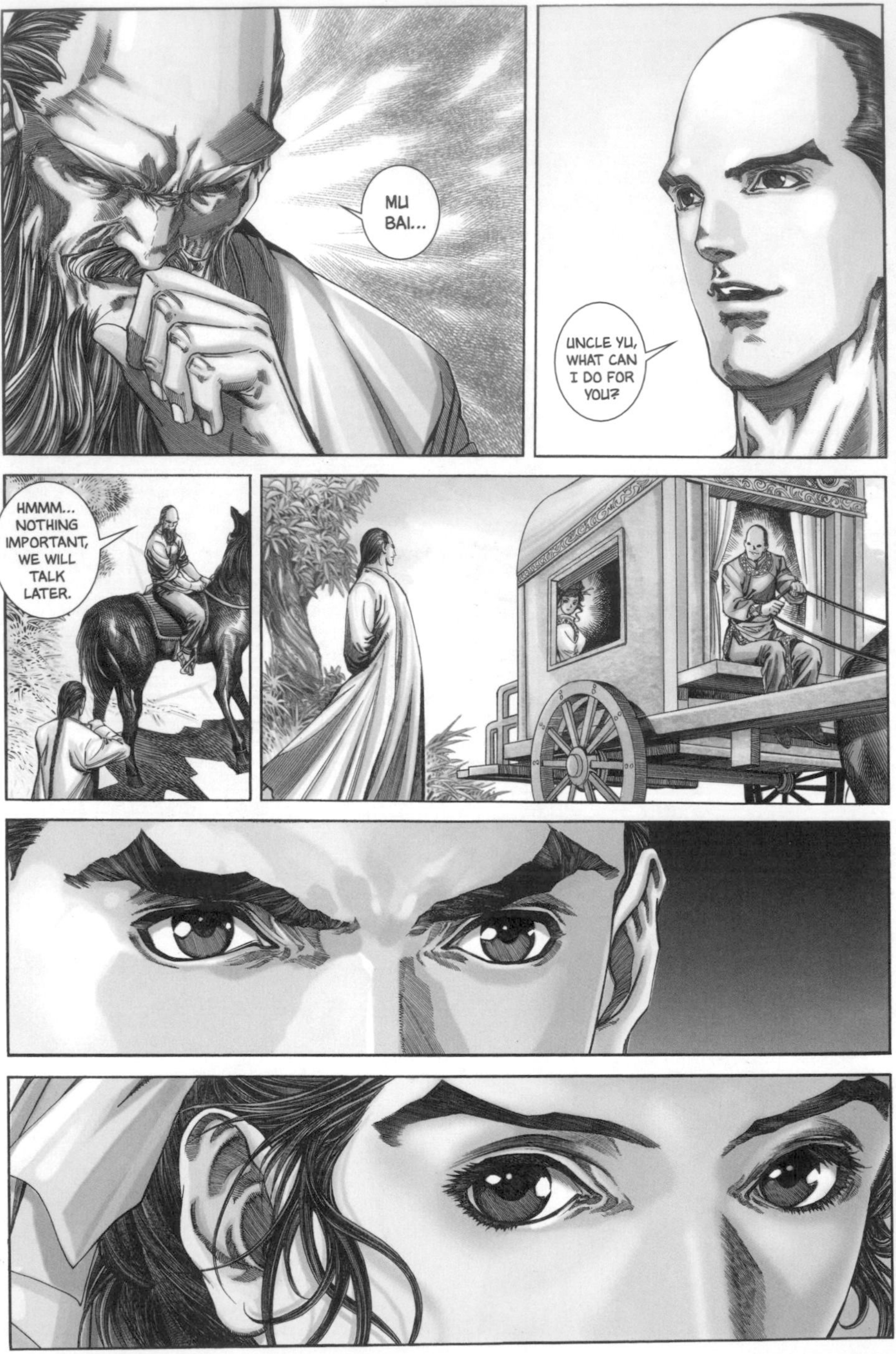
MU BAI...
UNCLE YU, WHAT CAN I DO FOR YOU?
HMMM... NOTHING IMPORTANT, WE WILL TALK LATER.

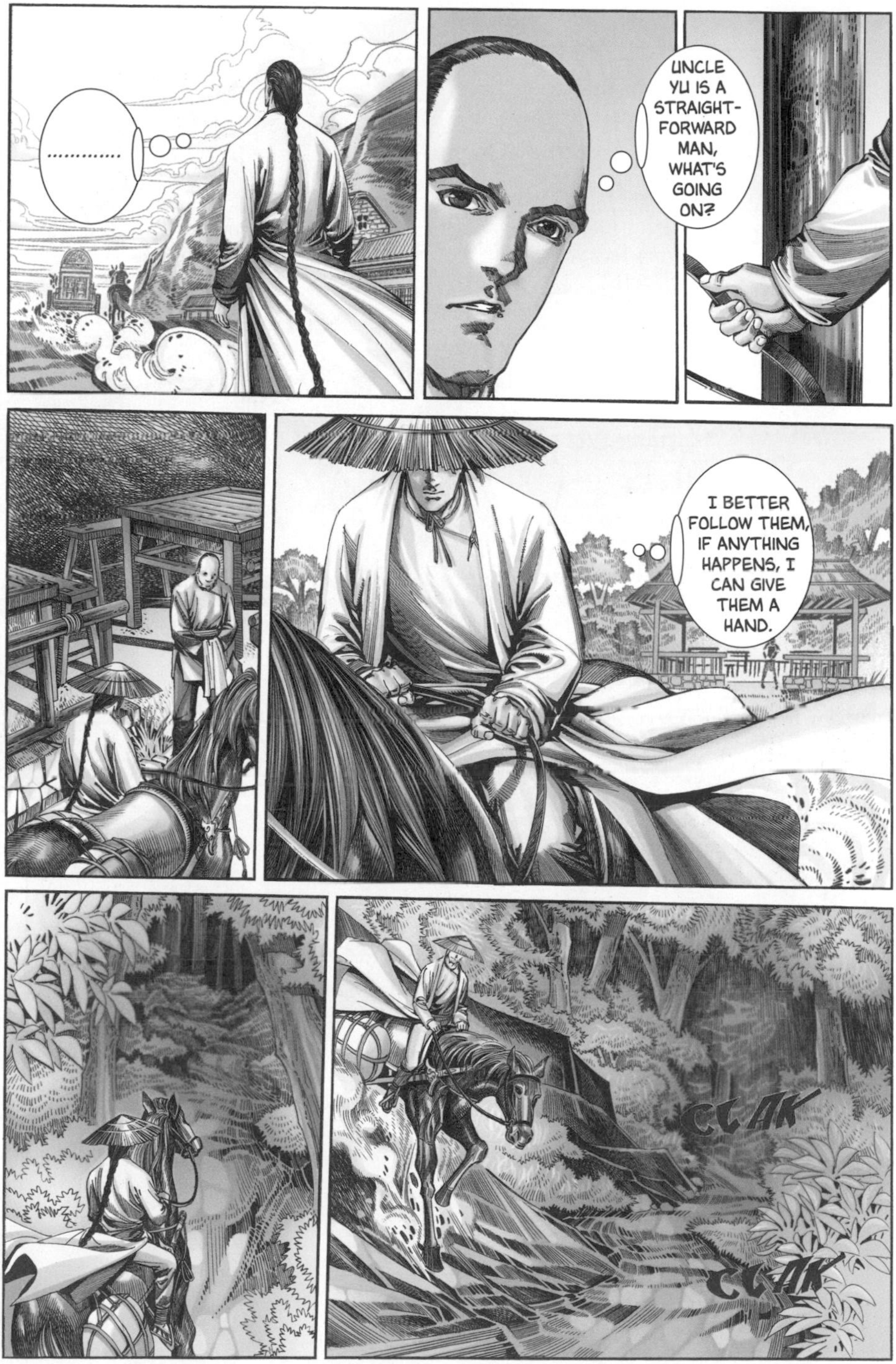
....
UNCLE YU IS A STRAIGHT-FORWARD MAN, WHAT'S GOING ON?
I BETTER FOLLOW THEM, IF ANYTHING HAPPENS, I CAN GIVE THEM A HAND.
CLAK
CLAK

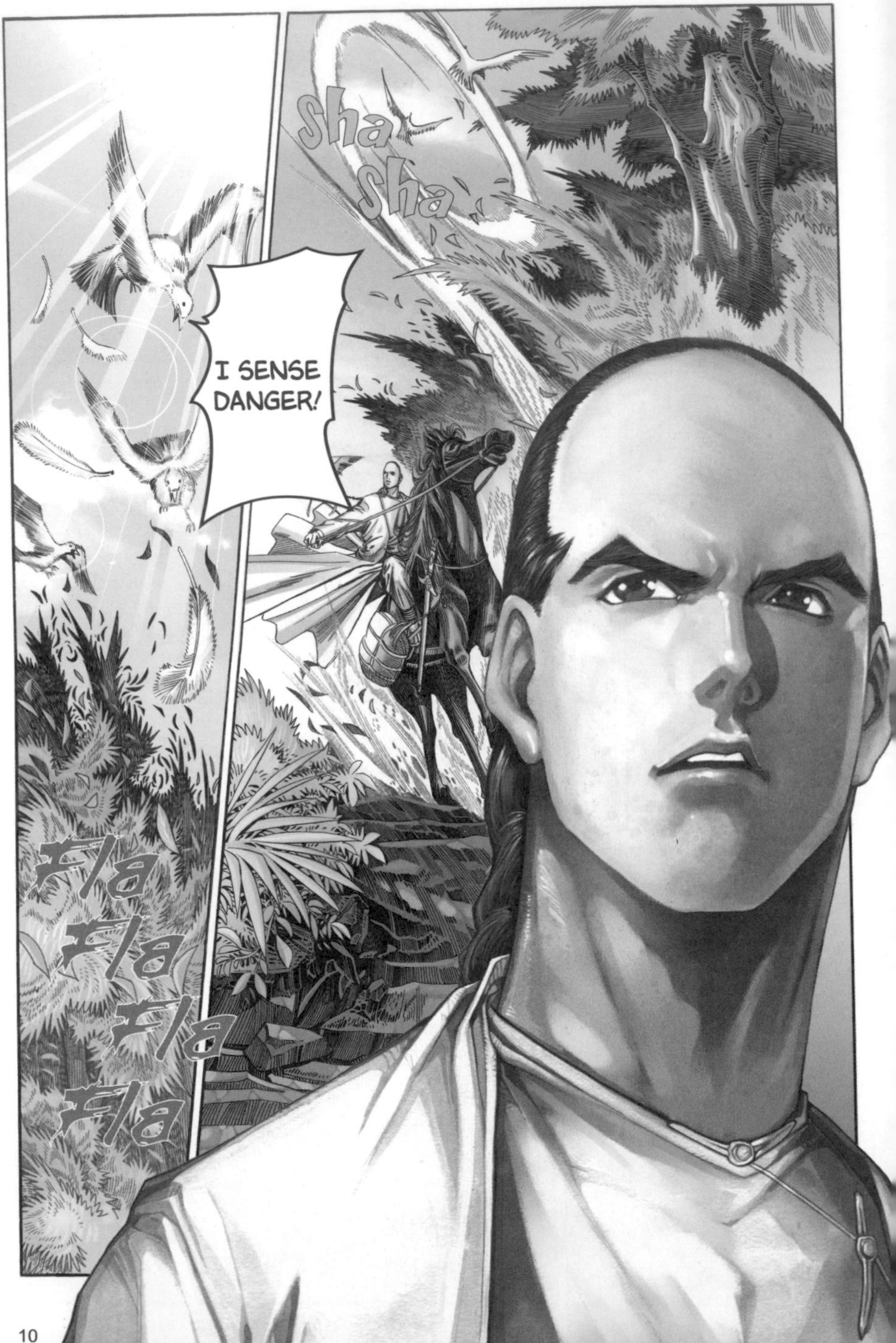
Sha
Sha
I SENSE DANGER!
Fla
Fla
Fla
Fla

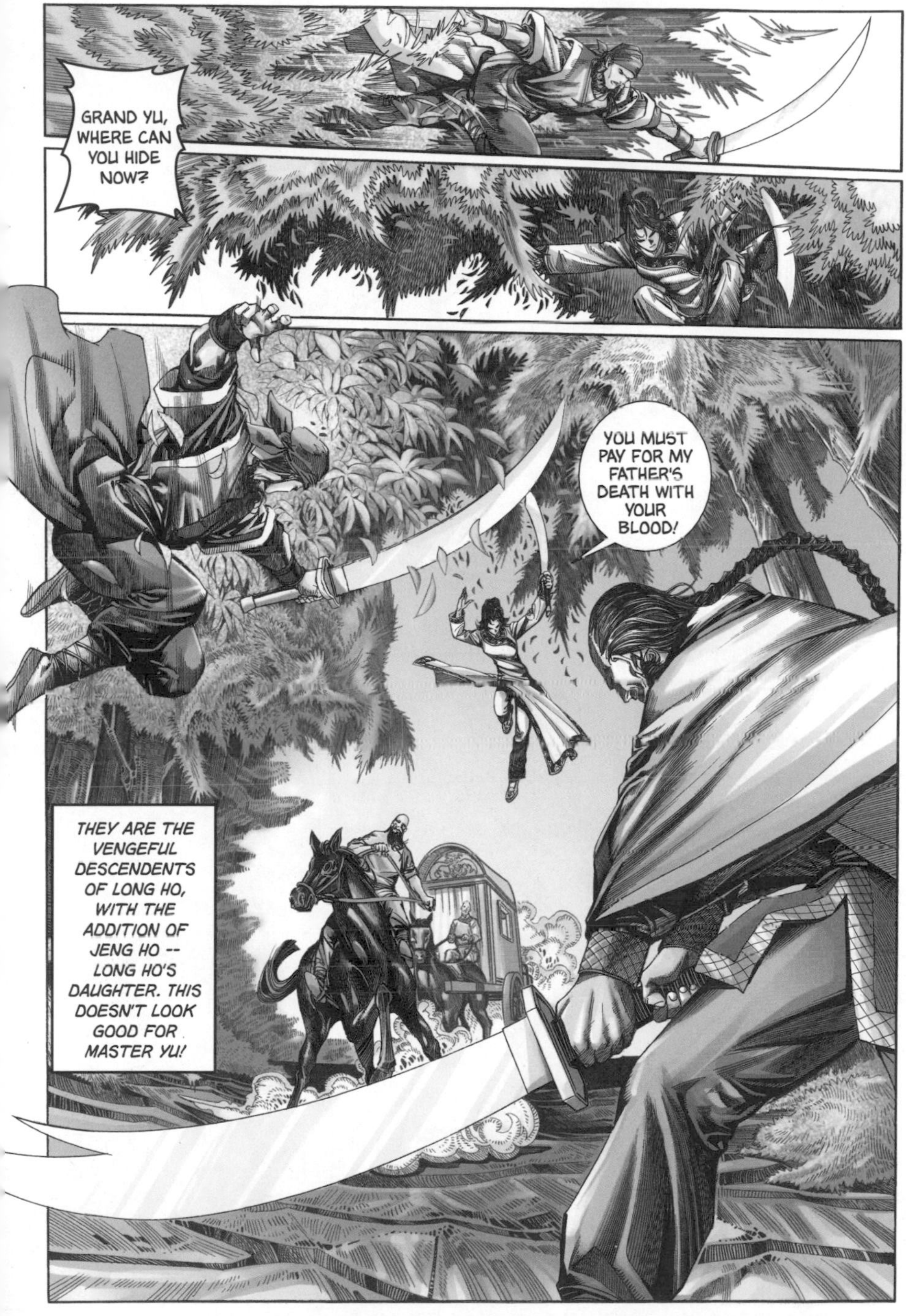
GRAND YU, WHERE CAN YOU HIDE NOW?
YOU MUST PAY FOR MY FATHER'S DEATH WITH YOUR BLOOD!
THEY ARE THE VENGEFUL DESCENDENTS OF LONG HO, WITH THE ADDITION OF JENG HO -- LONG HO'S DAUGHTER. THIS DOESN'T LOOK GOOD FOR MASTER YU!

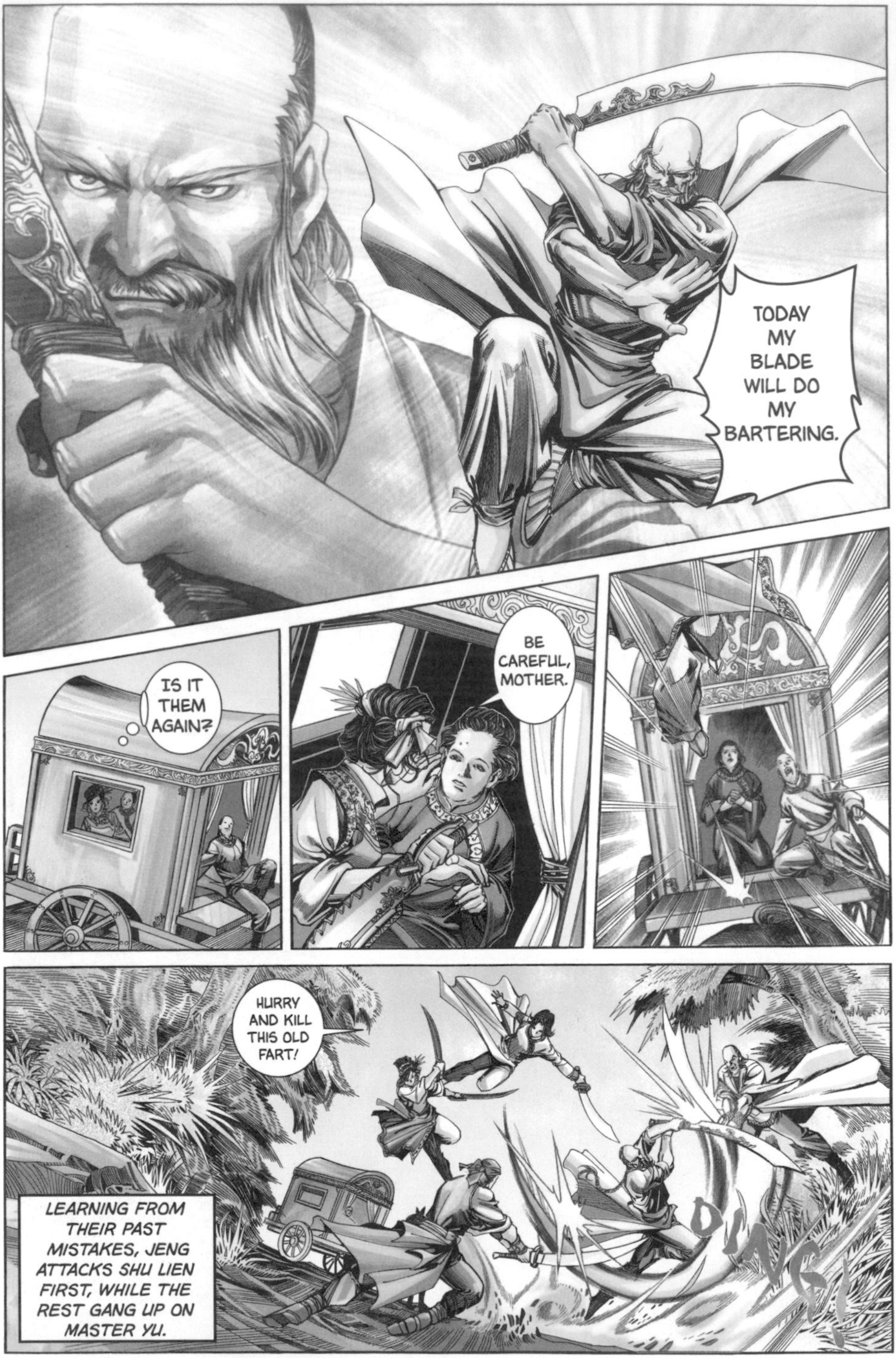
TODAY MY BLADE WILL DO MY BARTERING.
IS IT THEM AGAIN?
BE CAREFUL, MOTHER.
HURRY AND KILL THIS OLD FART!
LEARNING FROM THEIR PAST MISTAKES, JENG ATTACKS SHU LIEN FIRST, WHILE THE REST GANG UP ON MASTER YU.

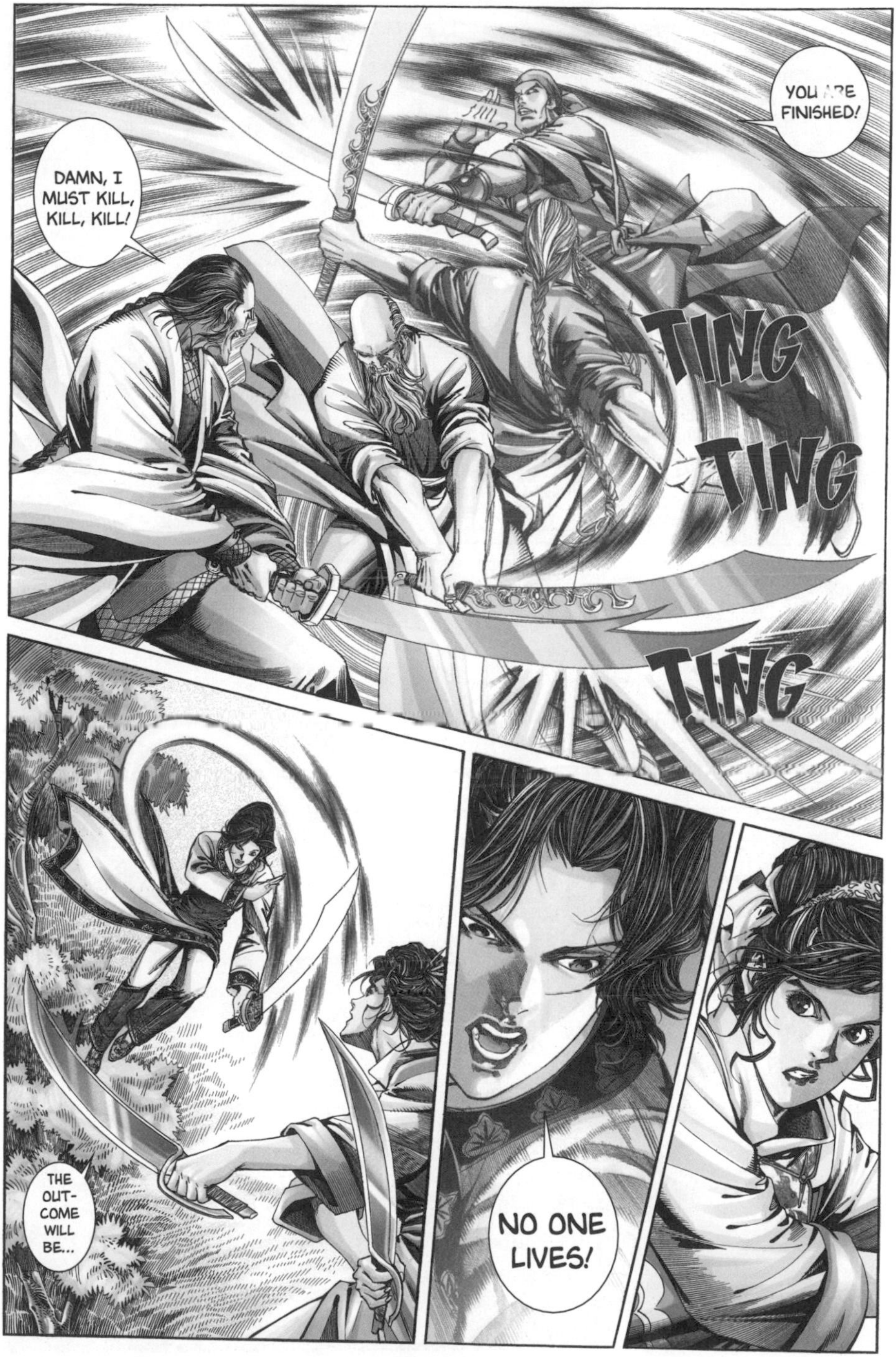
YOU ARE FINISHED!
DAMN, I MUST KILL, KILL, KILL!
TING
TING
TING
THE OUT-COME WILL BE...
NO ONE LIVES!

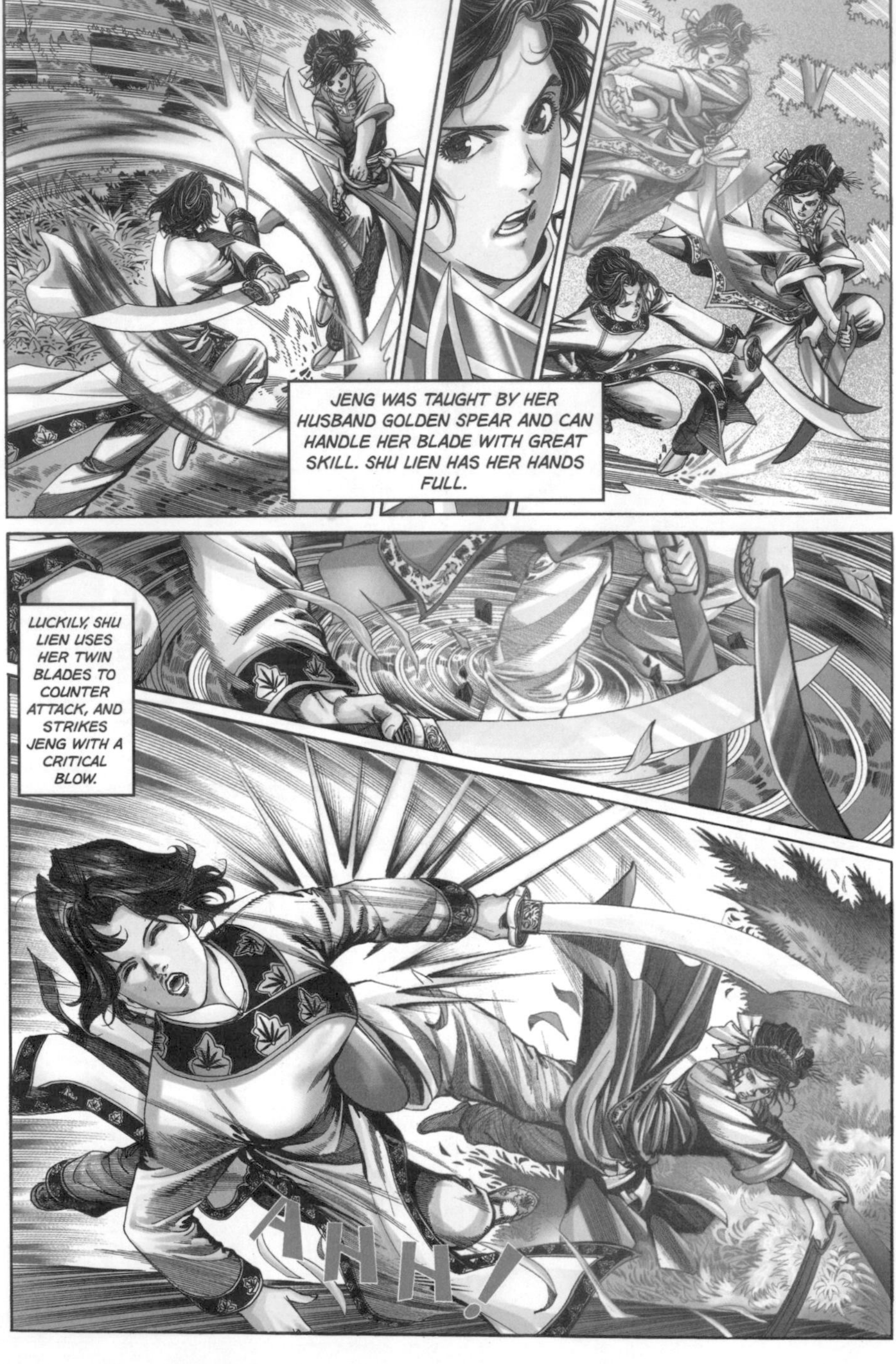
JENG WAS TAUGHT BY HER HUSBAND GOLDEN SPEAR AND CAN HANDLE HER BLADE WITH GREAT SKILL. SHU LIEN HAS HER HANDS FULL.
LUCKILY, SHU LIEN USES HER TWIN BLADES TO COUNTER ATTACK, AND STRIKES JENG WITH A CRITICAL BLOW.
AHH!

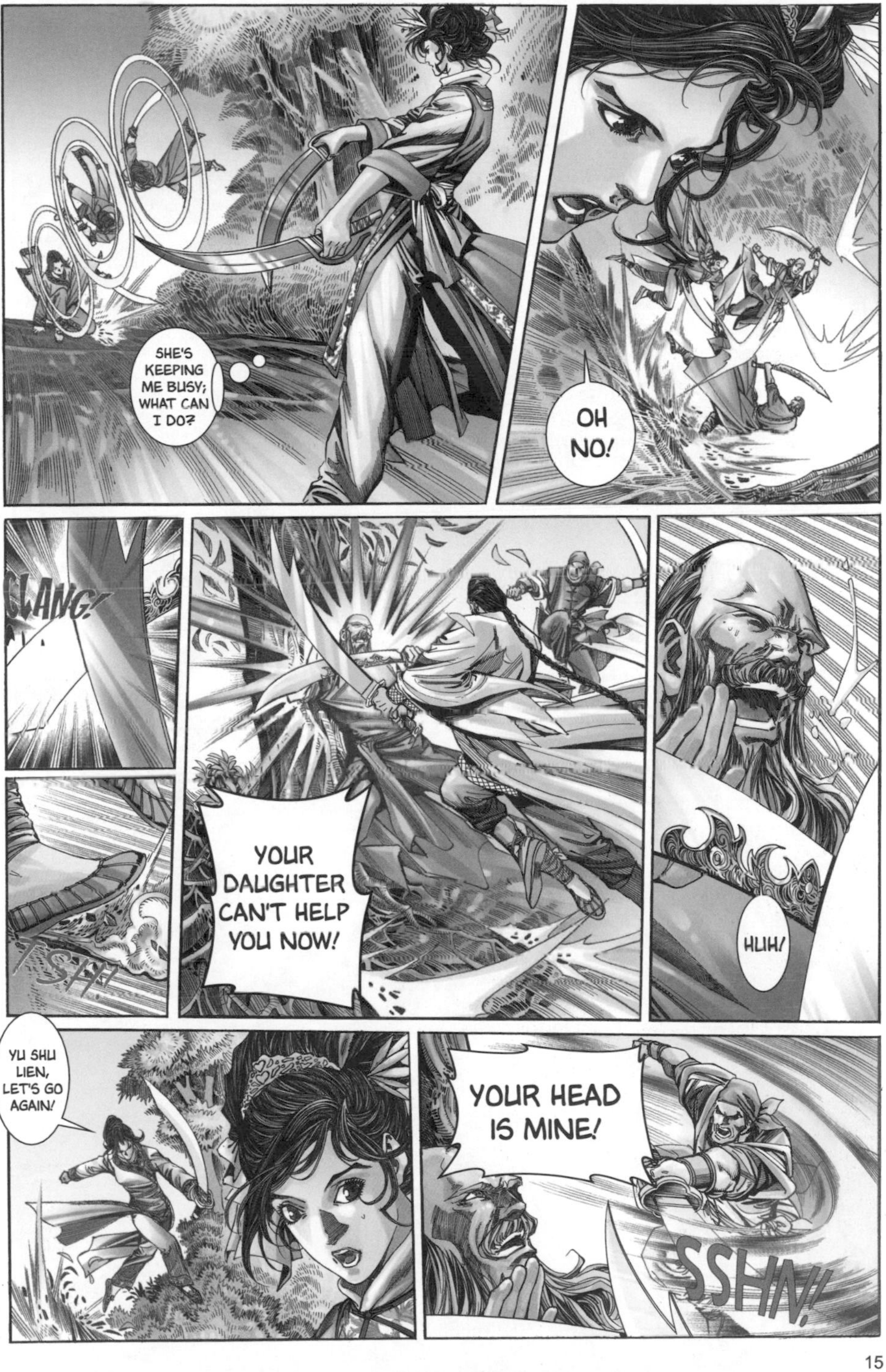
SHE'S KEEPING ME BUSY; WHAT CAN I DO?
OH NO!
CLANG!
TSHH!
YOUR DAUGHTER CAN'T HELP YOU NOW!
HUH!
YU SHU LIEN, LET'S GO AGAIN!
YOUR HEAD IS MINE!
SSHN!

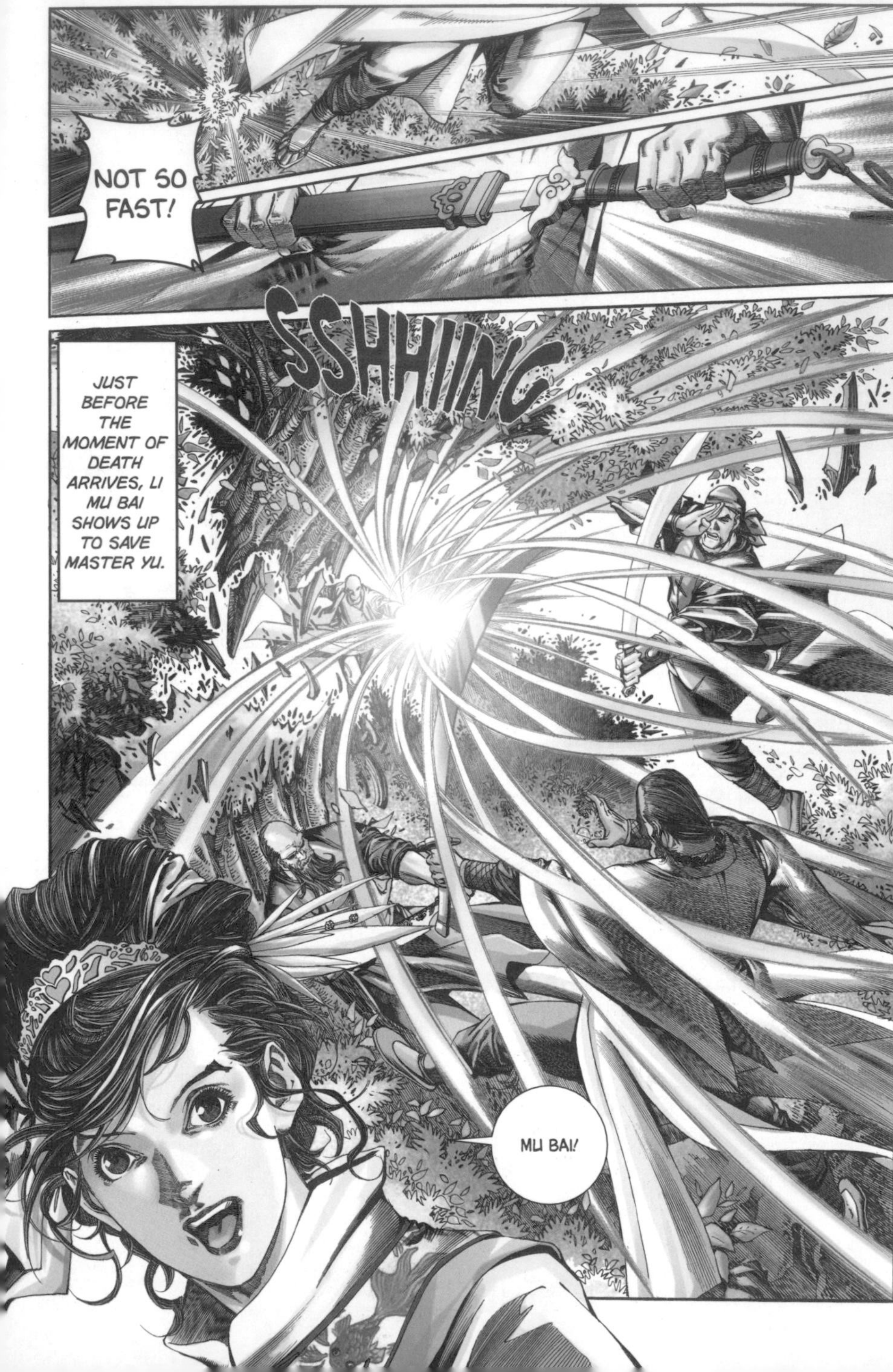
NOT SO FAST!
SSHHIING
JUST BEFORE THE MOMENT OF DEATH ARRIVES, LI MU BAI SHOWS UP TO SAVE MASTER YU.
MU BAI!

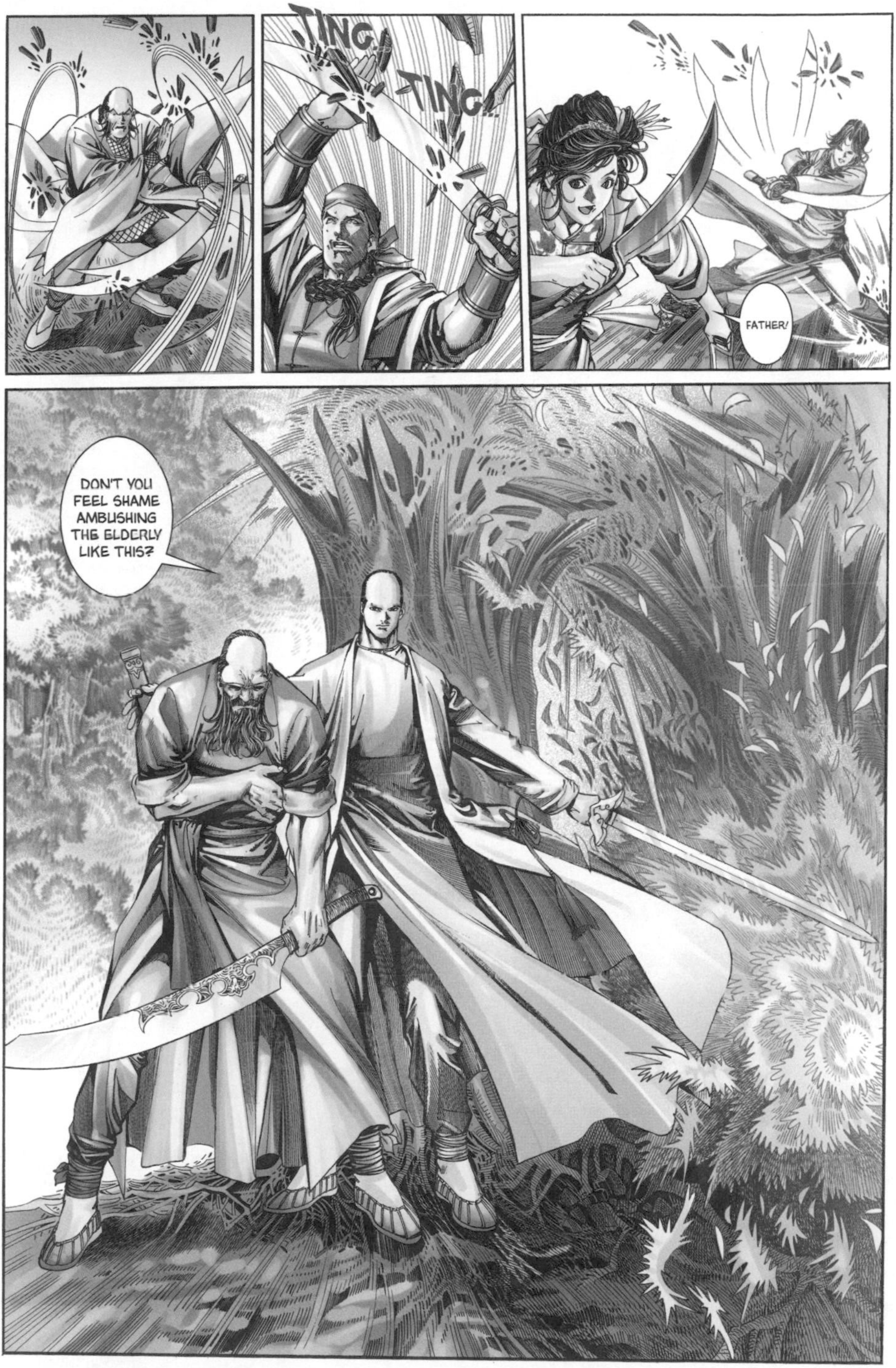

TING!
TING!
FATHER!
DON'T YOU FEEL SHAME AMBUSHING THE ELDERLY LIKE THIS?

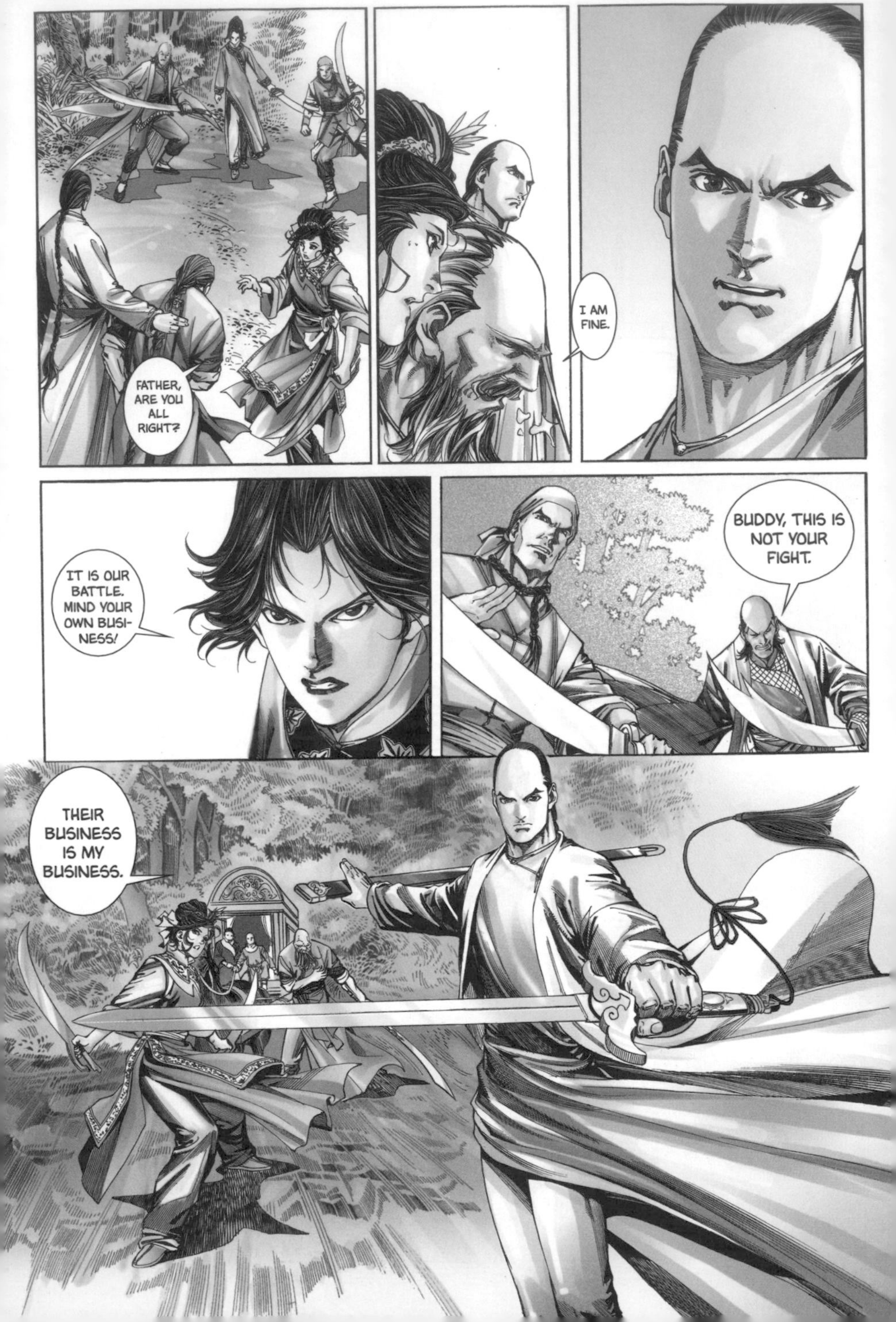
FATHER, ARE YOU ALL RIGHT?
I AM FINE.
IT IS OUR BATTLE. MIND YOUR OWN BUSI-NESS!
BUDDY, THIS IS NOT YOUR FIGHT.
THEIR BUSINESS IS MY BUSINESS.

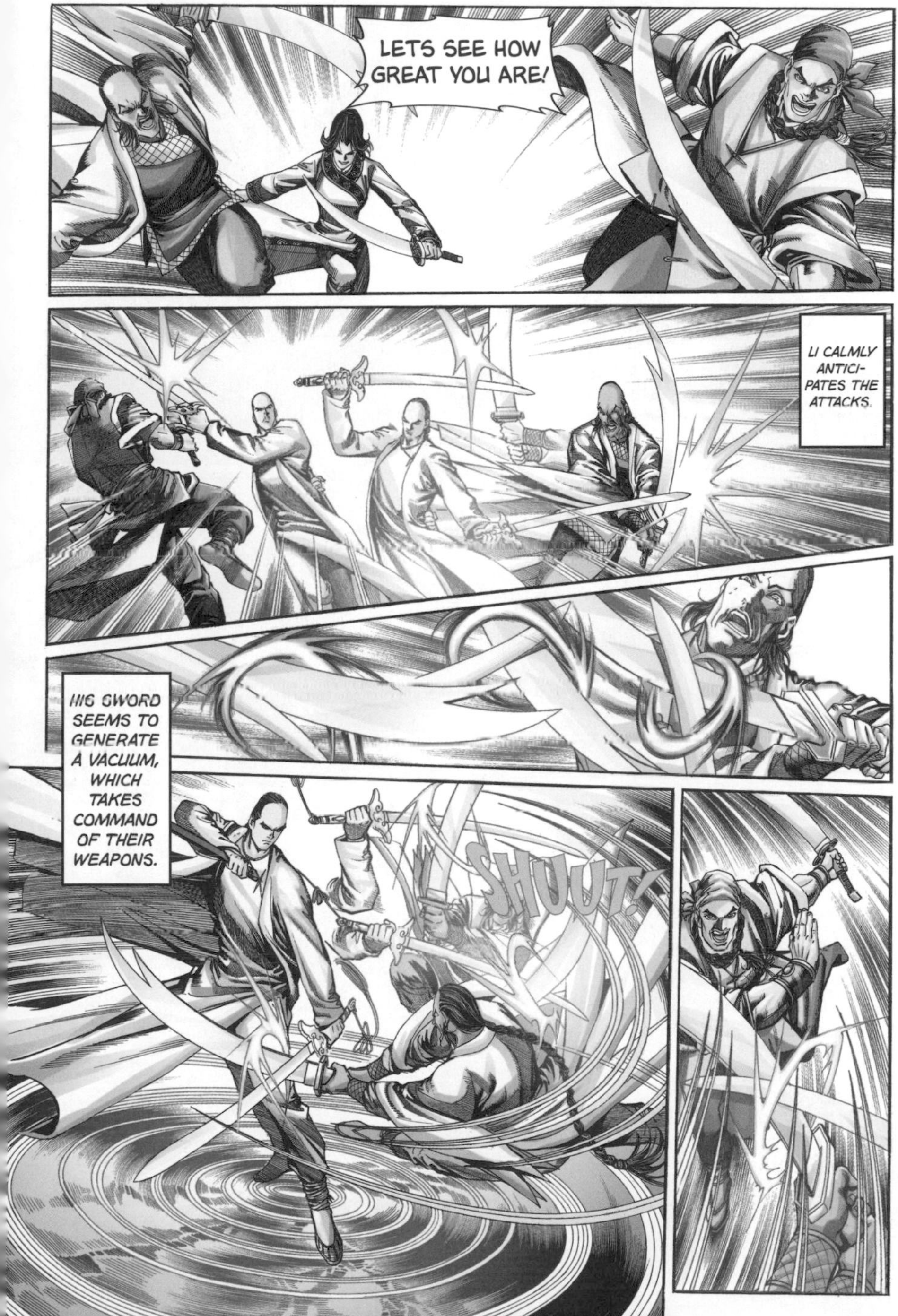
LETS SEE HOW GREAT YOU ARE!
LI CALMLY ANTICI-PATES THE ATTACKS.
HIS SWORD SEEMS TO GENERATE A VACUUM, WHICH TAKES COMMAND OF THEIR WEAPONS.
SHUUT!

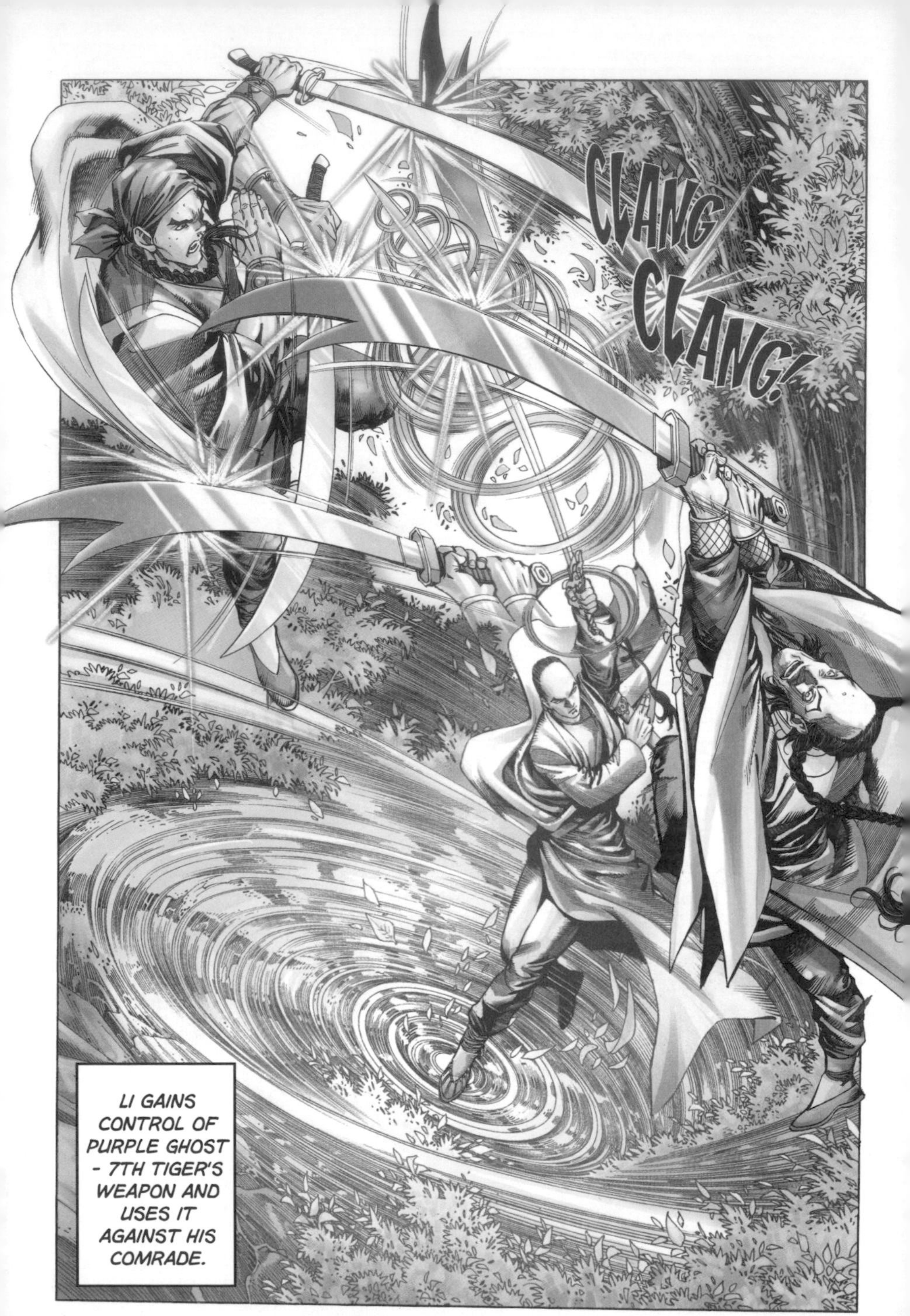
CLANG
CLANG
CLANG!
LI GAINS CONTROL OF PURPLE GHOST - 7TH TIGER'S WEAPON AND USES IT AGAINST HIS COMRADE.

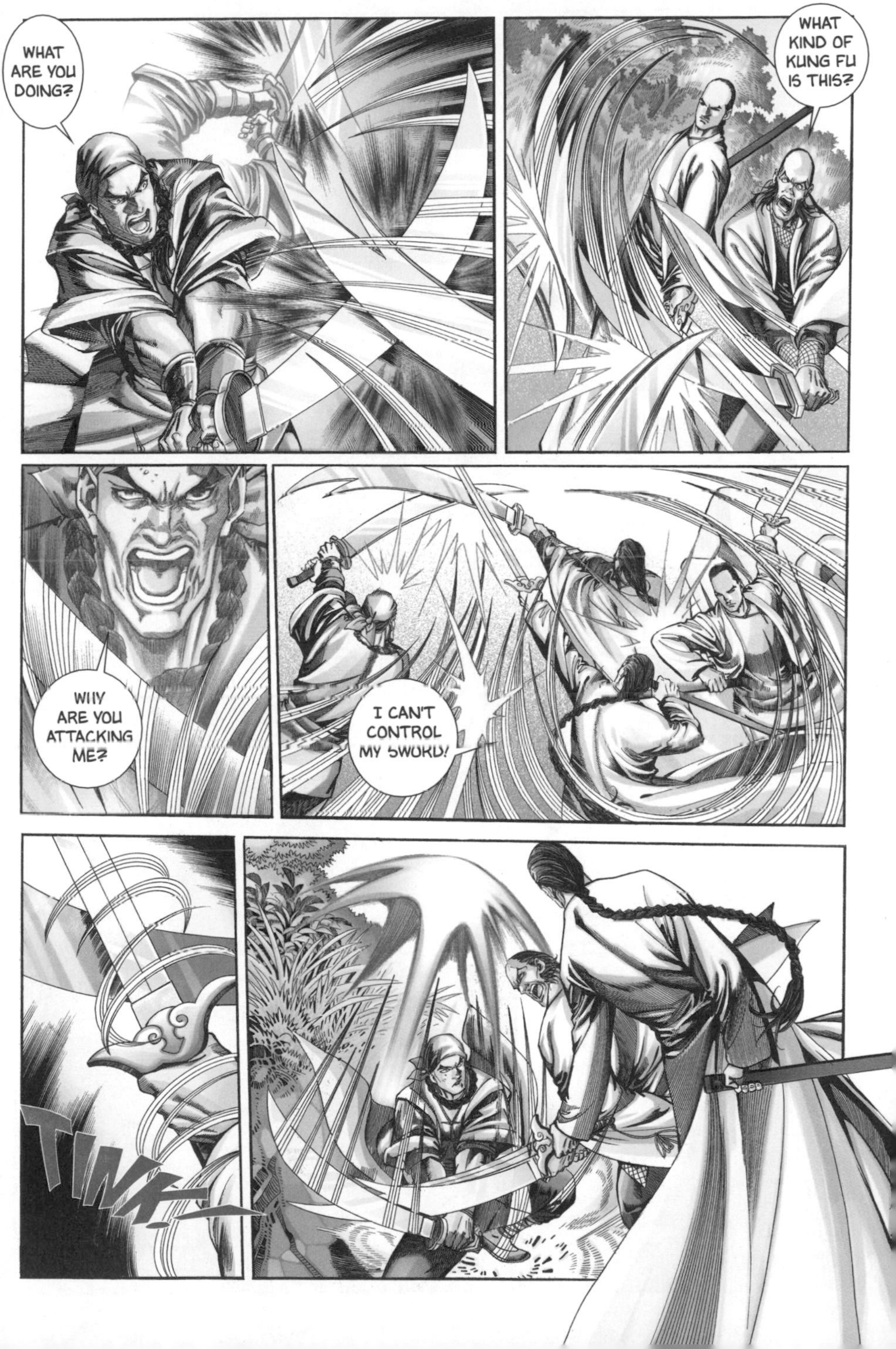
WHAT ARE YOU DOING?
WHAT KIND OF KUNG FU IS THIS?
WHY ARE YOU ATTACKING ME?
I CAN'T CONTROL MY SWORD!
TINK--!

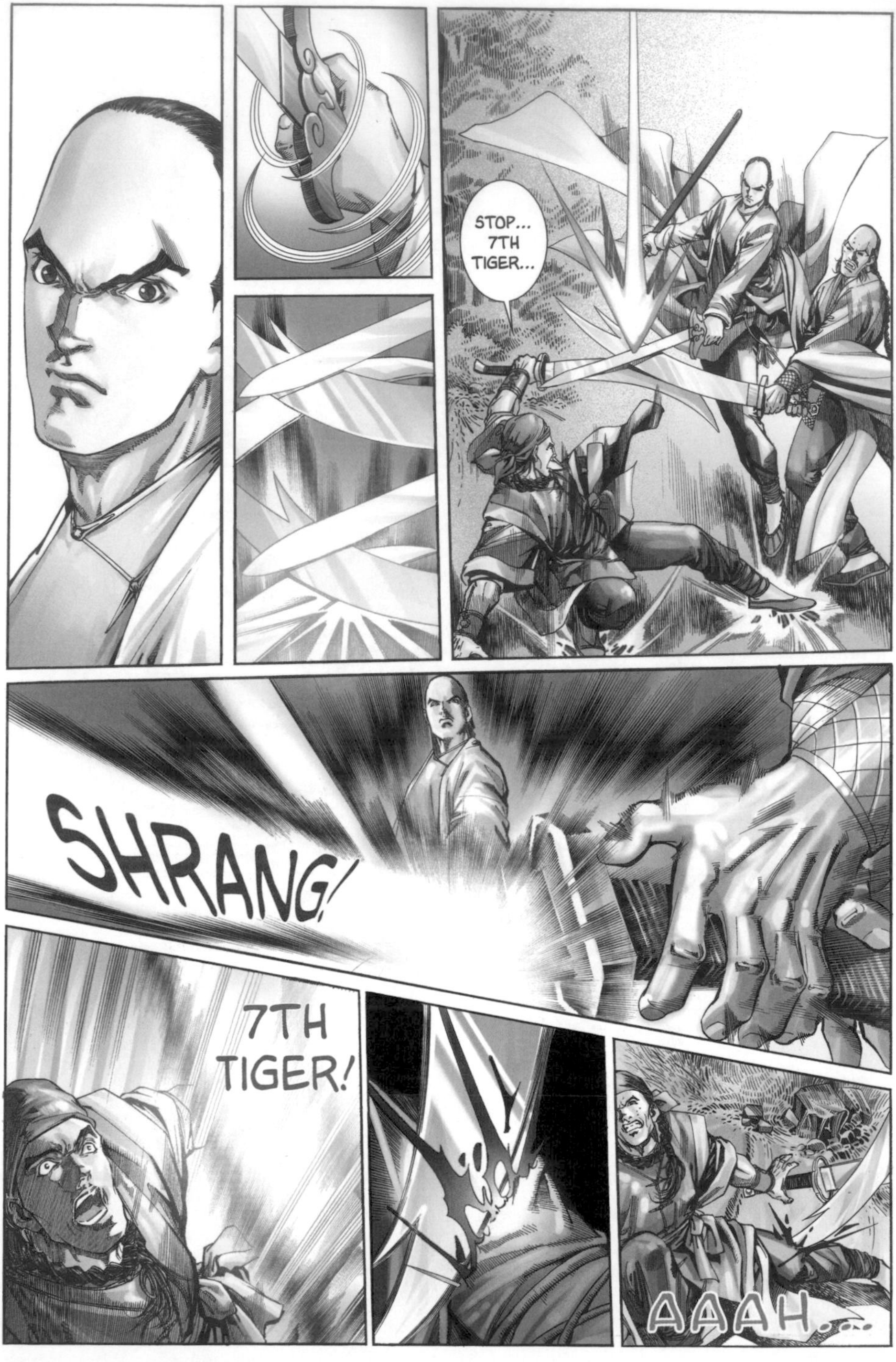
STOP... 7TH TIGER...
SHRANG!
7TH TIGER!
AAAH...

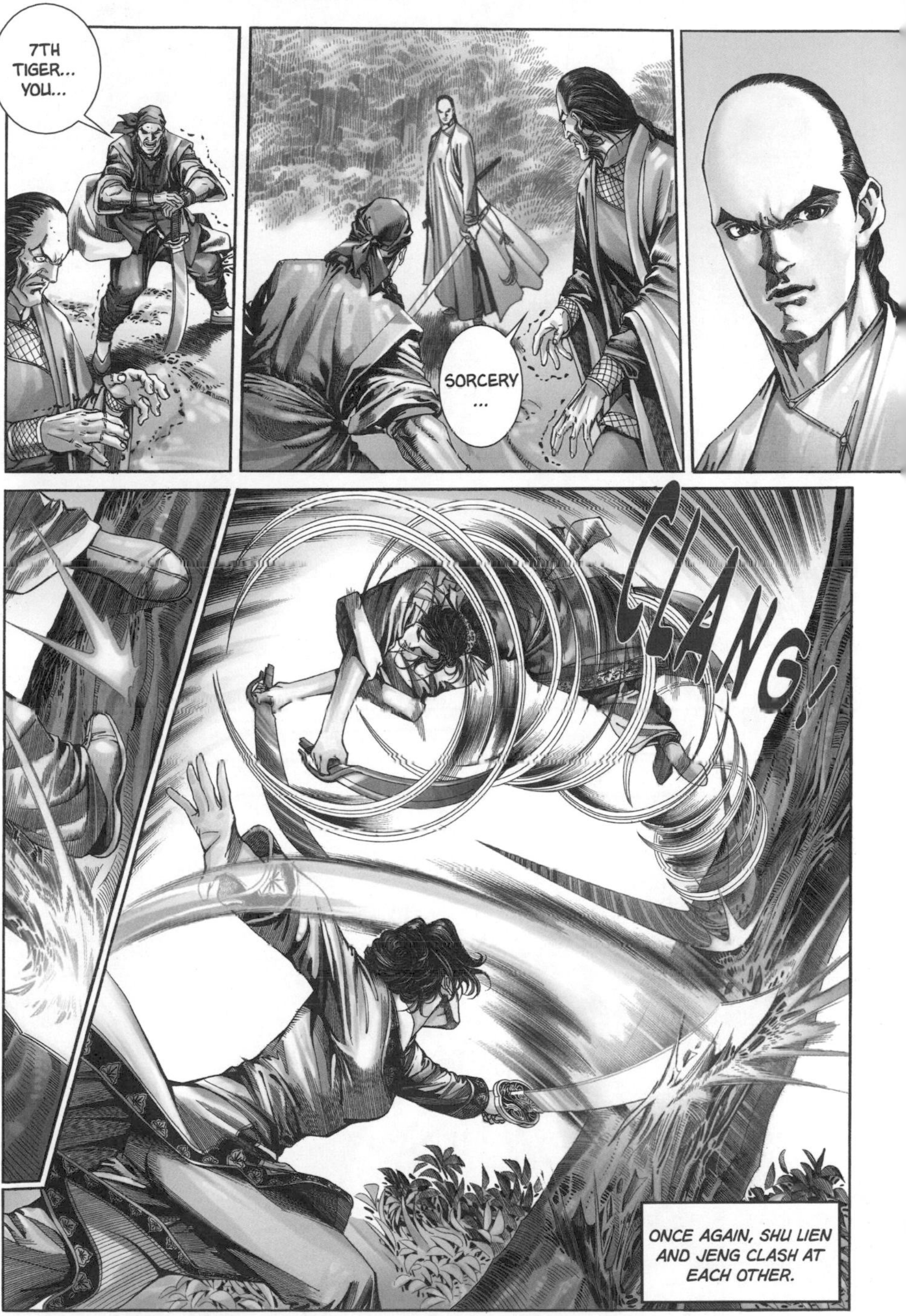
7TH TIGER... YOU...
SORCERY ...
CLANG!!
ONCE AGAIN, SHU LIEN AND JENG CLASH AT EACH OTHER.

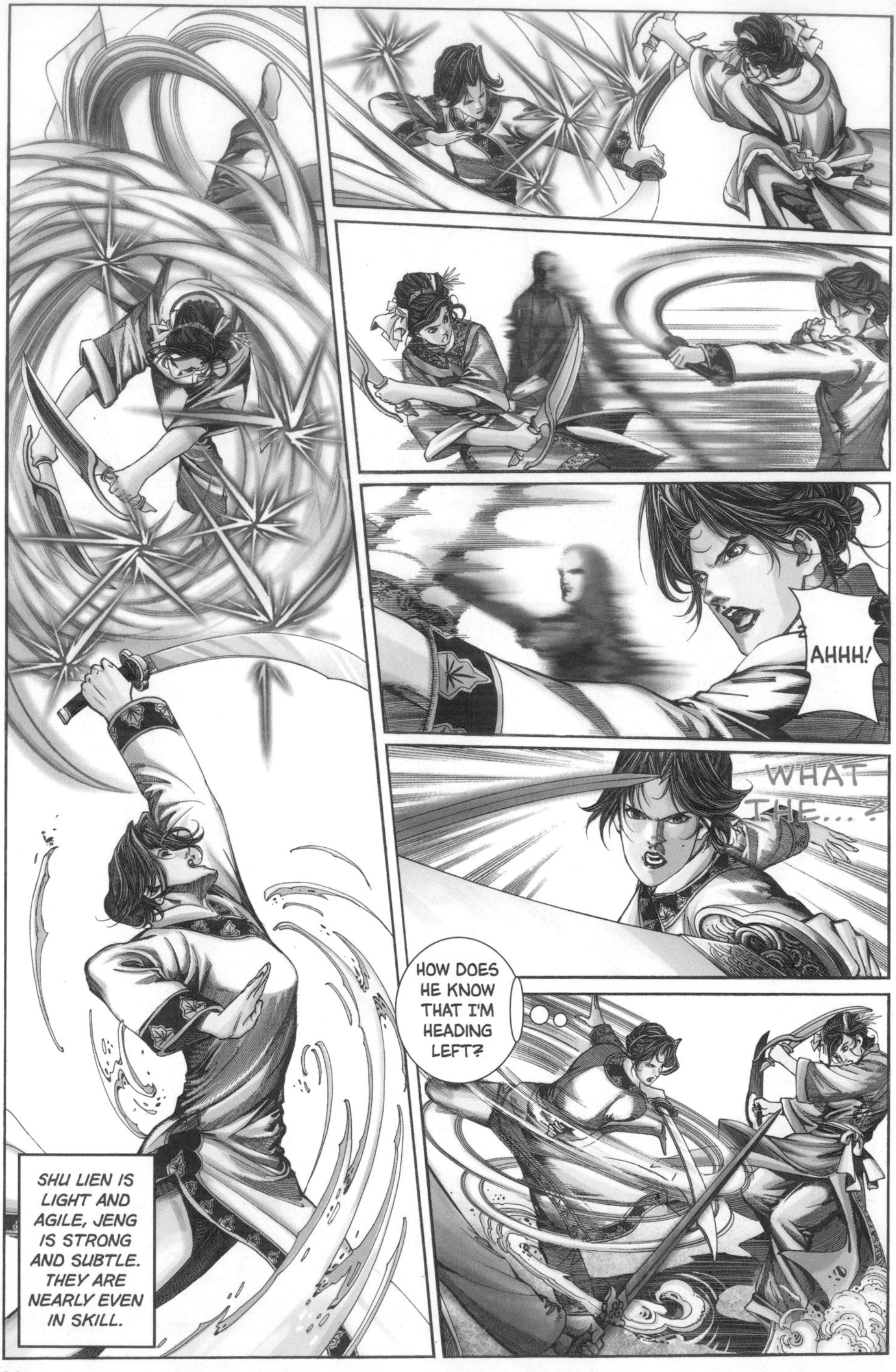
AHHH!
WHAT THE...?
HOW DOES HE KNOW THAT I'M HEADING LEFT?
SHU LIEN IS LIGHT AND AGILE, JENG IS STRONG AND SUBTLE. THEY ARE NEARLY EVEN IN SKILL.

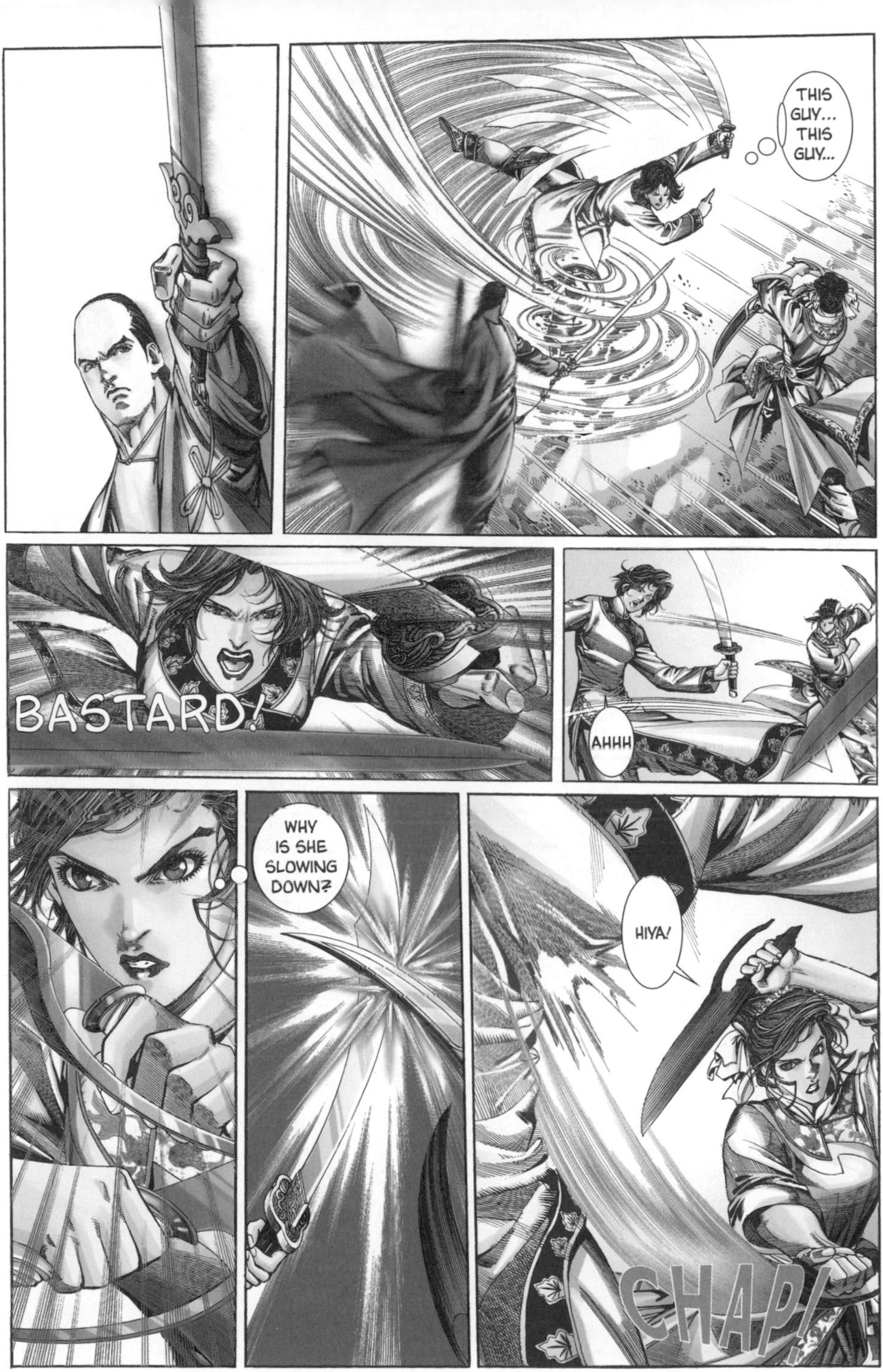
THIS GUY... THIS GUY...
BASTARD!
AHHH
WHY IS SHE SLOWING DOWN?
HIYA!
CHAP!

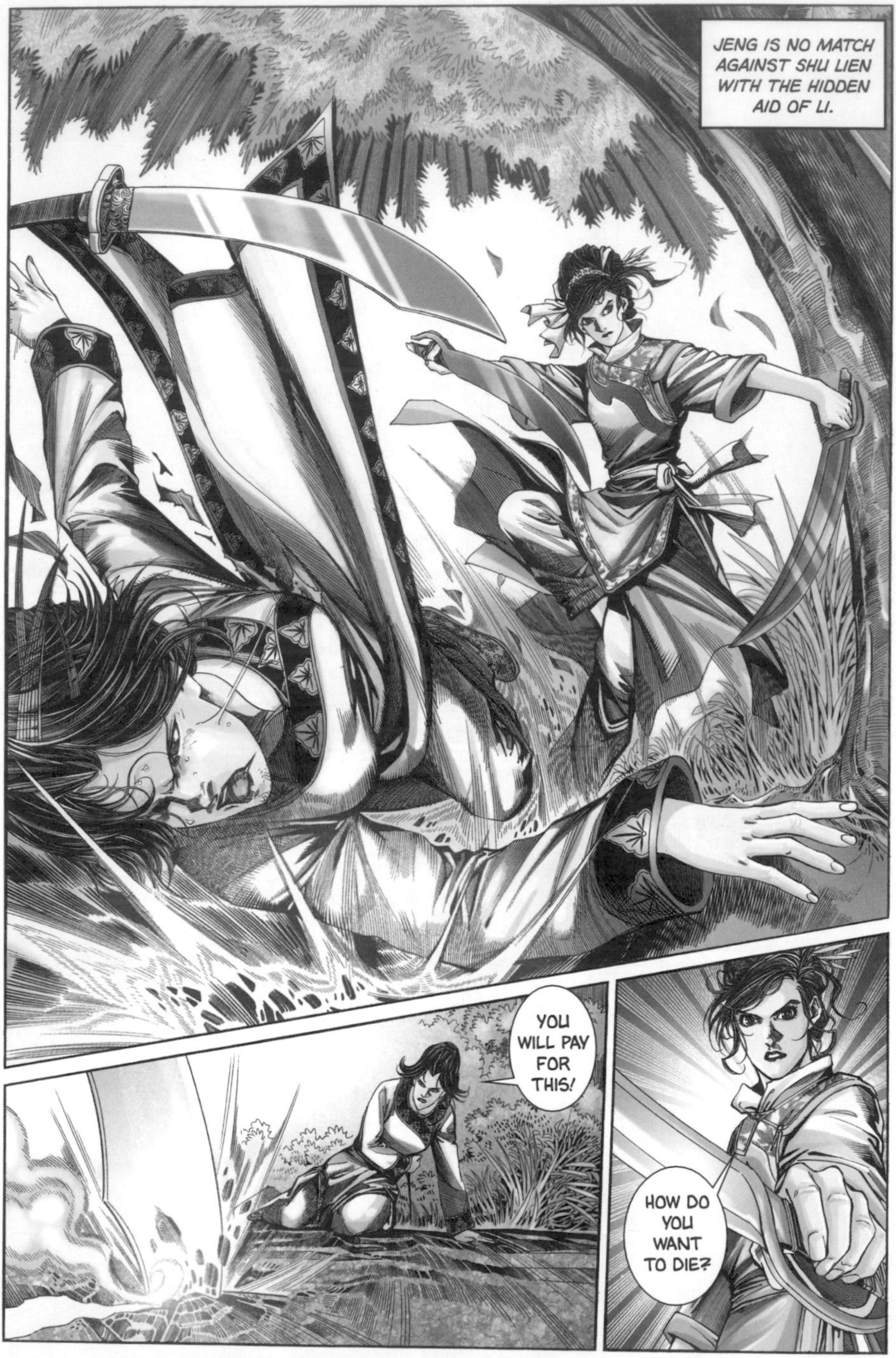
JENG IS NO MATCH AGAINST SHU LIEN WITH THE HIDDEN AID OF LI.
YOU WILL PAY FOR THIS!
HOW DO YOU WANT TO DIE?

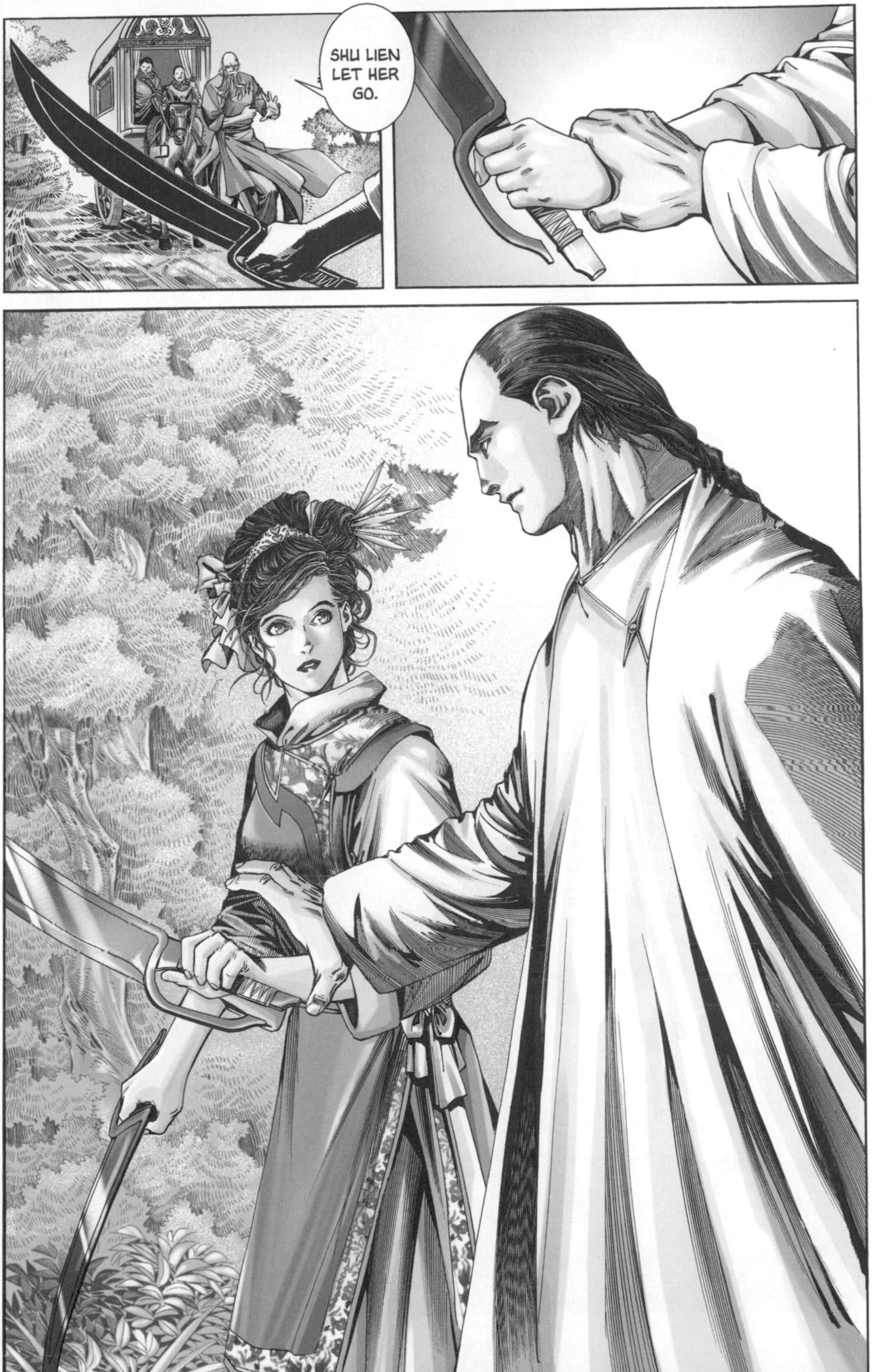
SHU LIEN LET HER GO.

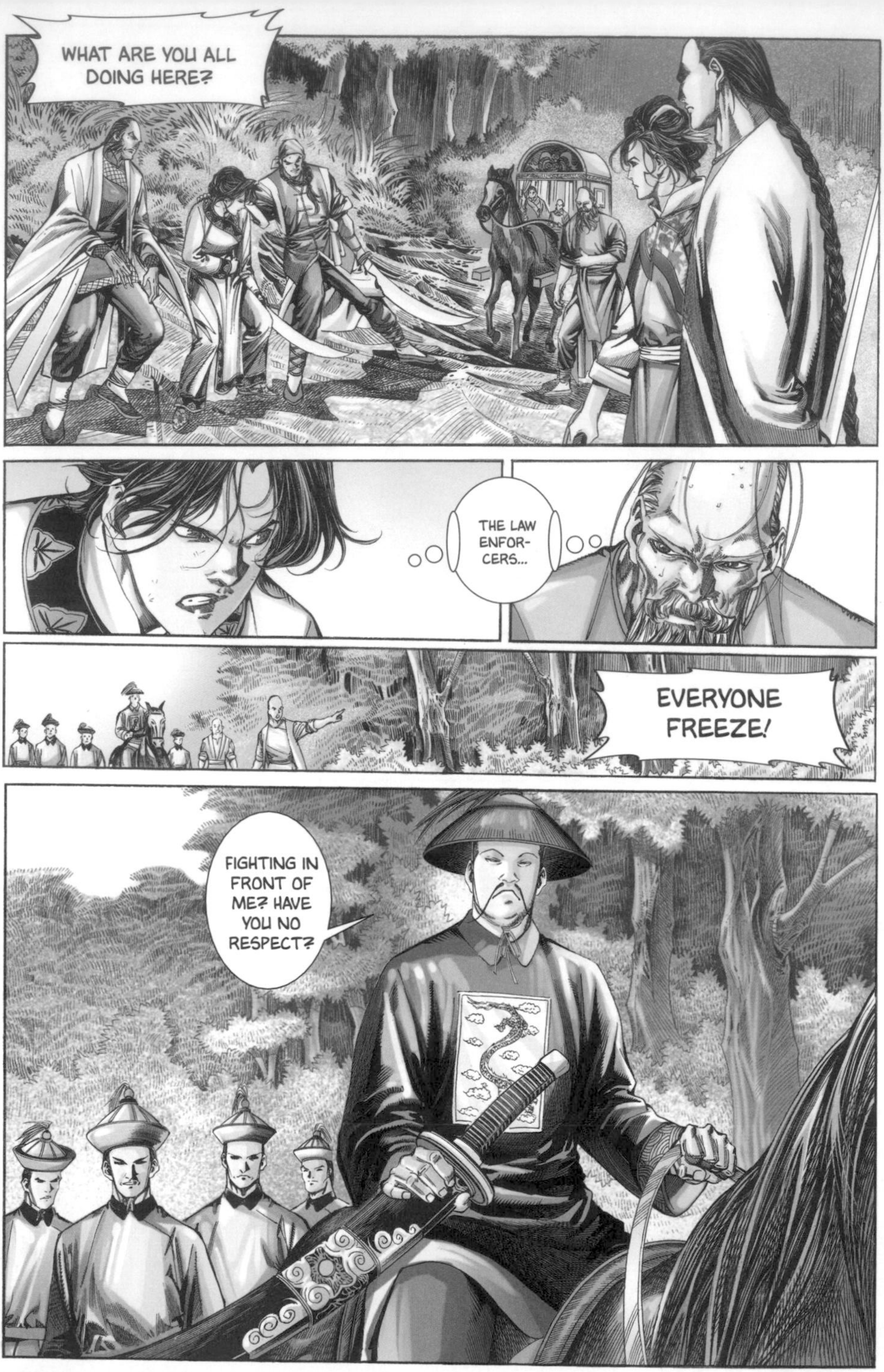
WHAT ARE YOU ALL DOING HERE?
THE LAW ENFORCERS...
EVERYONE FREEZE!
FIGHTING IN FRONT OF ME? HAVE YOU NO RESPECT?

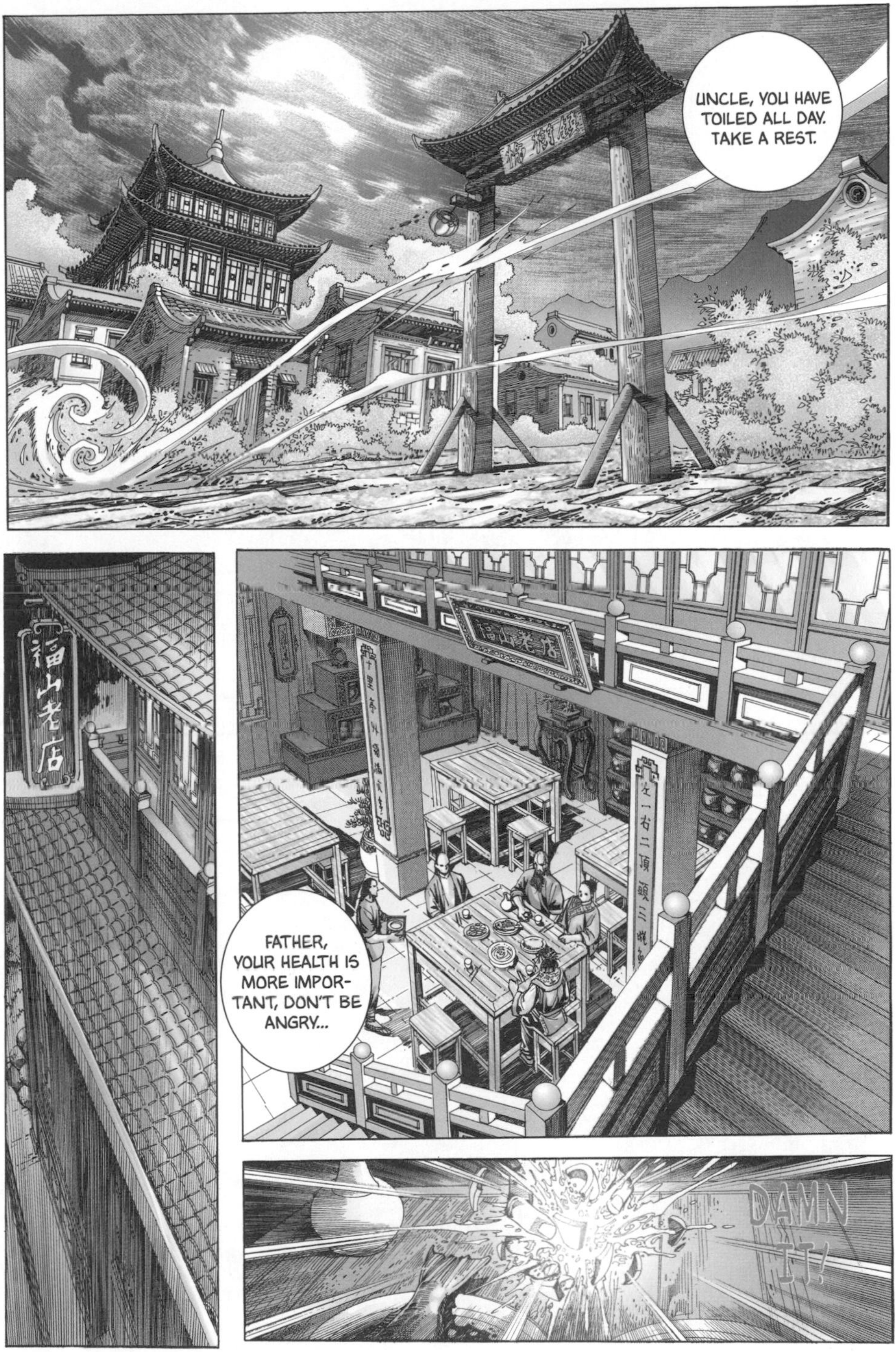
UNCLE, YOU HAVE TOILED ALL DAY. TAKE A REST.
福山老店
福山老店
FATHER, YOUR HEALTH IS MORE IMPOR-TANT, DON'T BE ANGRY...
DAMN IT!

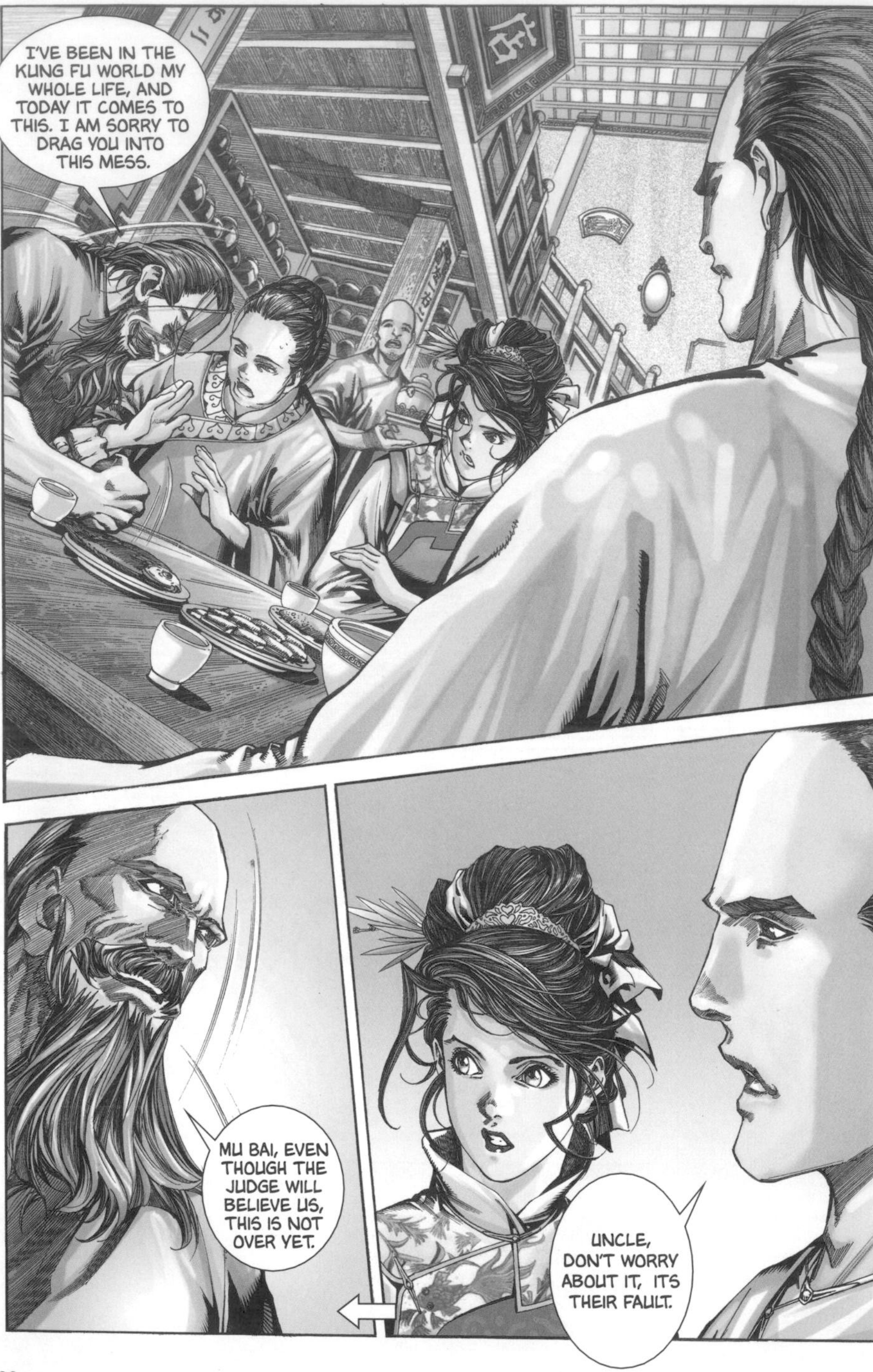
I'VE BEEN IN THE KUNG FU WORLD MY WHOLE LIFE, AND TODAY IT COMES TO THIS. I AM SORRY TO DRAG YOU INTO THIS MESS.
MU BAI, EVEN THOUGH THE JUDGE WILL BELIEVE US, THIS IS NOT OVER YET.
UNCLE, DON'T WORRY ABOUT IT, ITS THEIR FAULT.

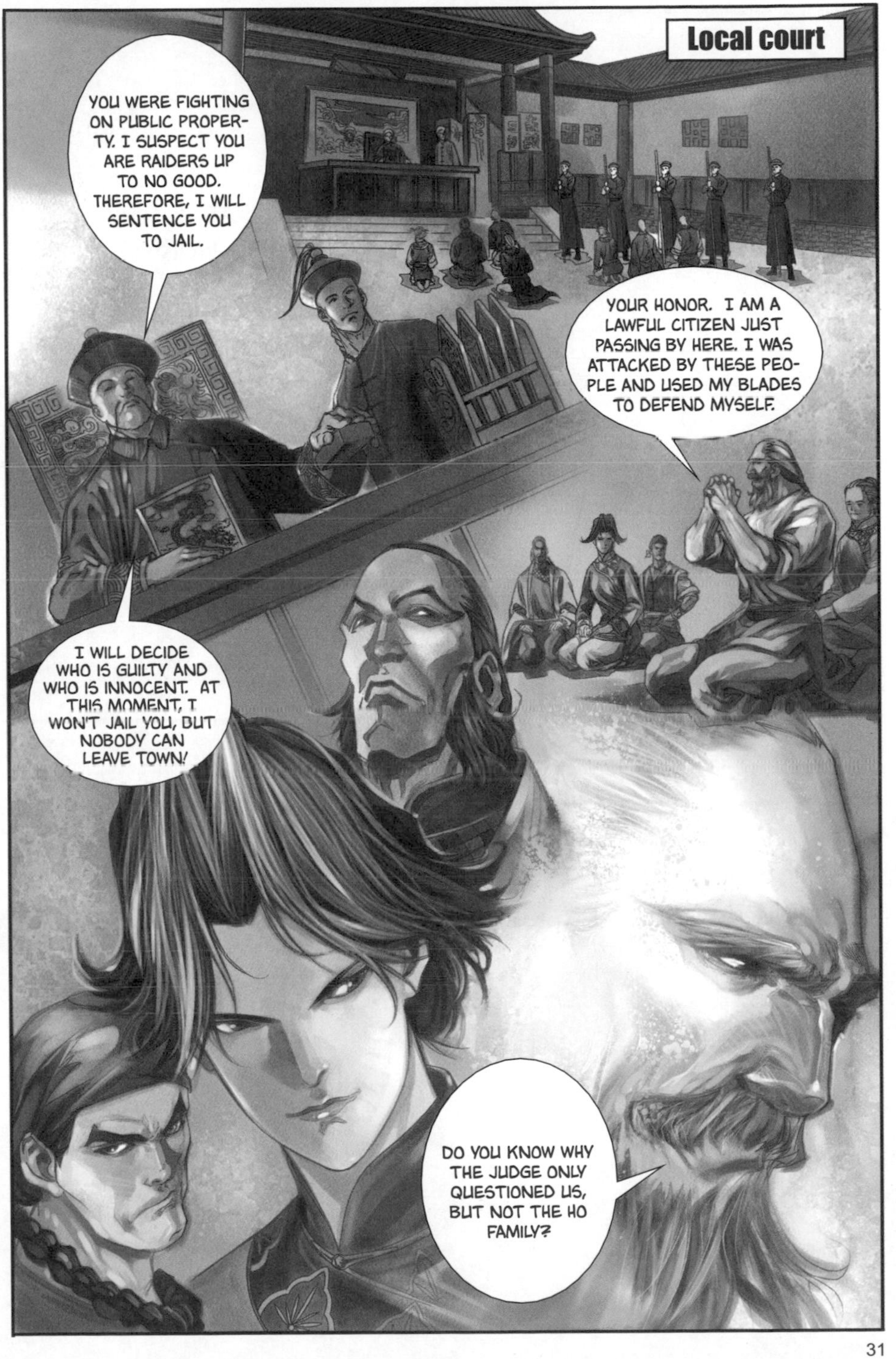
Local court
YOU WERE FIGHTING ON PUBLIC PROPERTY. I SUSPECT YOU ARE RAIDERS UP TO NO GOOD. THEREFORE, I WILL SENTENCE YOU TO JAIL.
YOUR HONOR. I AM A LAWFUL CITIZEN JUST PASSING BY HERE. I WAS ATTACKED BY THESE PEOPLE AND USED MY BLADES TO DEFEND MYSELF.
I WILL DECIDE WHO IS GUILTY AND WHO IS INNOCENT. AT THIS MOMENT, I WON'T JAIL YOU, BUT NOBODY CAN LEAVE TOWN!
DO YOU KNOW WHY THE JUDGE ONLY QUESTIONED US, BUT NOT THE HO FAMILY?

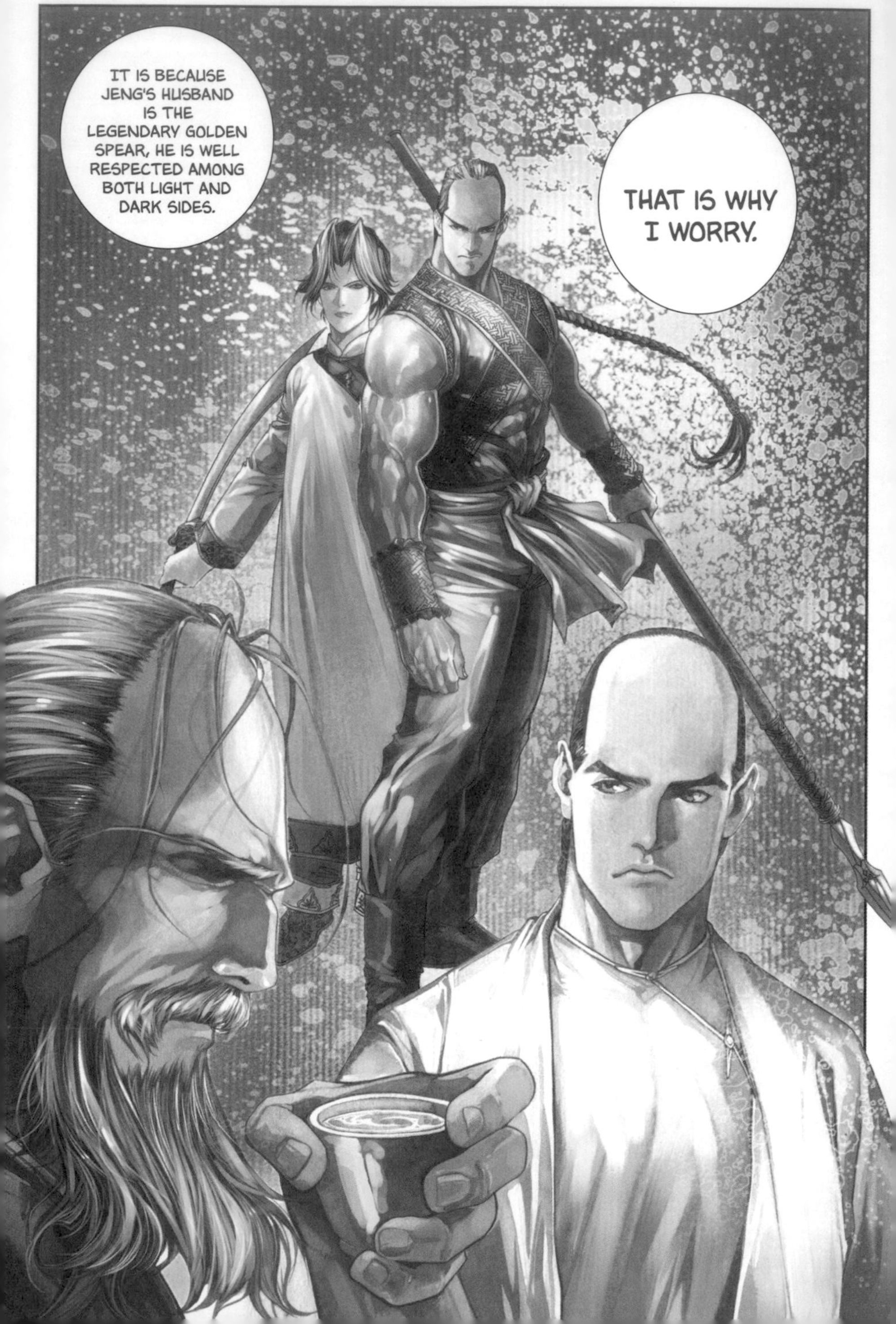
IT IS BECAUSE JENG'S HUSBAND IS THE LEGENDARY GOLDEN SPEAR, HE IS WELL RESPECTED AMONG BOTH LIGHT AND DARK SIDES.
THAT IS WHY I WORRY.

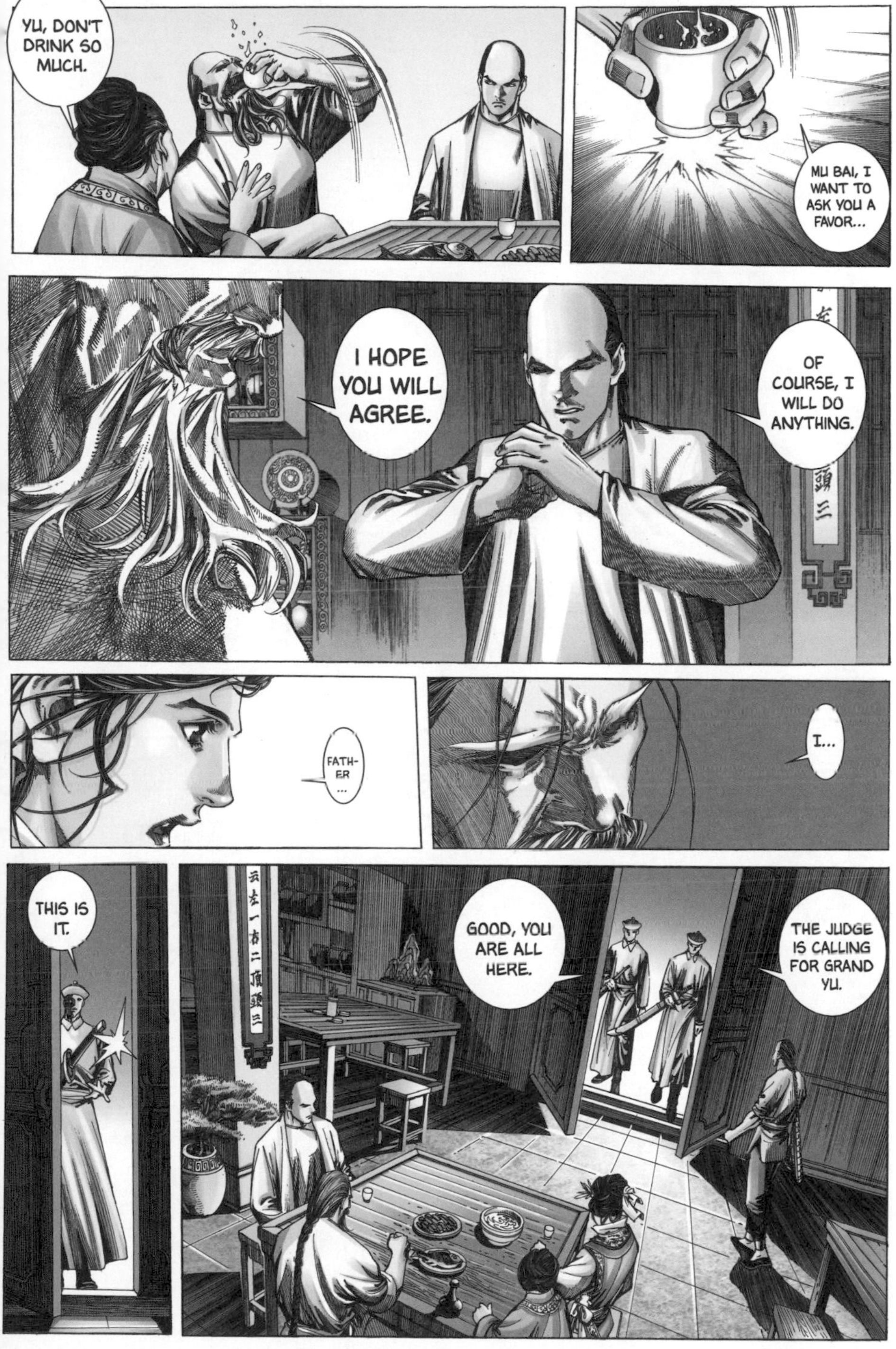
YU, DON'T DRINK SO MUCH.
MU BAI, I WANT TO ASK YOU A FAVOR...
I HOPE YOU WILL AGREE.
OF COURSE, I WILL DO ANYTHING.
FATHER...
I...
THIS IS IT.
GOOD, YOU ARE ALL HERE.
THE JUDGE IS CALLING FOR GRAND YU.

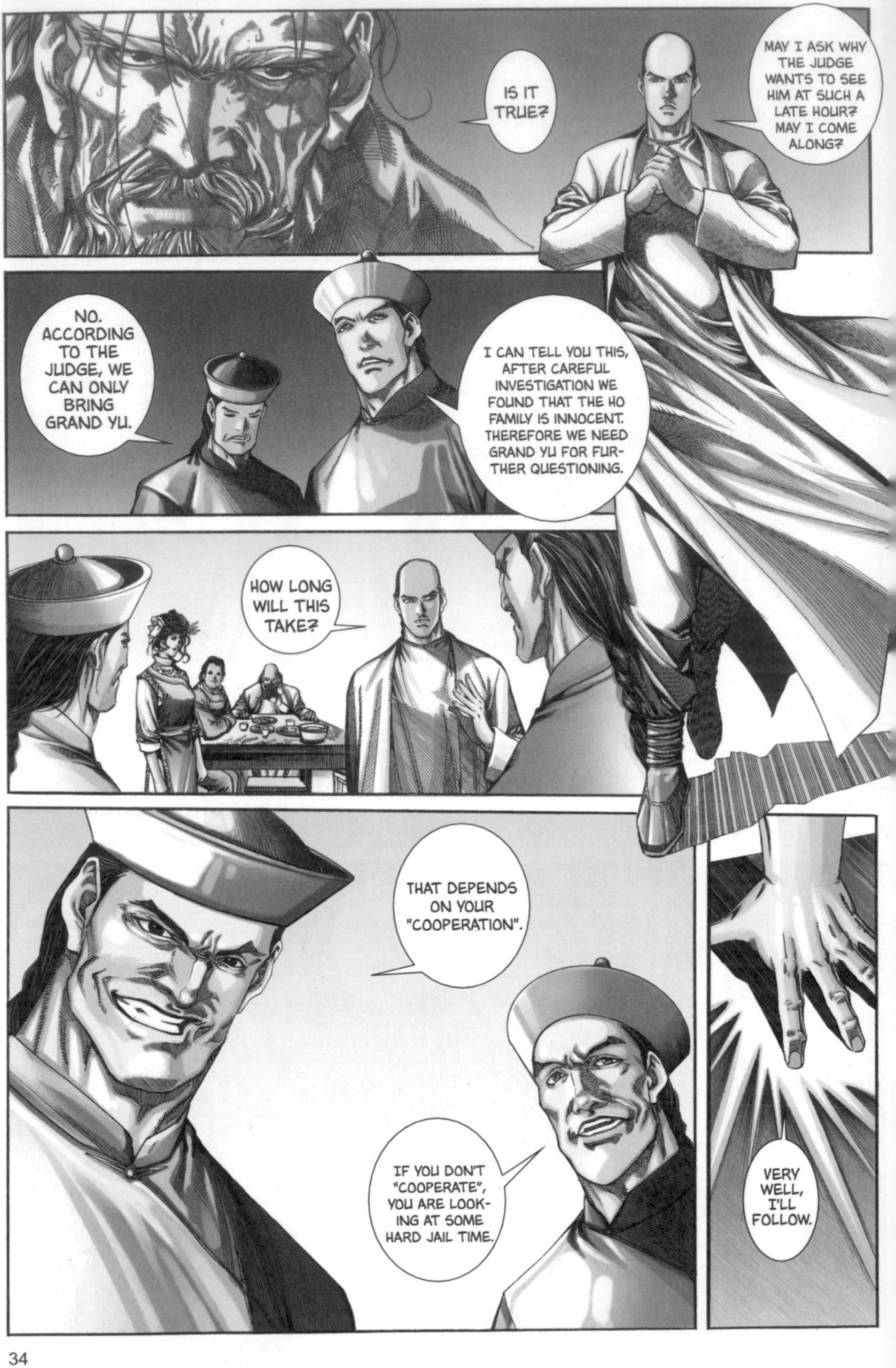
IS IT TRUE?
MAY I ASK WHY THE JUDGE WANTS TO SEE HIM AT SUCH A LATE HOUR? MAY I COME ALONG?
NO. ACCORDING TO THE JUDGE, WE CAN ONLY BRING GRAND YU.
I CAN TELL YOU THIS, AFTER CAREFUL INVESTIGATION WE FOUND THAT THE HO FAMILY IS INNOCENT. THEREFORE WE NEED GRAND YU FOR FURTHER QUESTIONING.
HOW LONG WILL THIS TAKE?
THAT DEPENDS ON YOUR "COOPERATION".
IF YOU DON'T "COOPERATE", YOU ARE LOOKING AT SOME HARD JAIL TIME.
VERY WELL, I'LL FOLLOW.

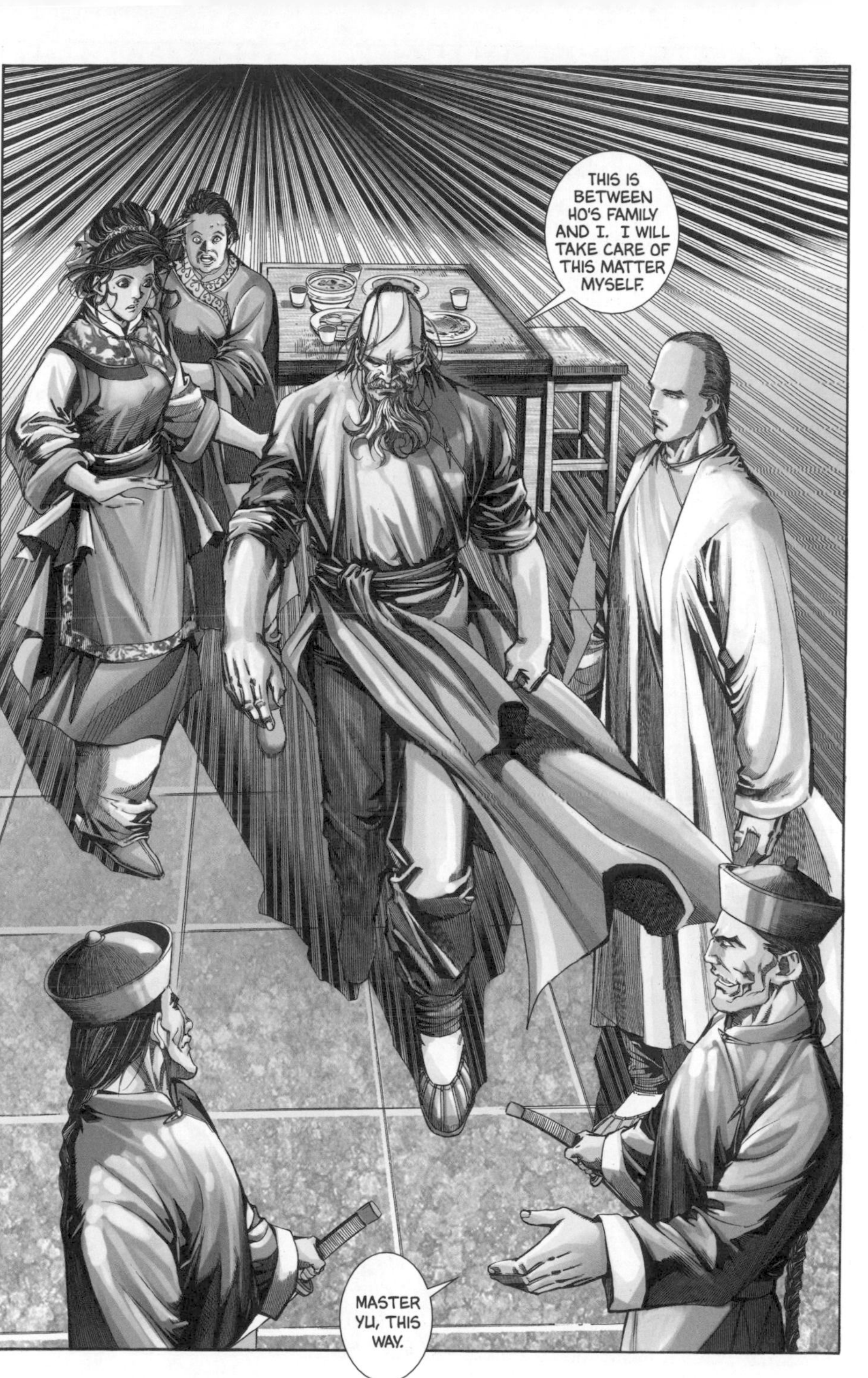
THIS IS BETWEEN HO'S FAMILY AND I. I WILL TAKE CARE OF THIS MATTER MYSELF.
MASTER YU, THIS WAY.

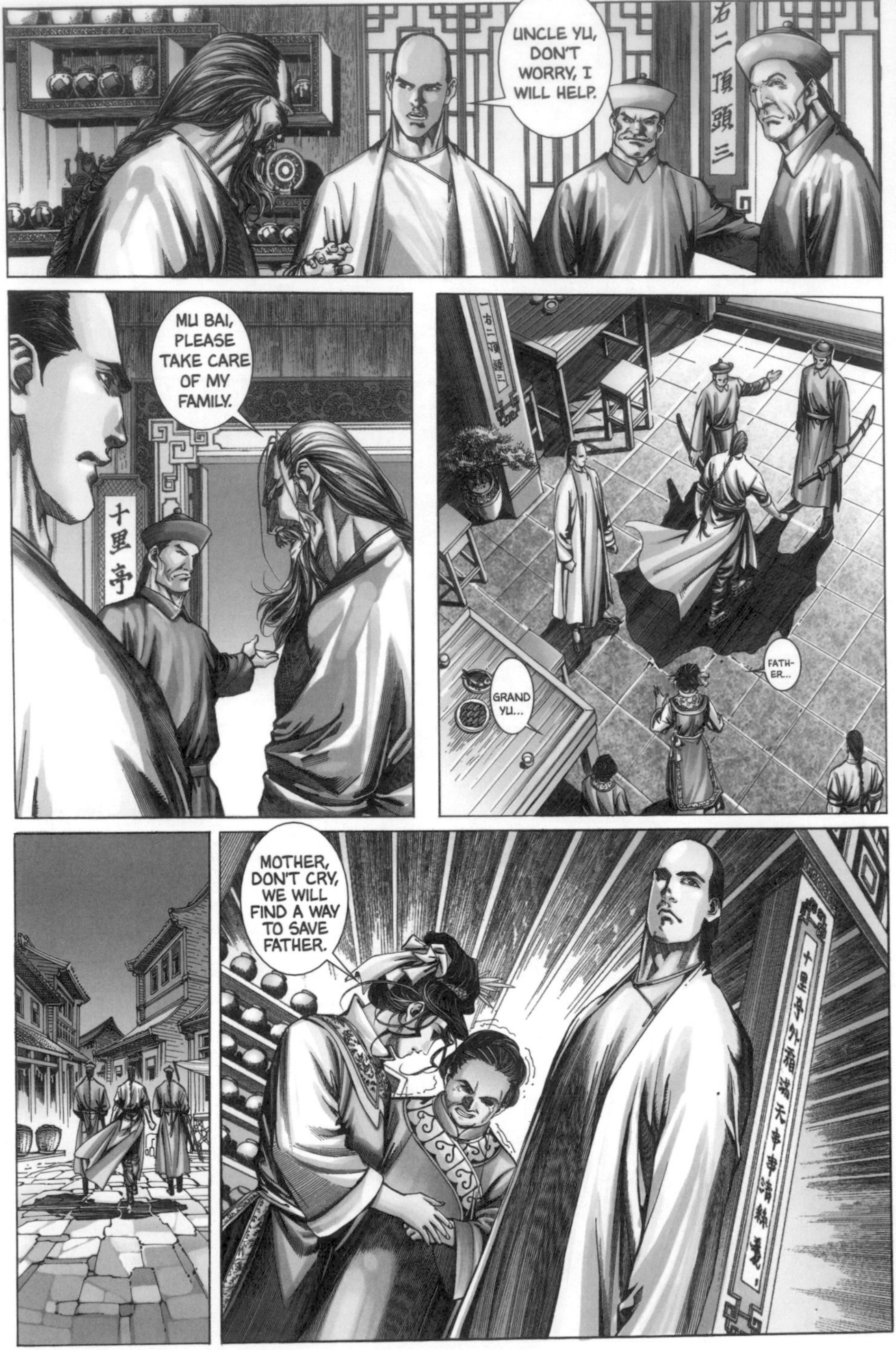
UNCLE YU, DON'T WORRY, I WILL HELP.
右二頂頭三
MU BAI, PLEASE TAKE CARE OF MY FAMILY.
十里亭
GRAND YU...
FATHER...
MOTHER, DON'T CRY, WE WILL FIND A WAY TO SAVE FATHER.

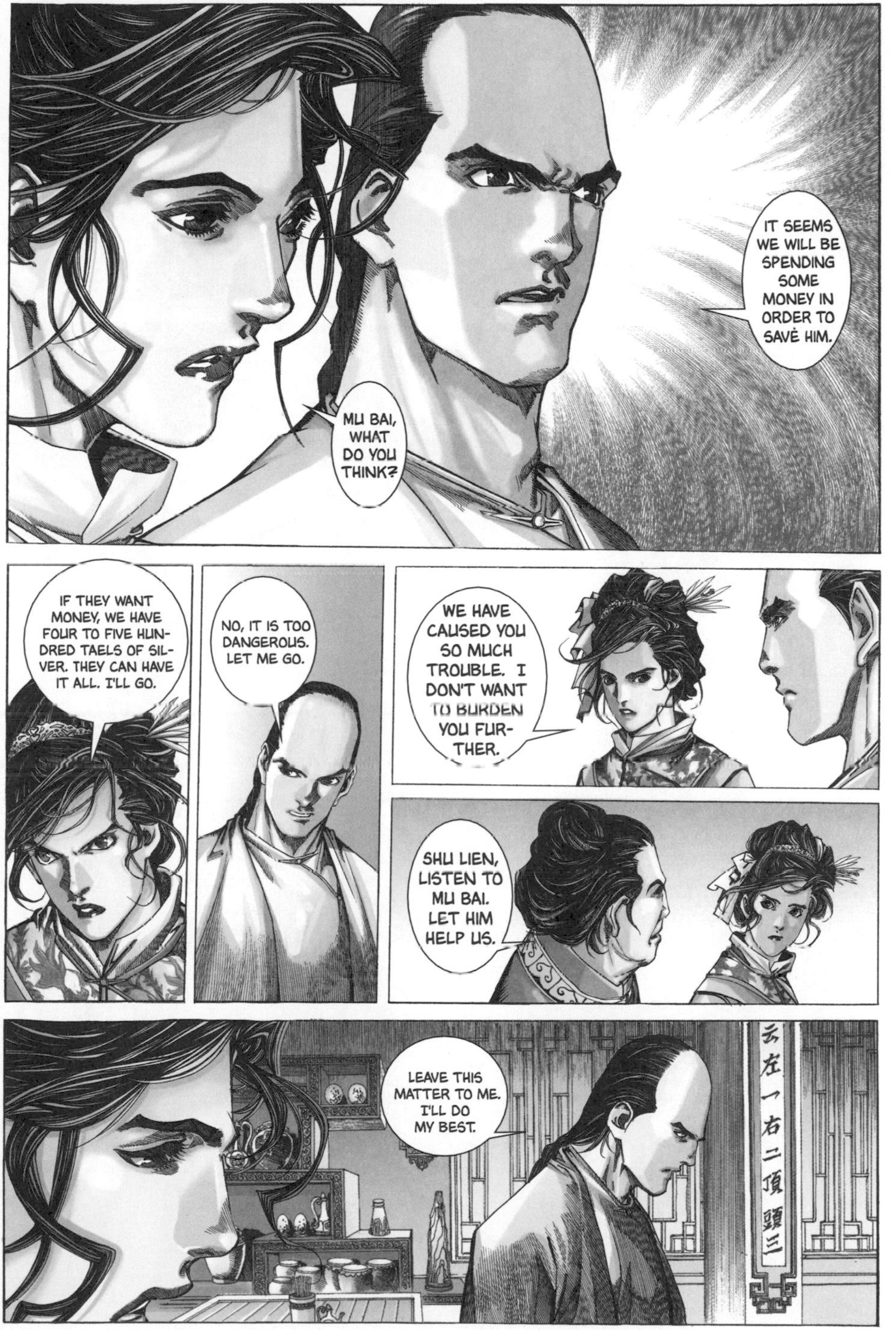
IT SEEMS WE WILL BE SPENDING SOME MONEY IN ORDER TO SAVE HIM.
MU BAI, WHAT DO YOU THINK?
IF THEY WANT MONEY, WE HAVE FOUR TO FIVE HUNDRED TAELS OF SILVER. THEY CAN HAVE IT ALL. I'LL GO.
NO, IT IS TOO DANGEROUS. LET ME GO.
WE HAVE CAUSED YOU SO MUCH TROUBLE. I DON'T WANT TO BURDEN YOU FURTHER.
SHU LIEN, LISTEN TO MU BAI. LET HIM HELP US.
LEAVE THIS MATTER TO ME. I'LL DO MY BEST.
云左一右二頂頭三

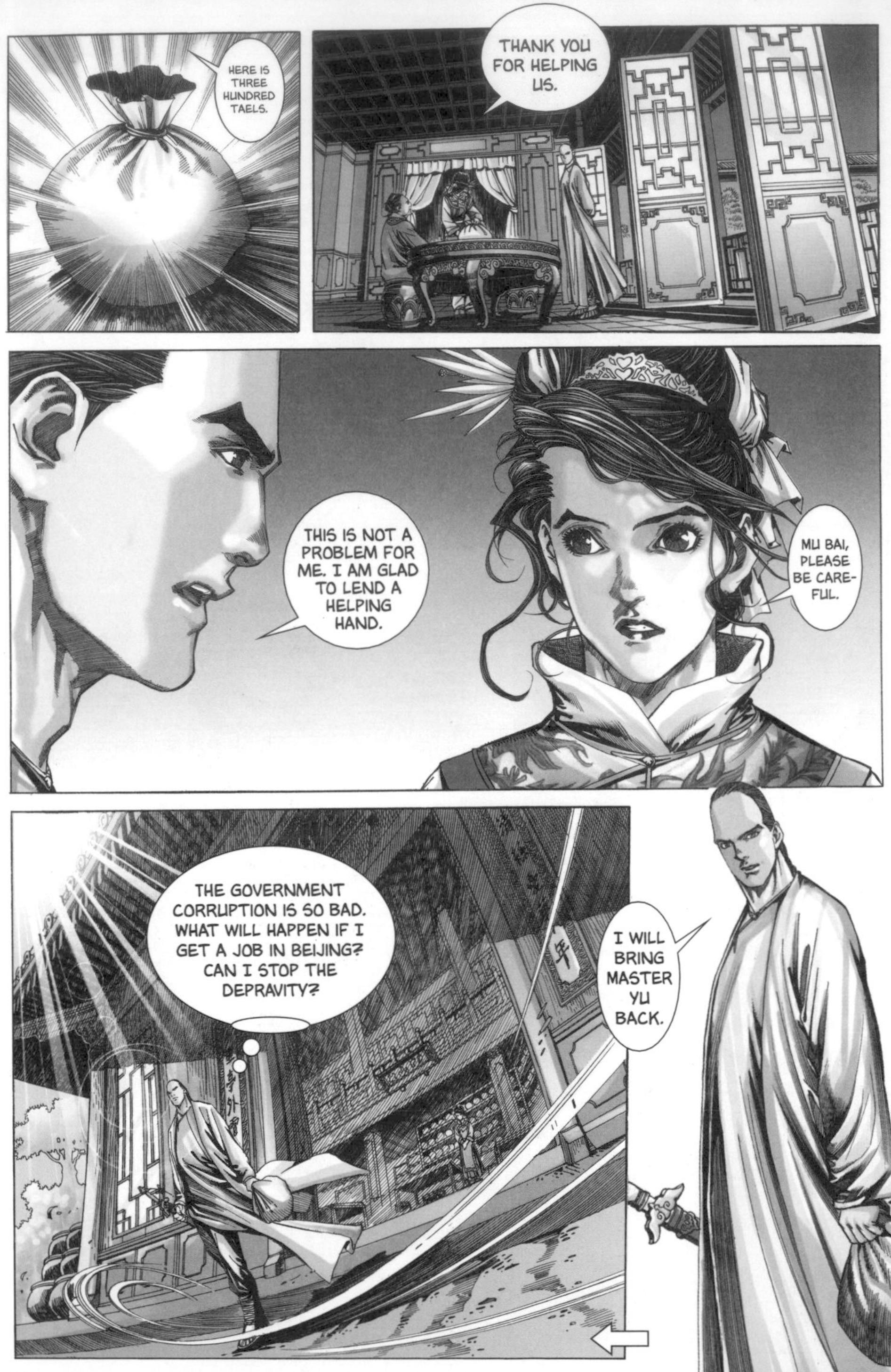
HERE IS THREE HUNDRED TAELS.
THANK YOU FOR HELPING US.
THIS IS NOT A PROBLEM FOR ME. I AM GLAD TO LEND A HELPING HAND.
MU BAI, PLEASE BE CARE-FUL.
THE GOVERNMENT CORRUPTION IS SO BAD. WHAT WILL HAPPEN IF I GET A JOB IN BEIJING? CAN I STOP THE DEPRAVITY?
I WILL BRING MASTER YU BACK.

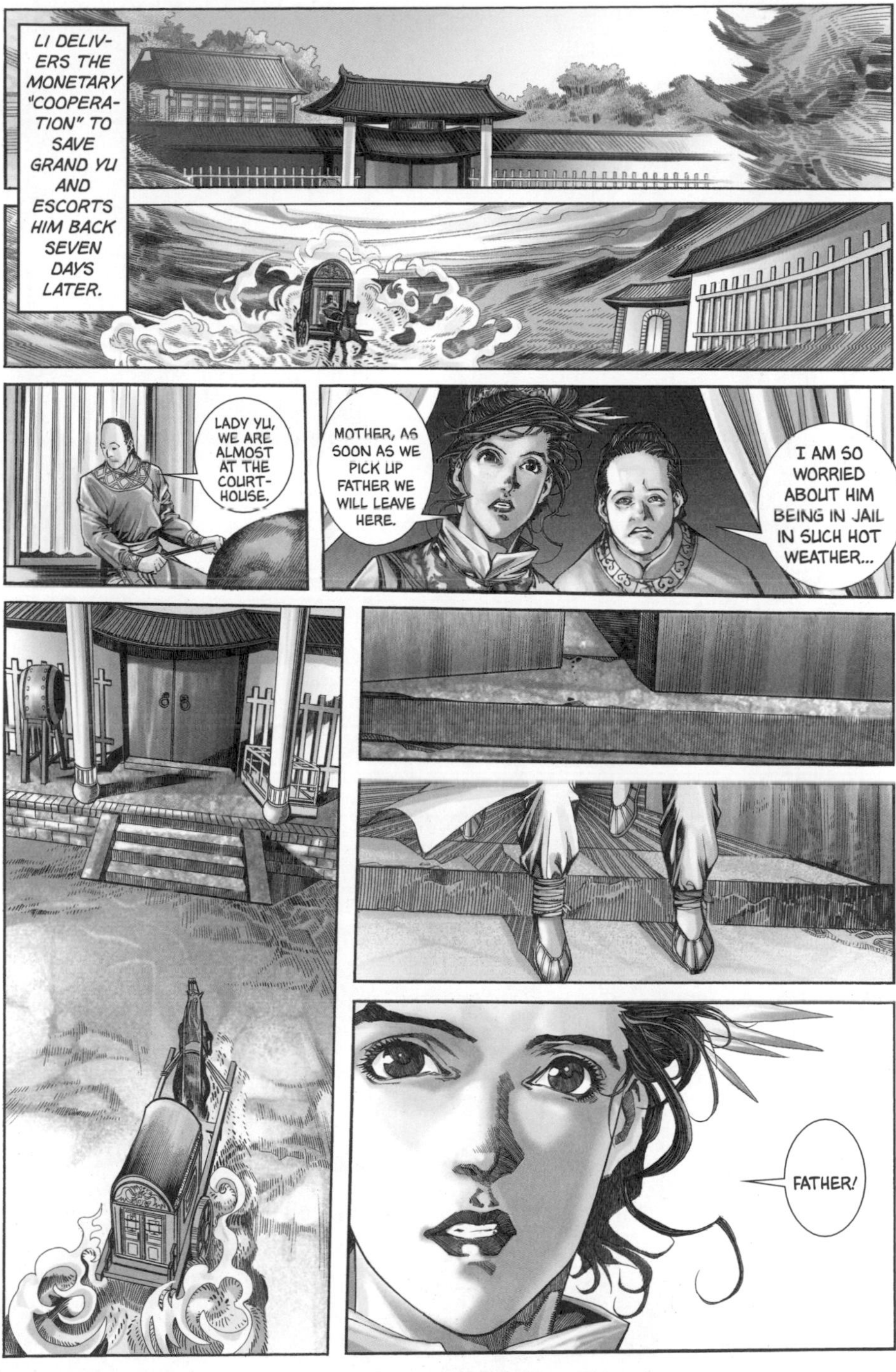
LI DELIVERS THE MONETARY "COOPERATION" TO SAVE GRAND YU AND ESCORTS HIM BACK SEVEN DAYS LATER.
LADY YU, WE ARE ALMOST AT THE COURTHOUSE.
MOTHER, AS SOON AS WE PICK UP FATHER WE WILL LEAVE HERE.
I AM SO WORRIED ABOUT HIM BEING IN JAIL IN SUCH HOT WEATHER...
FATHER!

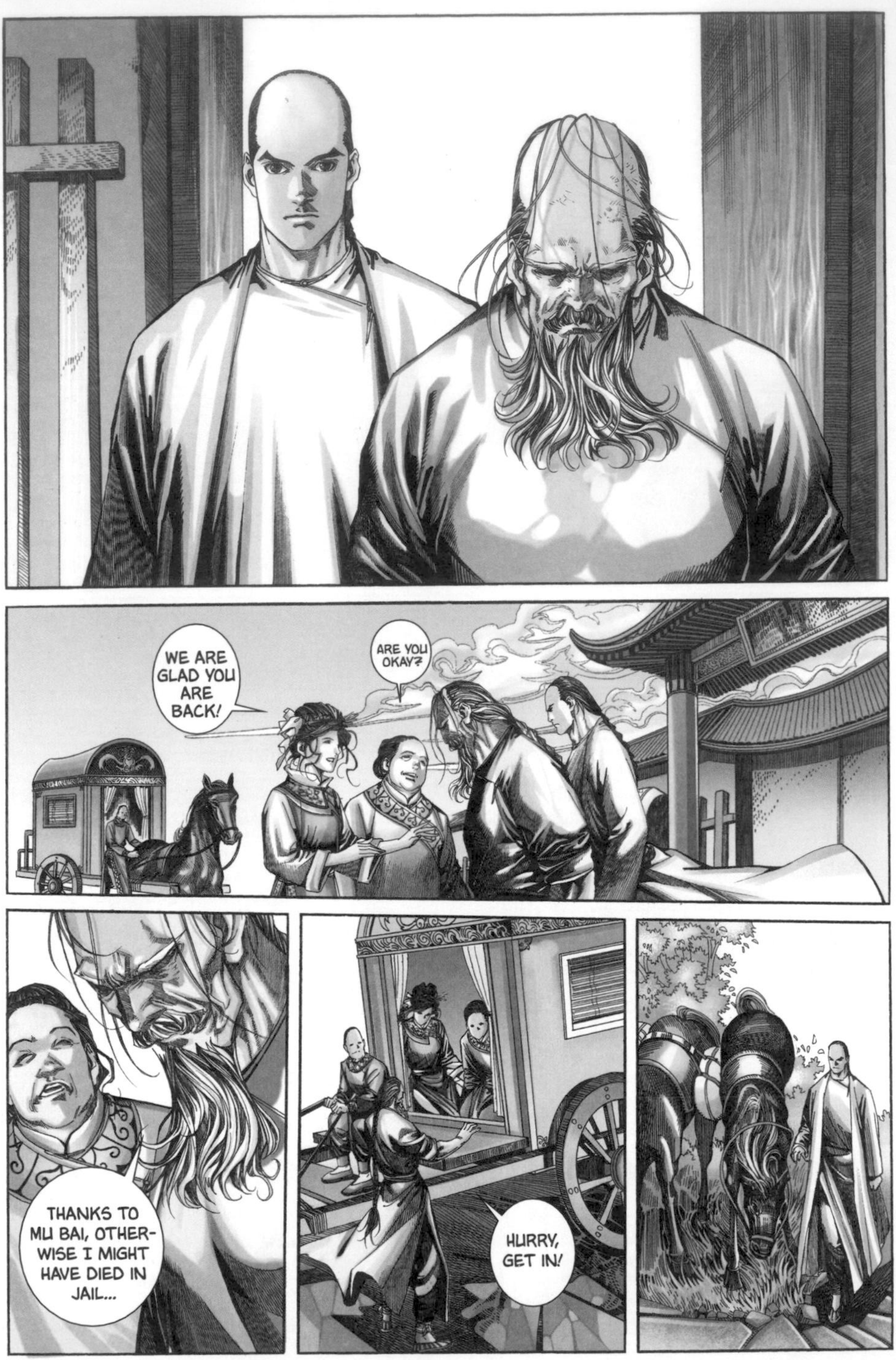
WE ARE GLAD YOU ARE BACK!
ARE YOU OKAY?
THANKS TO MU BAI, OTHER-WISE I MIGHT HAVE DIED IN JAIL...
HURRY, GET IN!

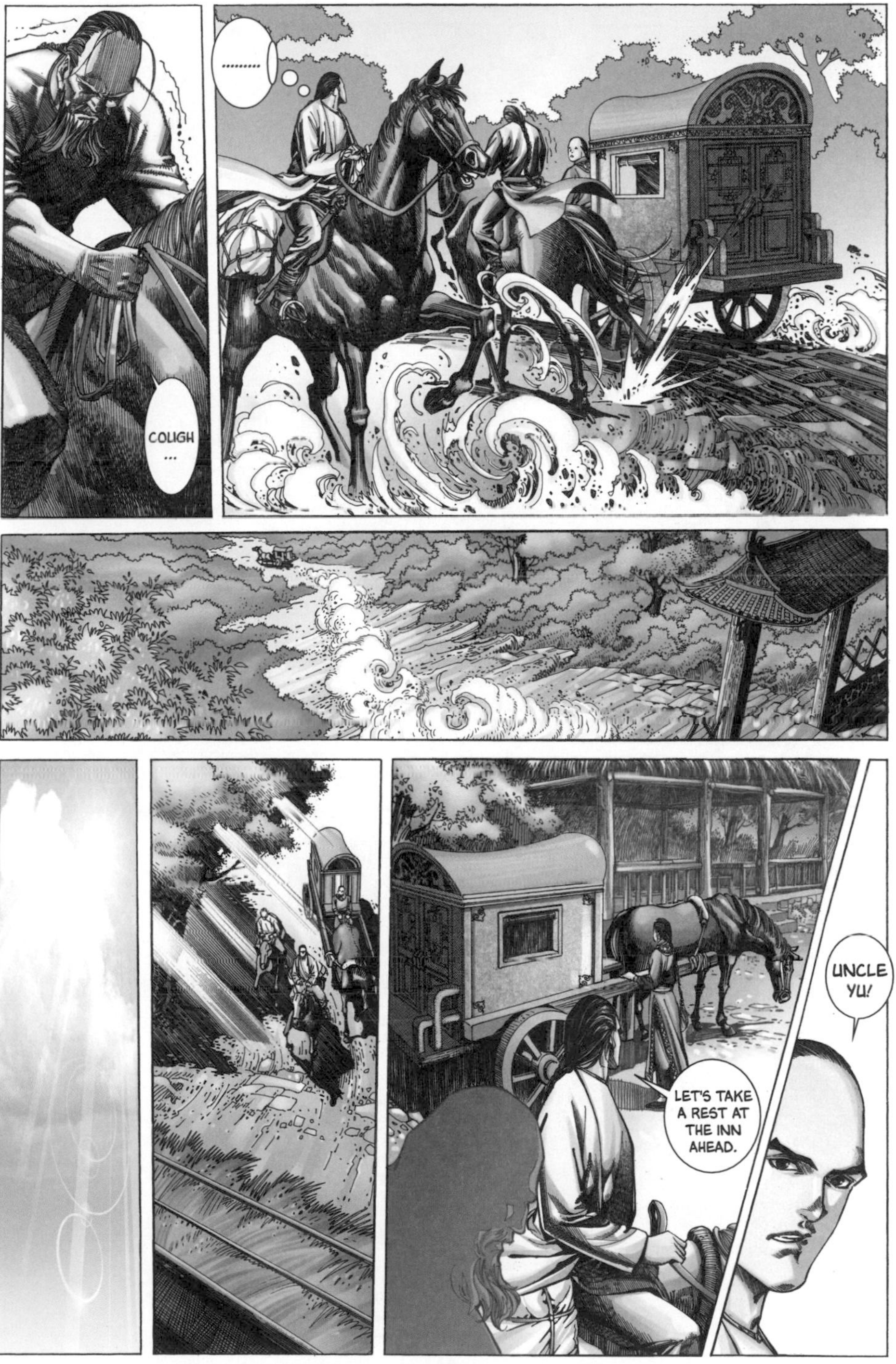
COUGH ...
....
UNCLE YU!
LET'S TAKE A REST AT THE INN AHEAD.

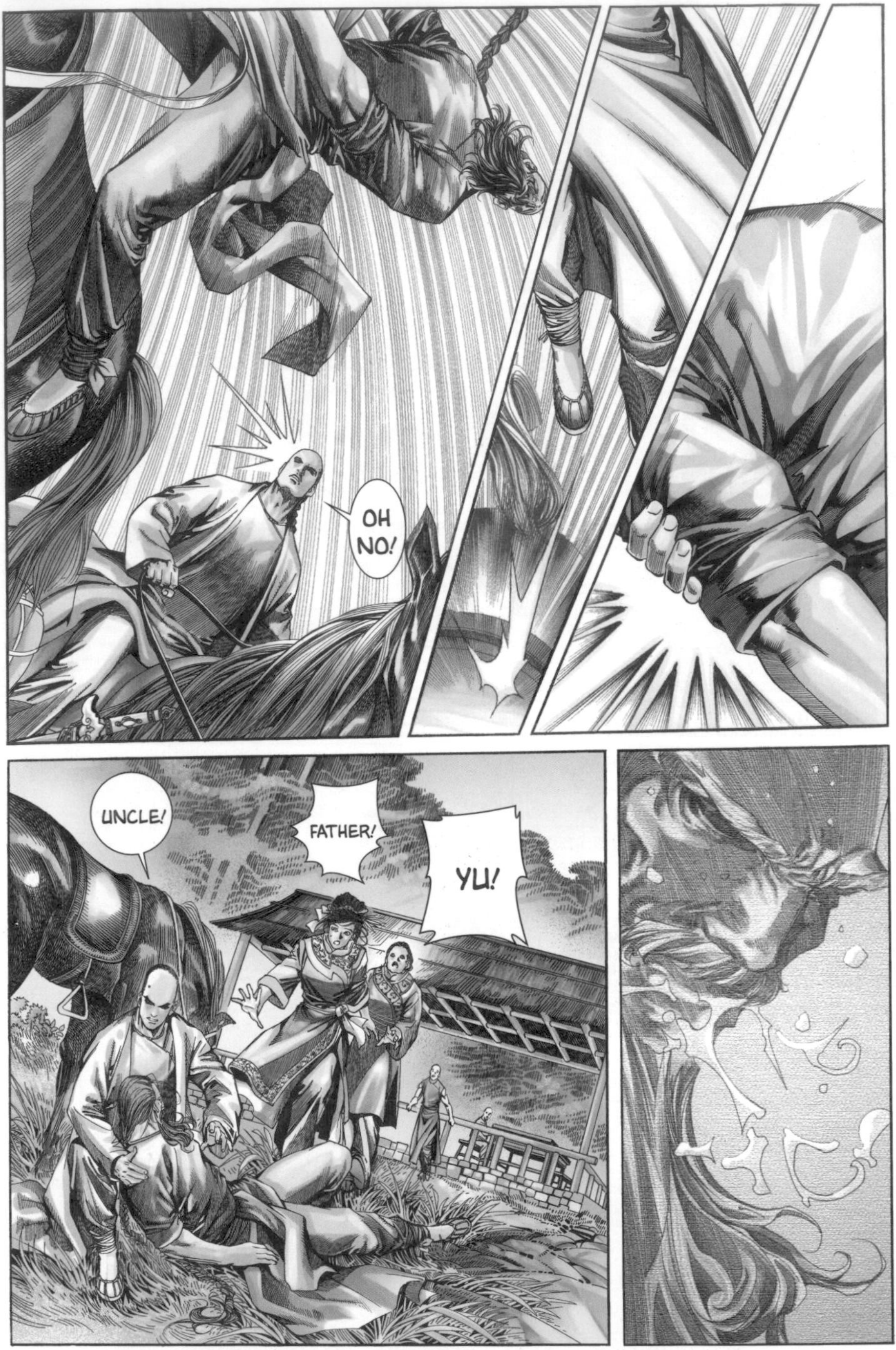
OH NO!
UNCLE!
FATHER!
YU!

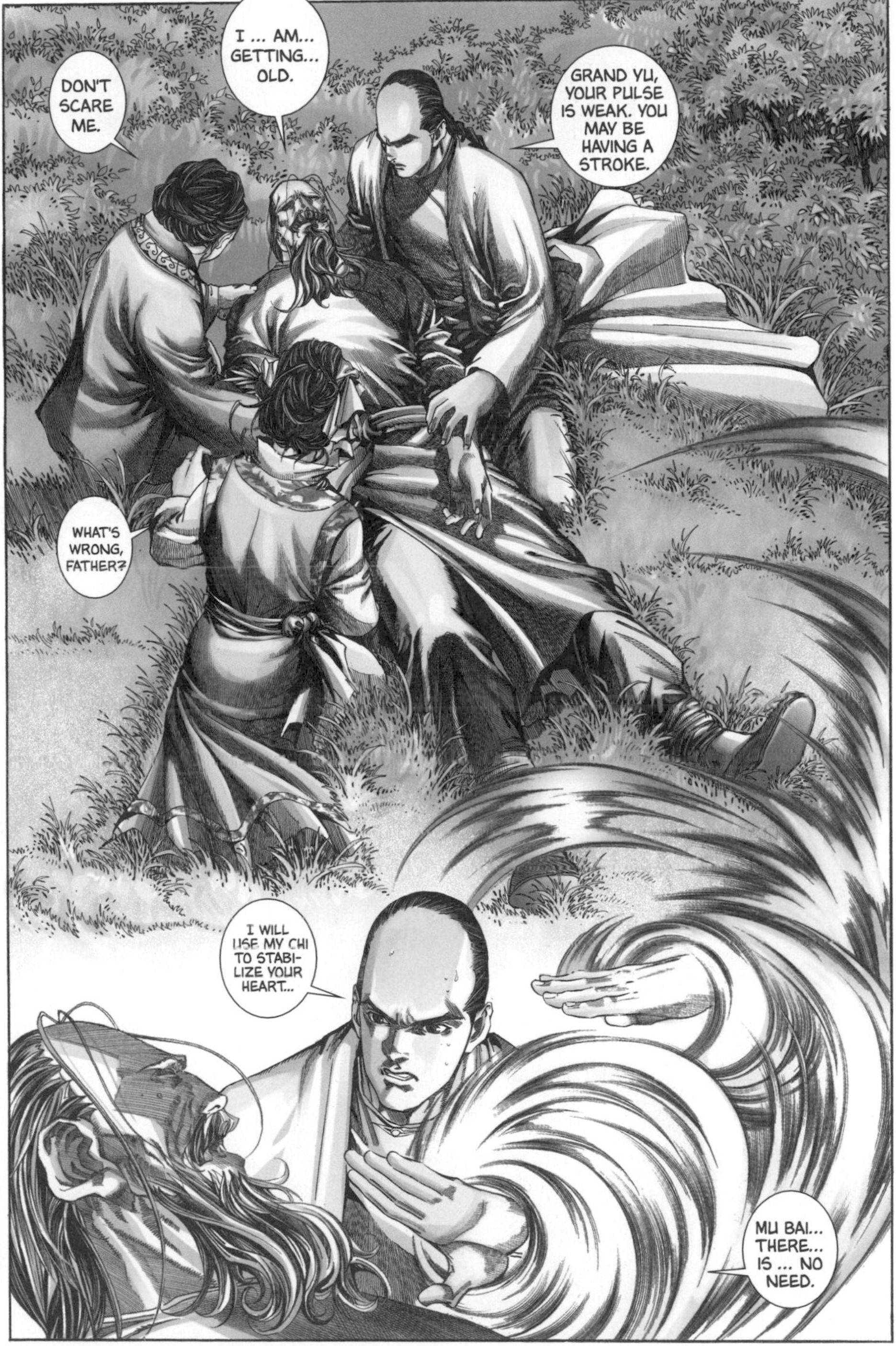
DON'T SCARE ME.
I ... AM... GETTING... OLD.
GRAND YU, YOUR PULSE IS WEAK. YOU MAY BE HAVING A STROKE.
WHAT'S WRONG, FATHER?
I WILL USE MY CHI TO STABILIZE YOUR HEART...
MU BAI... THERE... IS ... NO NEED.

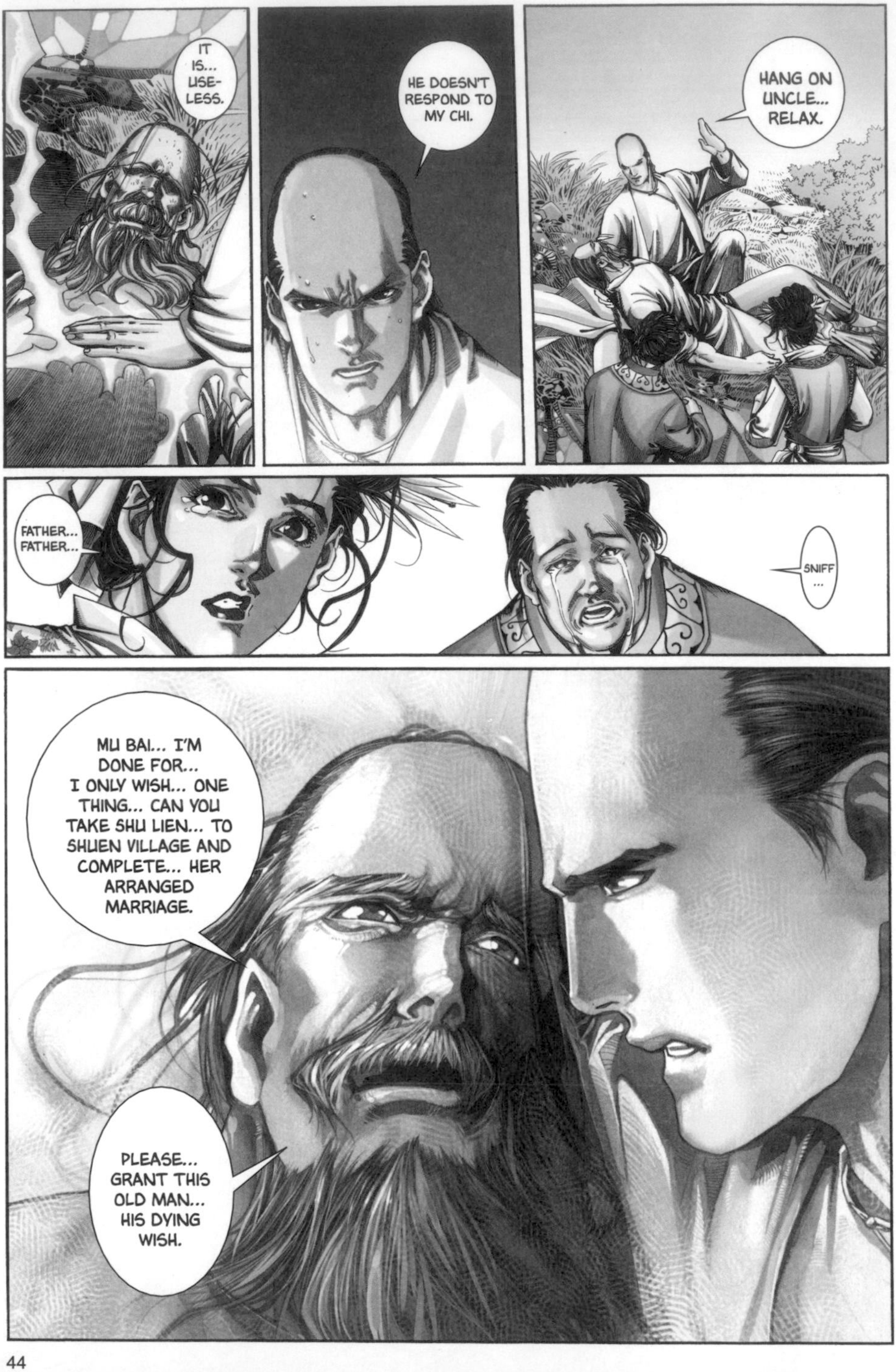
IT IS... USE-LESS.
HE DOESN'T RESPOND TO MY CHI.
HANG ON UNCLE... RELAX.
FATHER... FATHER...
SNIFF ...
MU BAI... I'M DONE FOR... I ONLY WISH... ONE THING... CAN YOU TAKE SHU LIEN... TO SHUEN VILLAGE AND COMPLETE... HER ARRANGED MARRIAGE.
PLEASE... GRANT THIS OLD MAN... HIS DYING WISH.

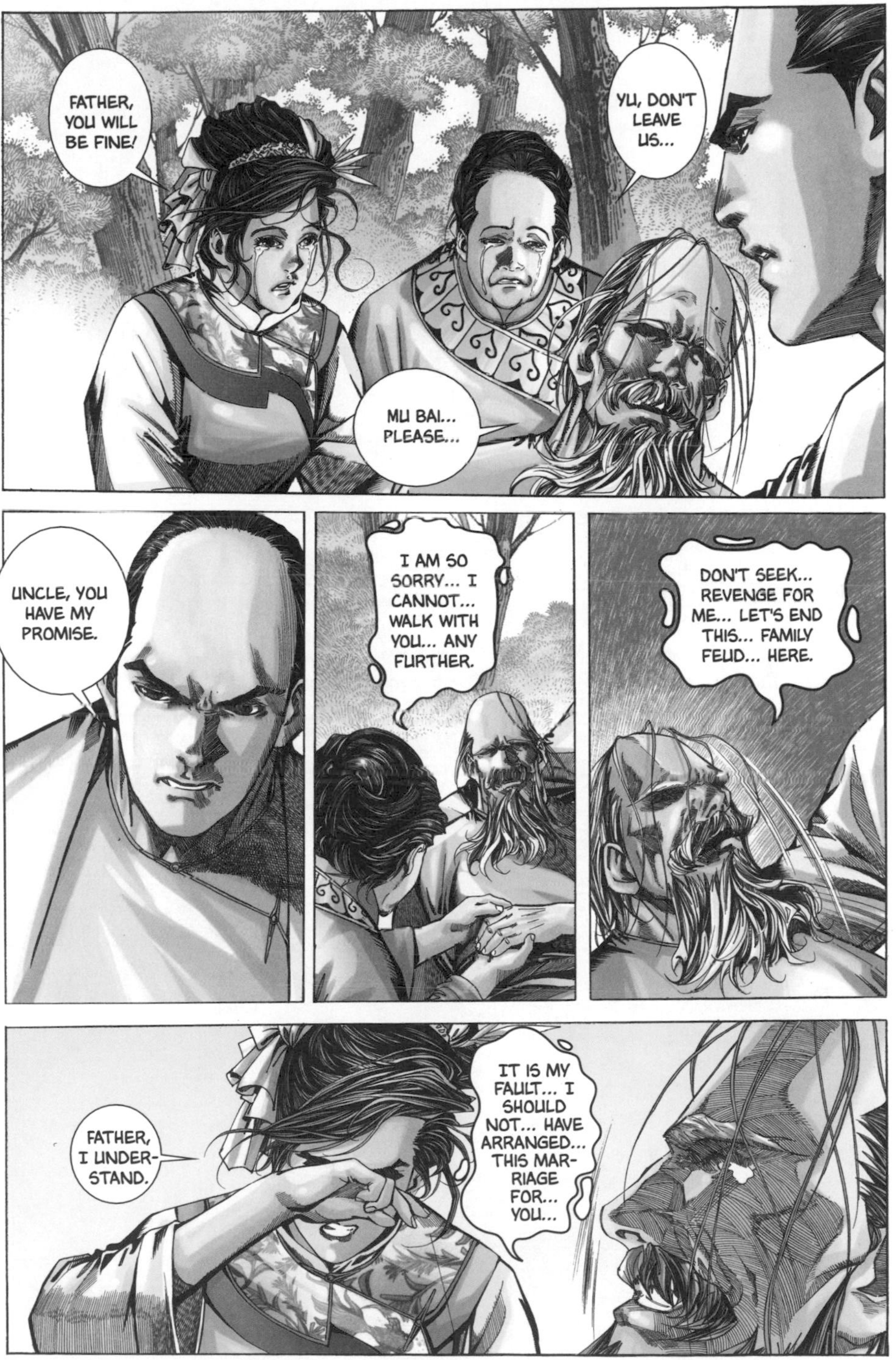

FATHER, YOU WILL BE FINE!
YU, DON'T LEAVE US...
MU BAI... PLEASE...
UNCLE, YOU HAVE MY PROMISE.
I AM SO SORRY... I CANNOT... WALK WITH YOU... ANY FURTHER.
DON'T SEEK... REVENGE FOR ME... LET'S END THIS... FAMILY FEUD... HERE.
IT IS MY FAULT... I SHOULD NOT... HAVE ARRANGED... THIS MAR-RIAGE FOR... YOU...
FATHER, I UNDER-STAND.

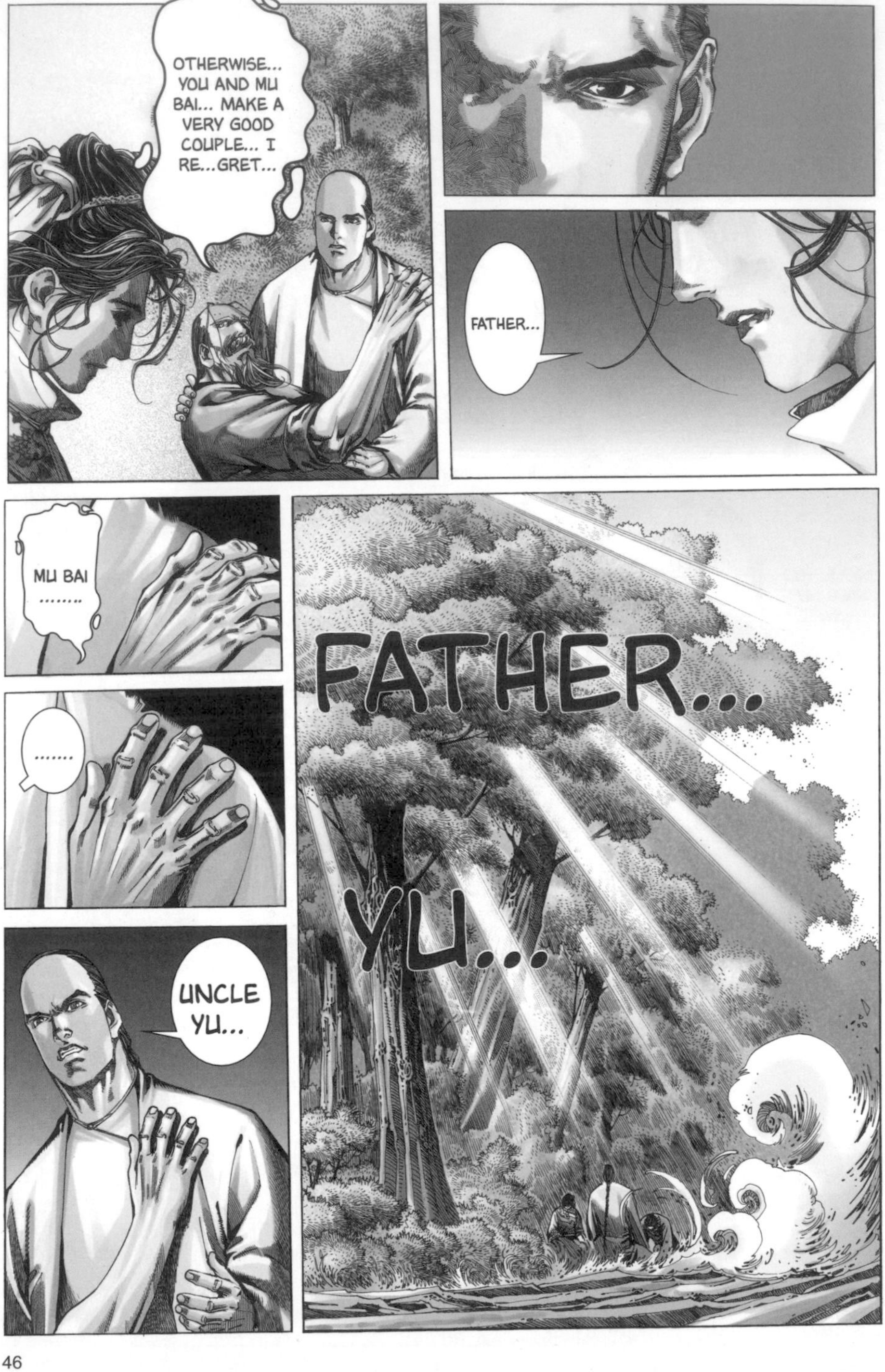
OTHERWISE... YOU AND MU BAI... MAKE A VERY GOOD COUPLE... I RE...GRET...
FATHER...
MU BAI ....
....
UNCLE YU...
FATHER...
YU...

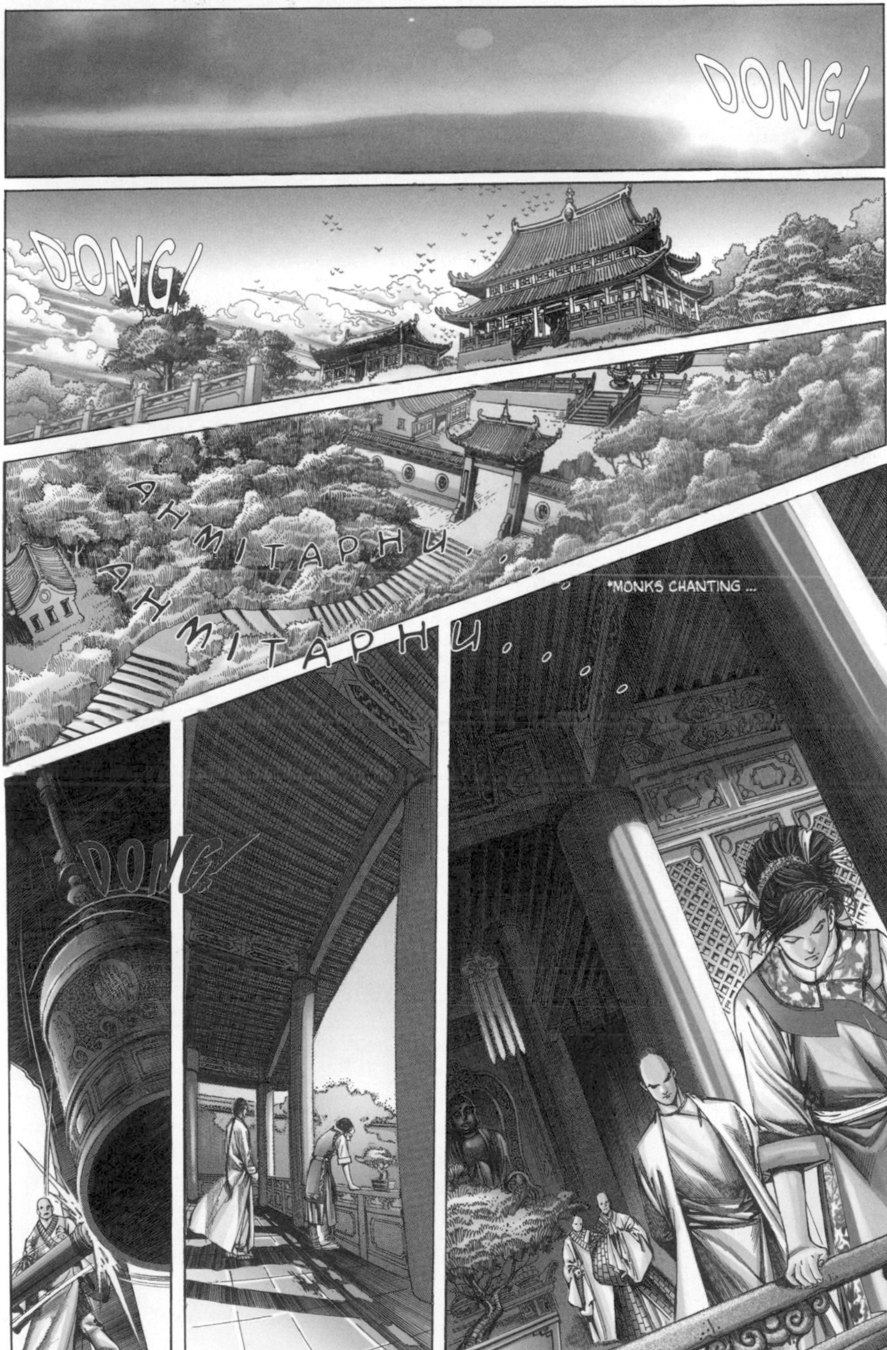
DONG!
DONG!
AHMITAPHU...
AHMITAPHU.....
*MONKS CHANTING ...
DONG

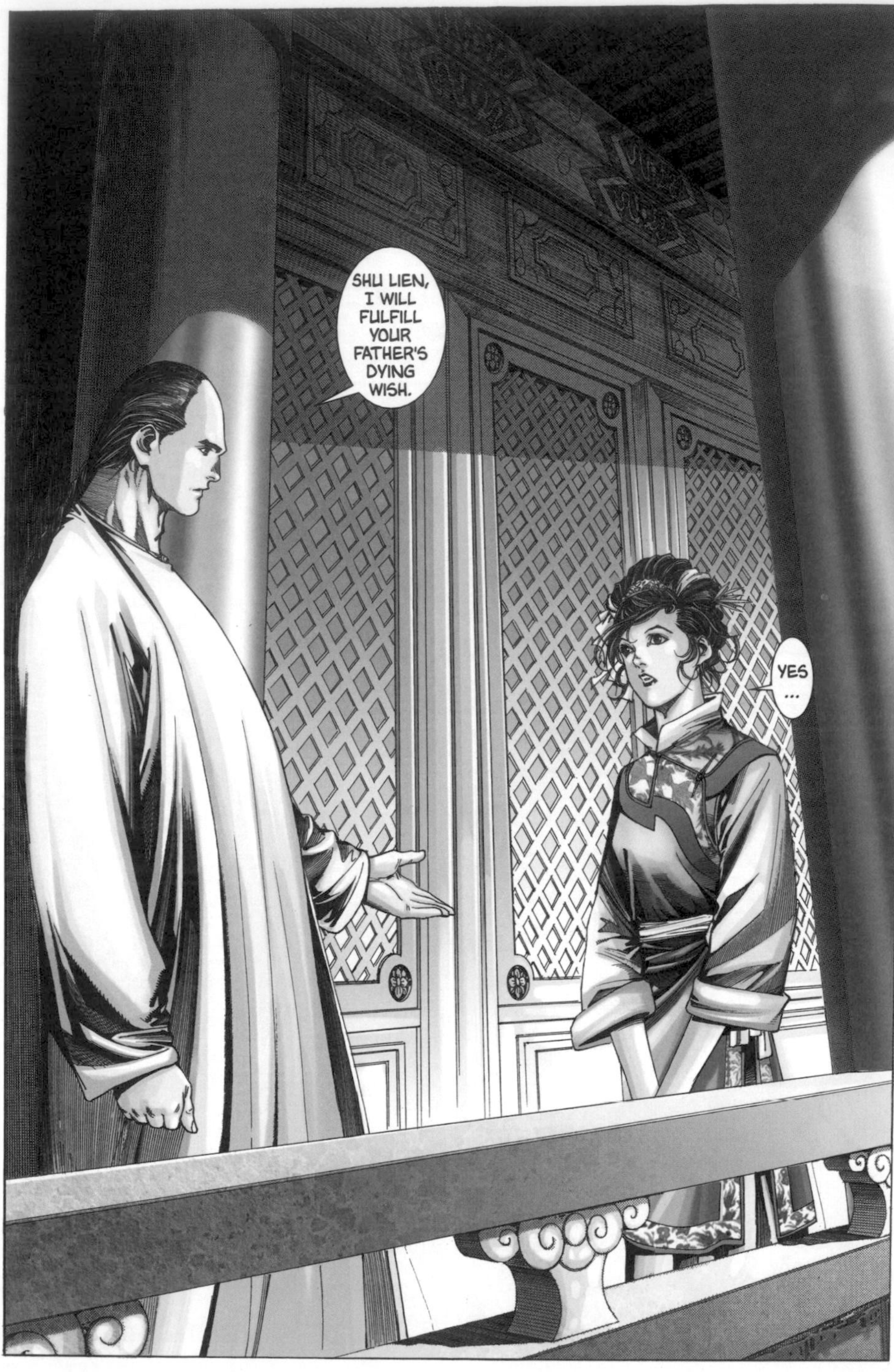
SHU LIEN, I WILL FULFILL YOUR FATHER'S DYING WISH.
YES ...

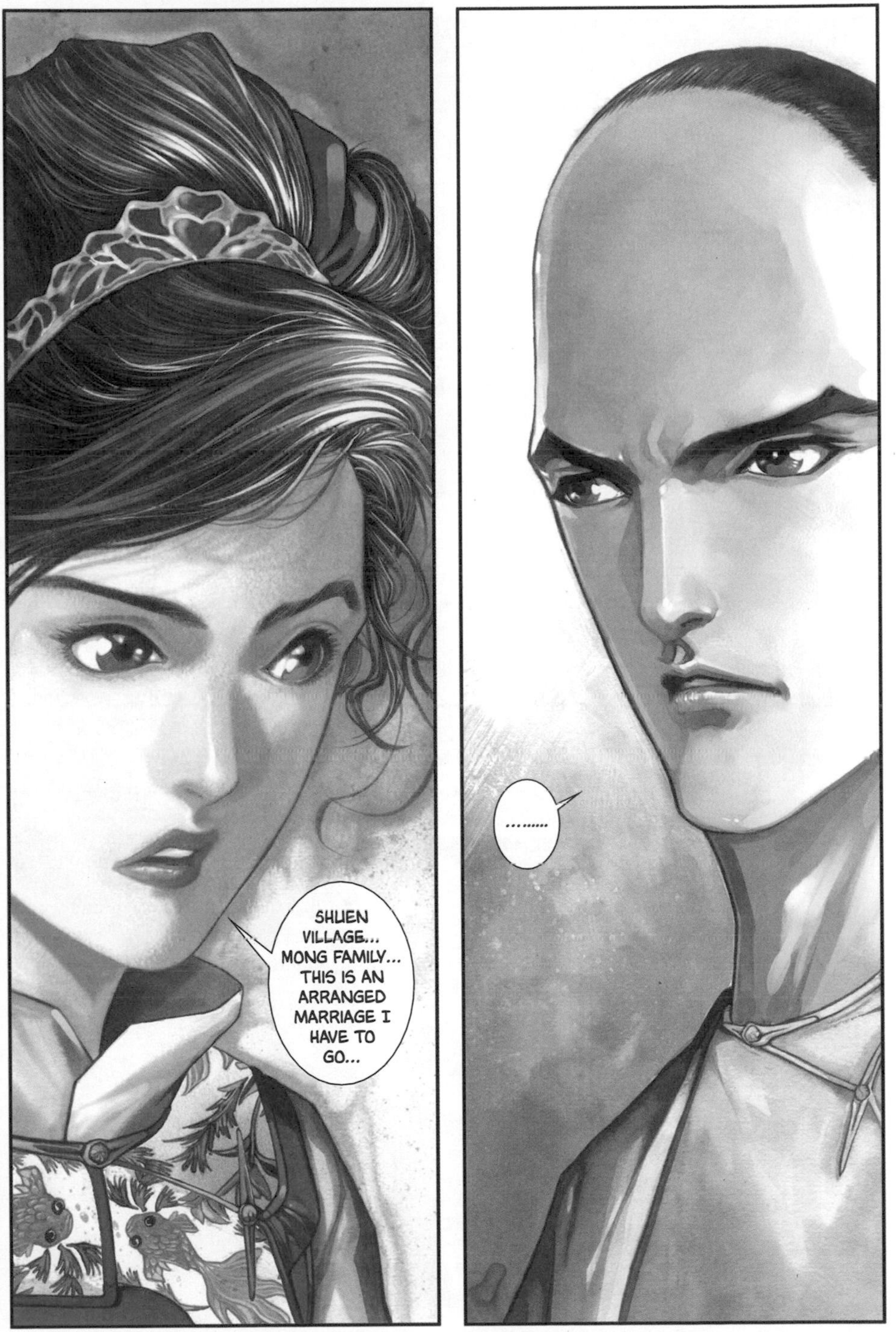
SHUEN VILLAGE... MONG FAMILY... THIS IS AN ARRANGED MARRIAGE I HAVE TO GO...
....

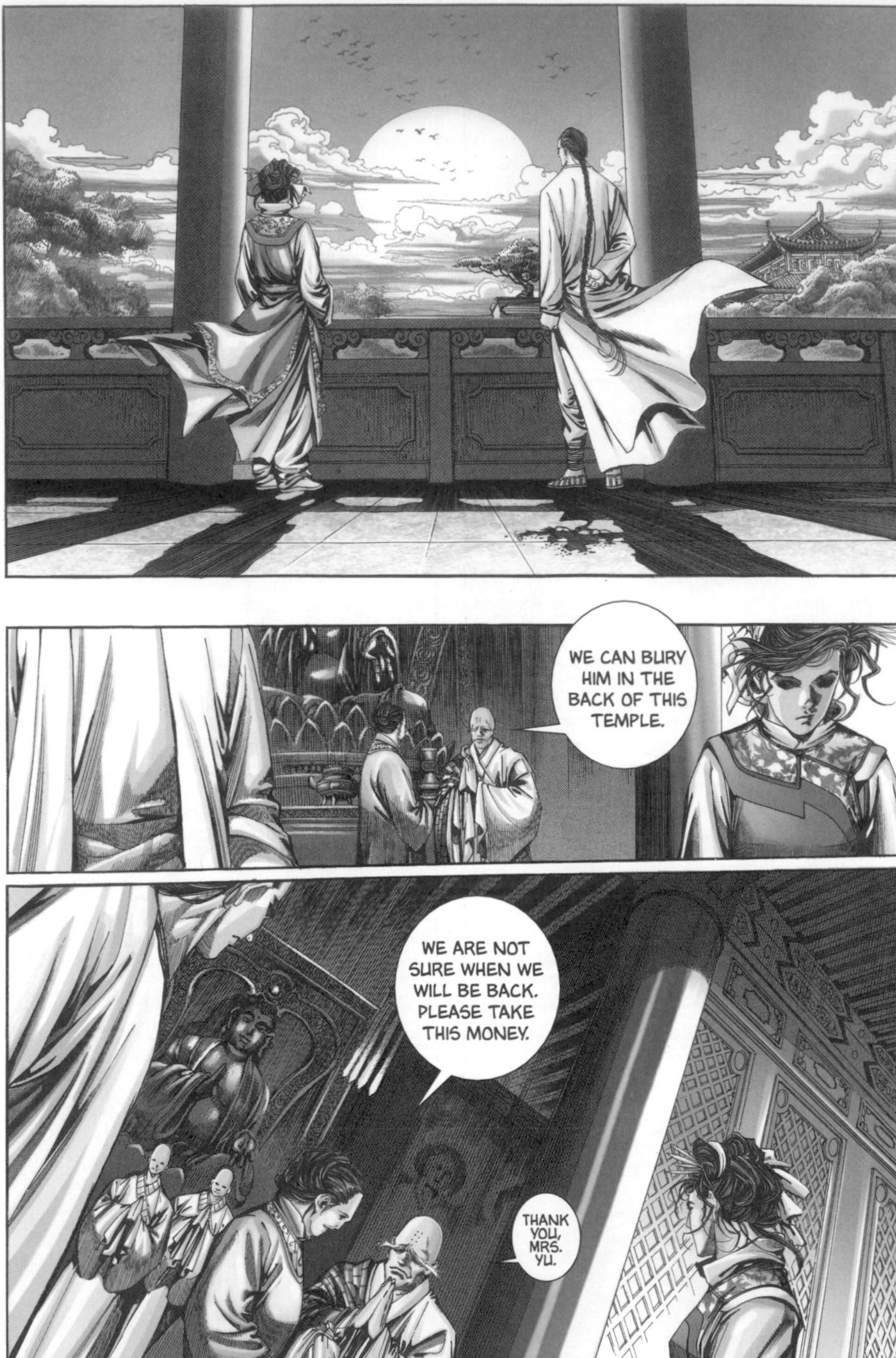
WE CAN BURY HIM IN THE BACK OF THIS TEMPLE.
WE ARE NOT SURE WHEN WE WILL BE BACK. PLEASE TAKE THIS MONEY.
THANK YOU, MRS. YU.

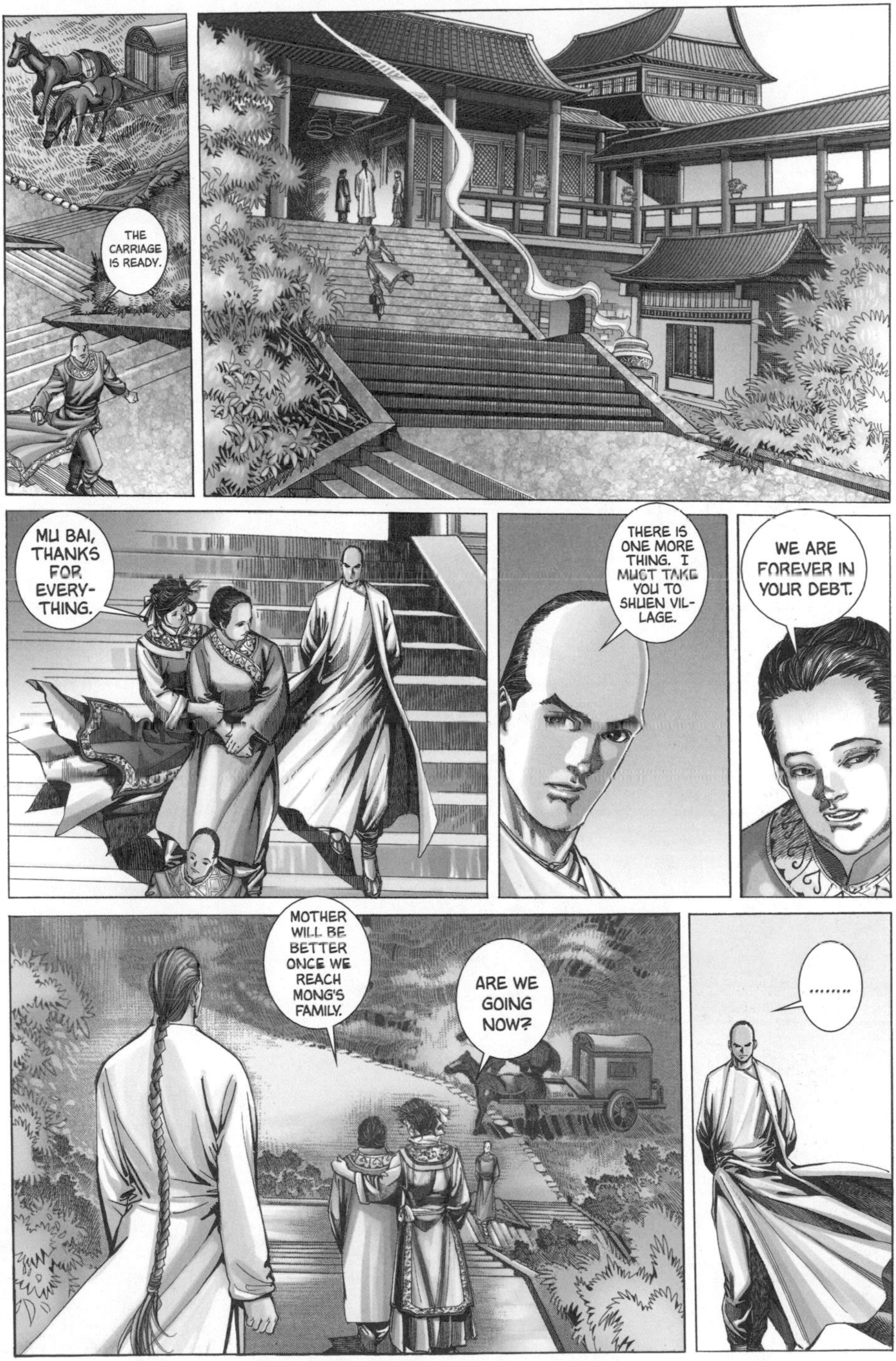

THE CARRIAGE IS READY.
MU BAI, THANKS FOR EVERY-THING.
THERE IS ONE MORE THING. I MUST TAKE YOU TO SHUEN VIL-LAGE.
WE ARE FOREVER IN YOUR DEBT.
MOTHER WILL BE BETTER ONCE WE REACH MONG'S FAMILY.
ARE WE GOING NOW?
....

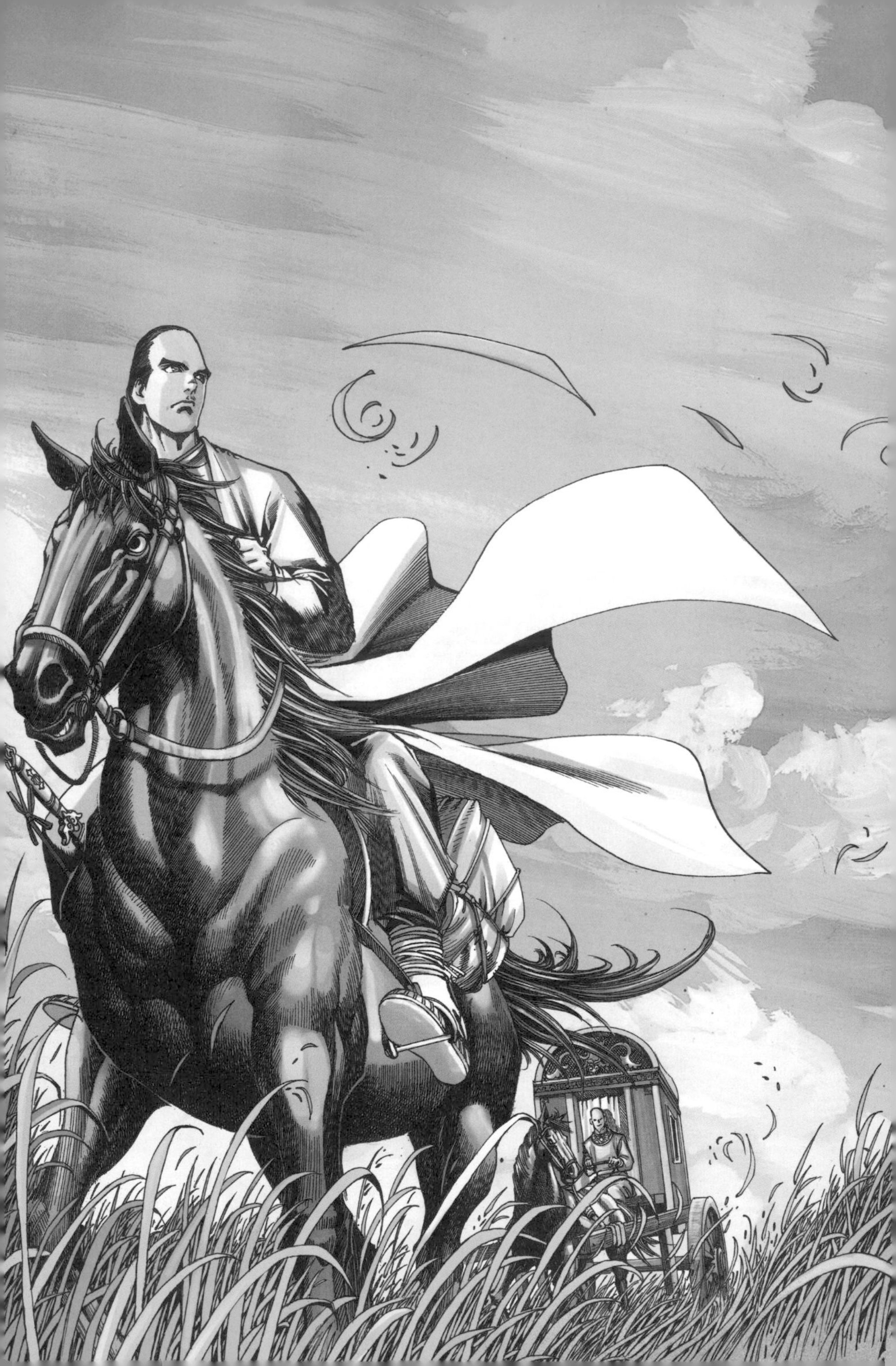

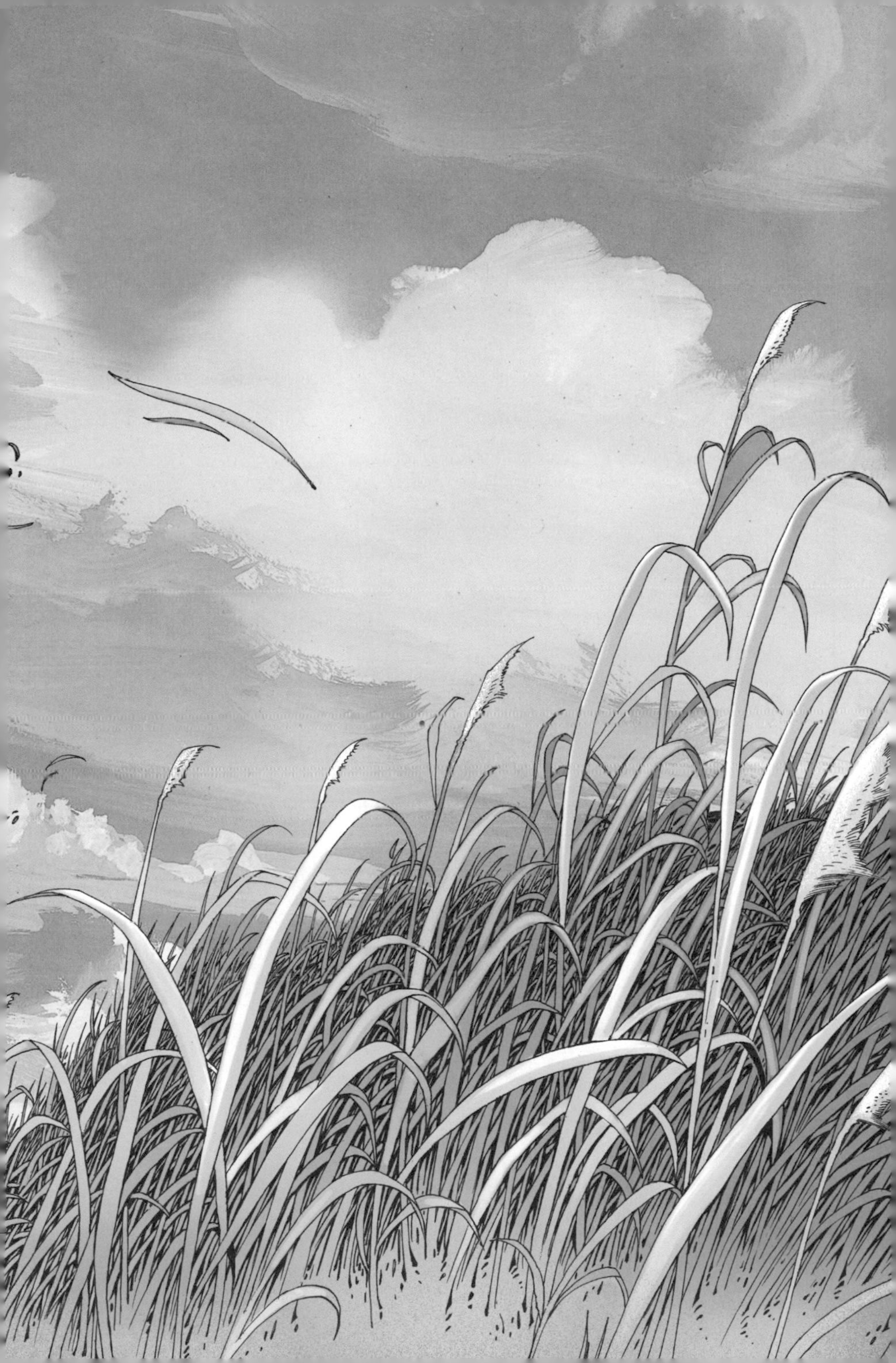

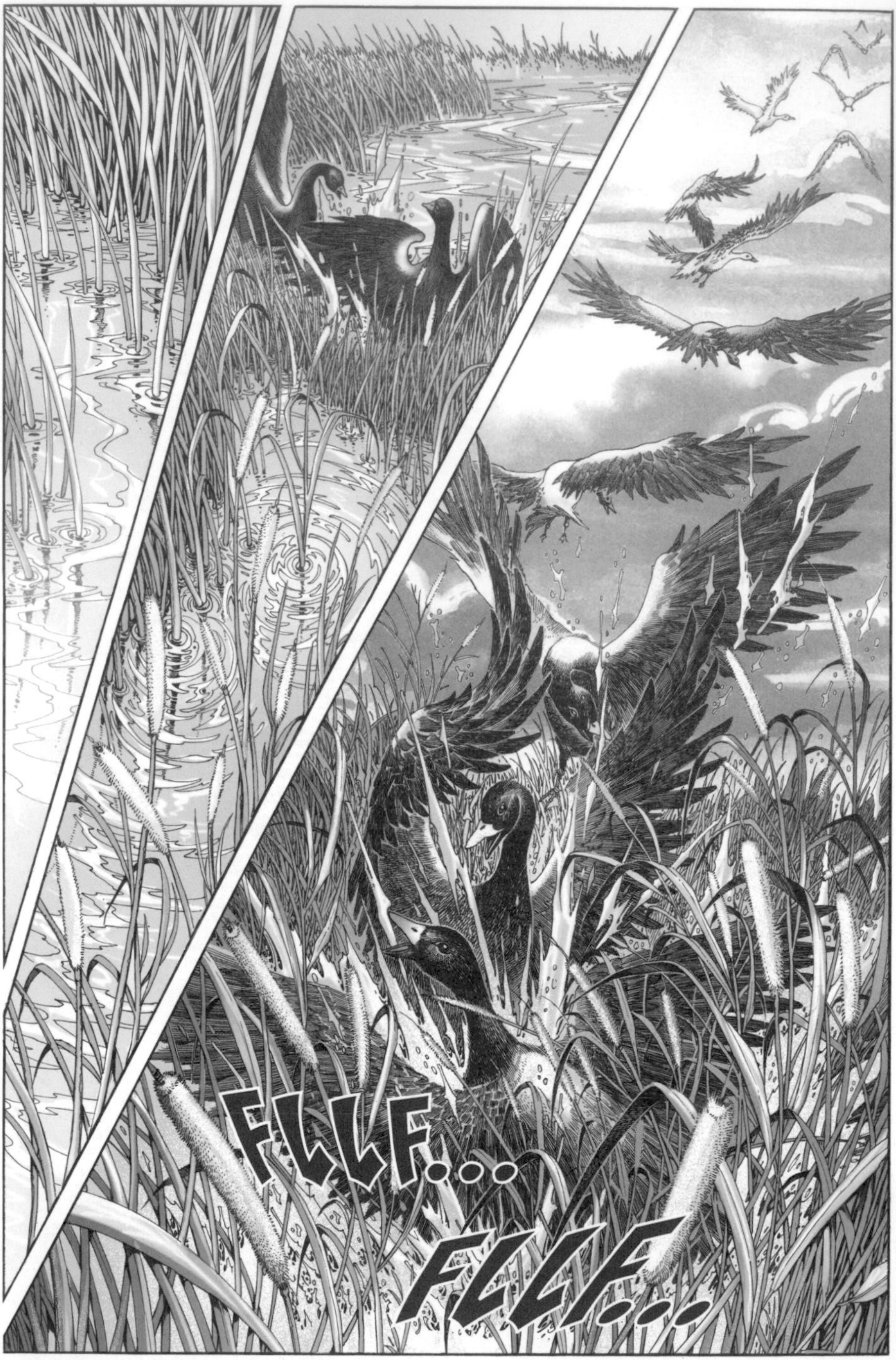
FLLF...
FLLF...

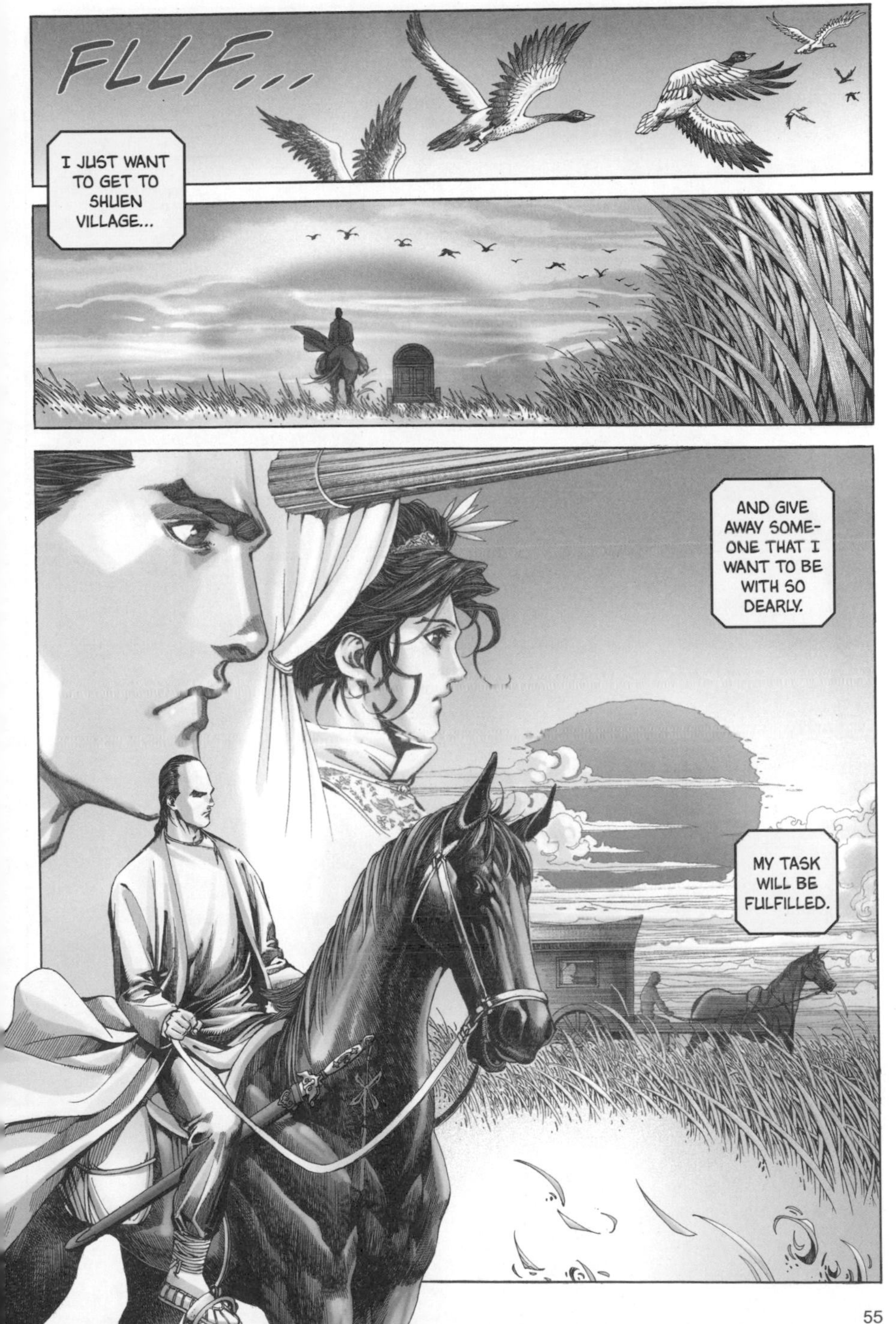
FLLF...
I JUST WANT TO GET TO SHUEN VILLAGE...
AND GIVE AWAY SOME-ONE THAT I WANT TO BE WITH SO DEARLY.
MY TASK WILL BE FULFILLED.

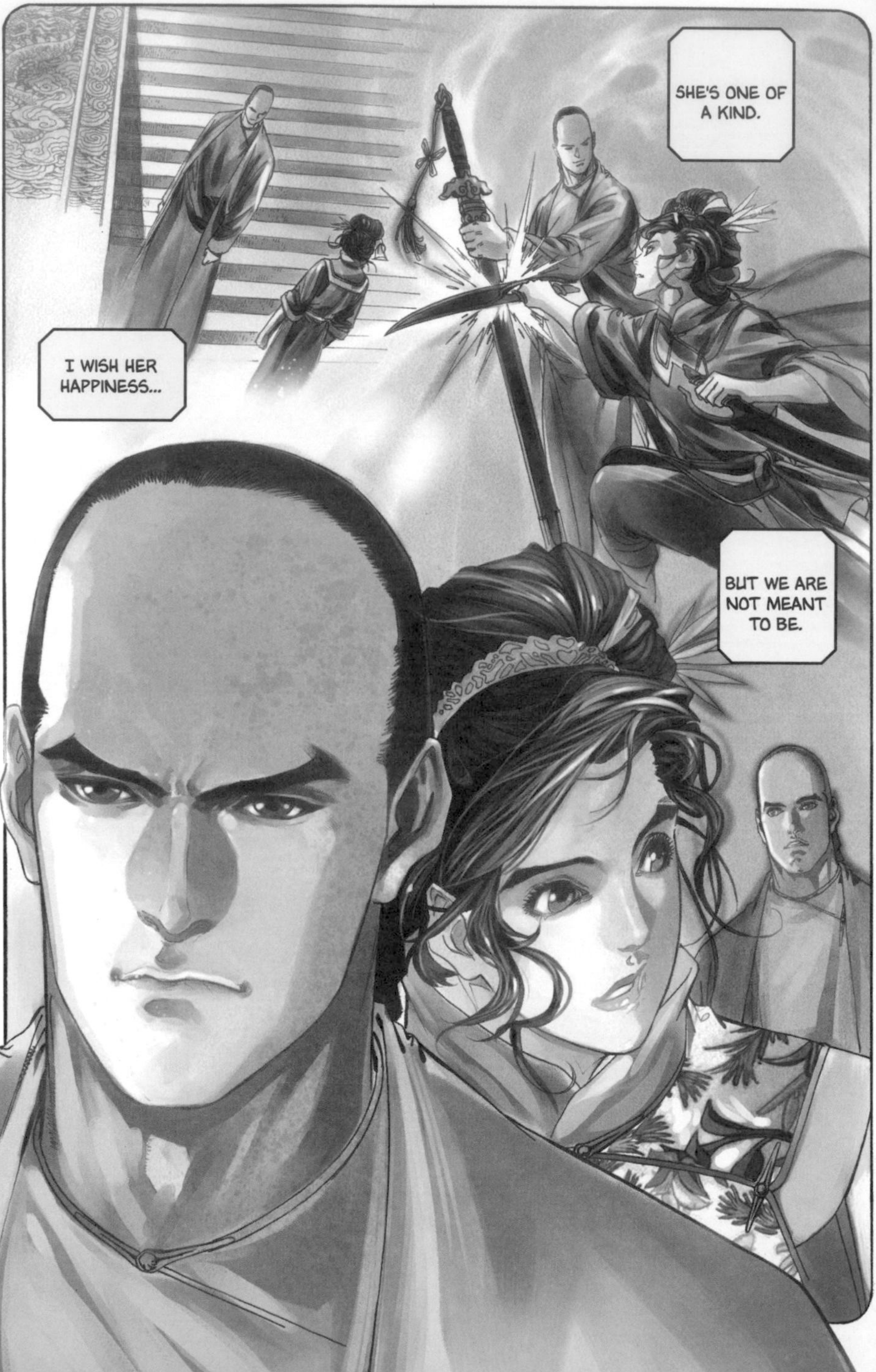
SHE'S ONE OF A KIND.
I WISH HER HAPPINESS...
BUT WE ARE NOT MEANT TO BE.

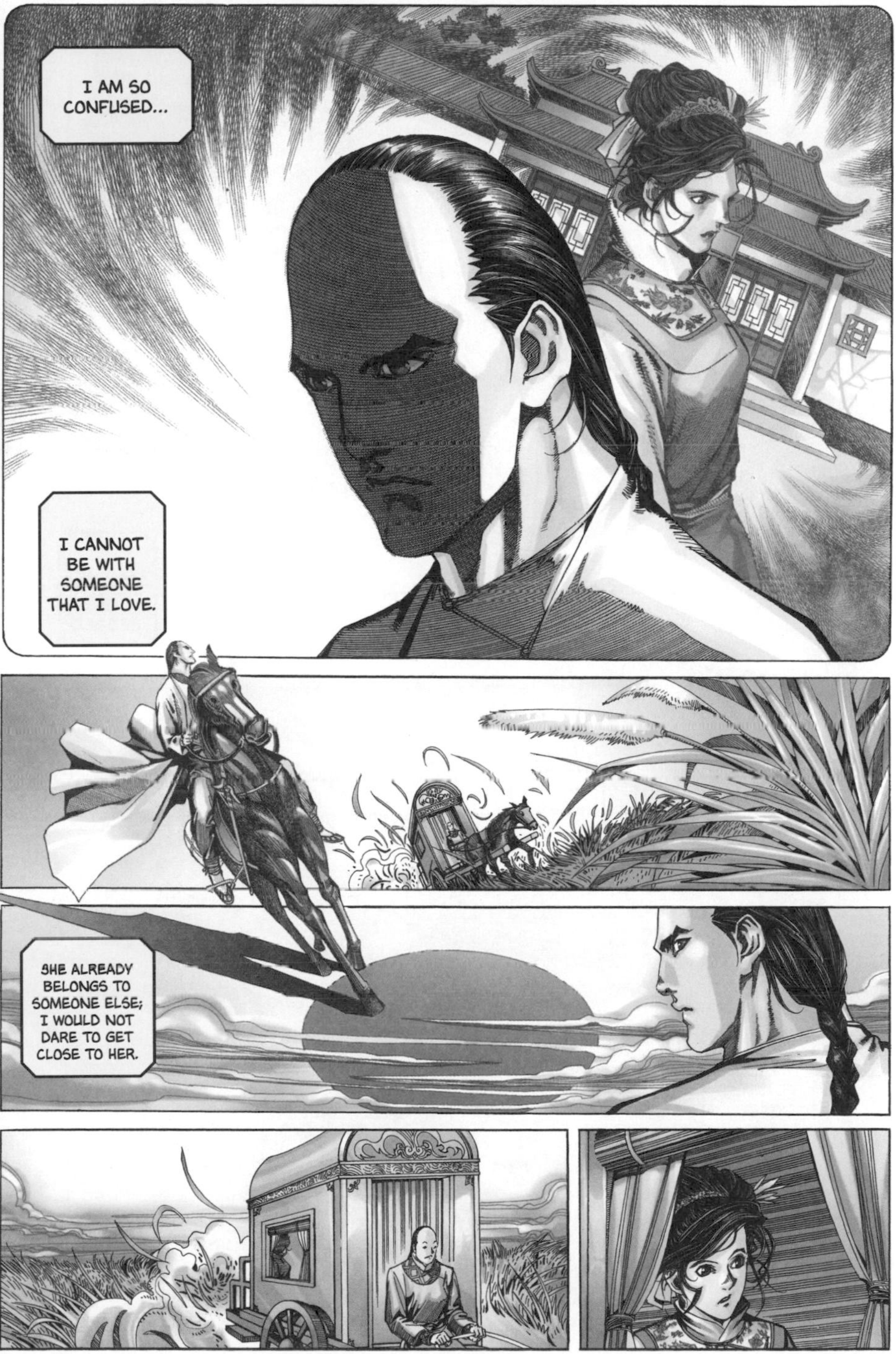
I AM SO CONFUSED...
I CANNOT BE WITH SOMEONE THAT I LOVE.
SHE ALREADY BELONGS TO SOMEONE ELSE; I WOULD NOT DARE TO GET CLOSE TO HER.

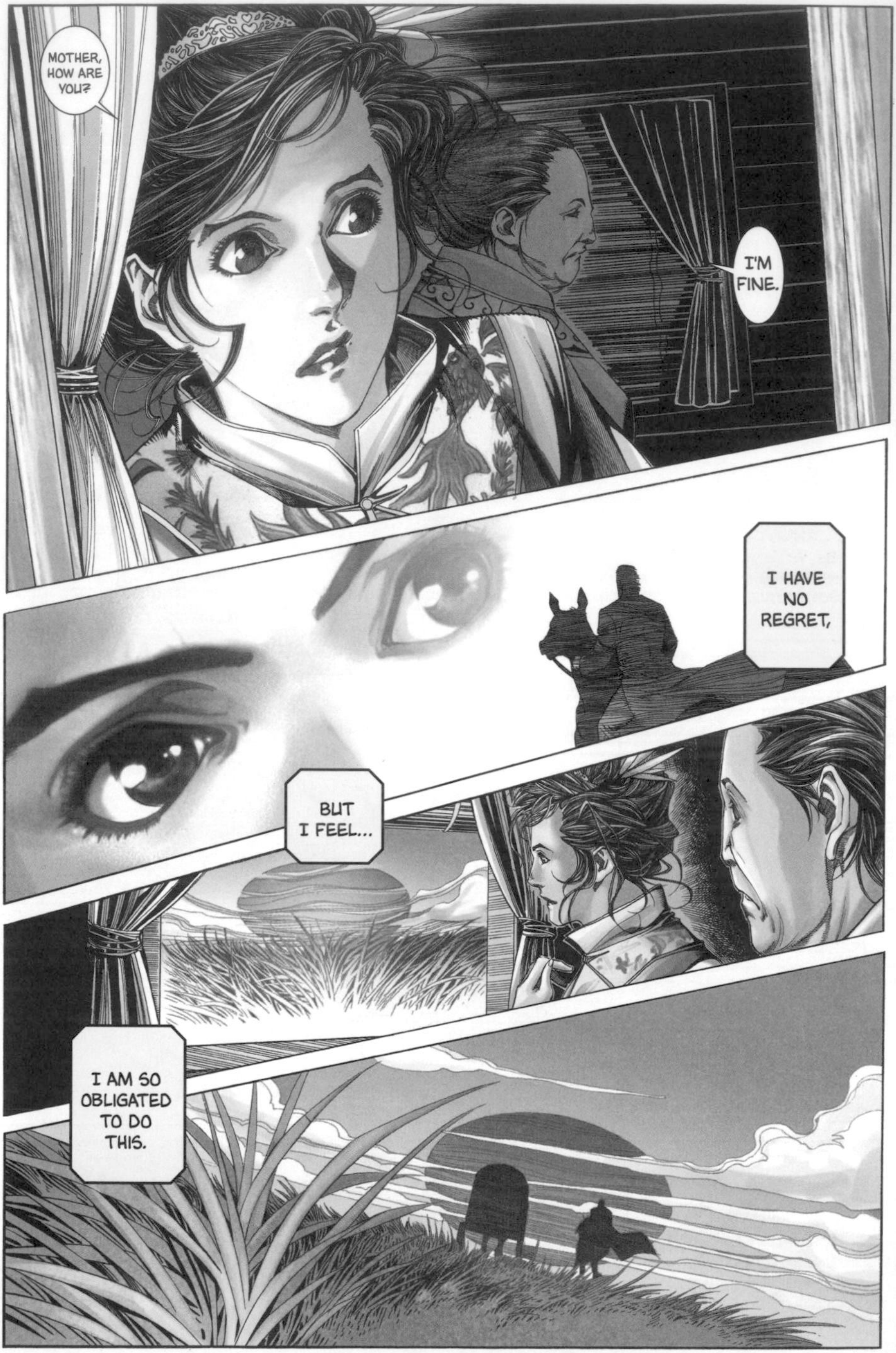
MOTHER, HOW ARE YOU?
I'M FINE.
I HAVE NO REGRET,
BUT I FEEL...
I AM SO OBLIGATED TO DO THIS.

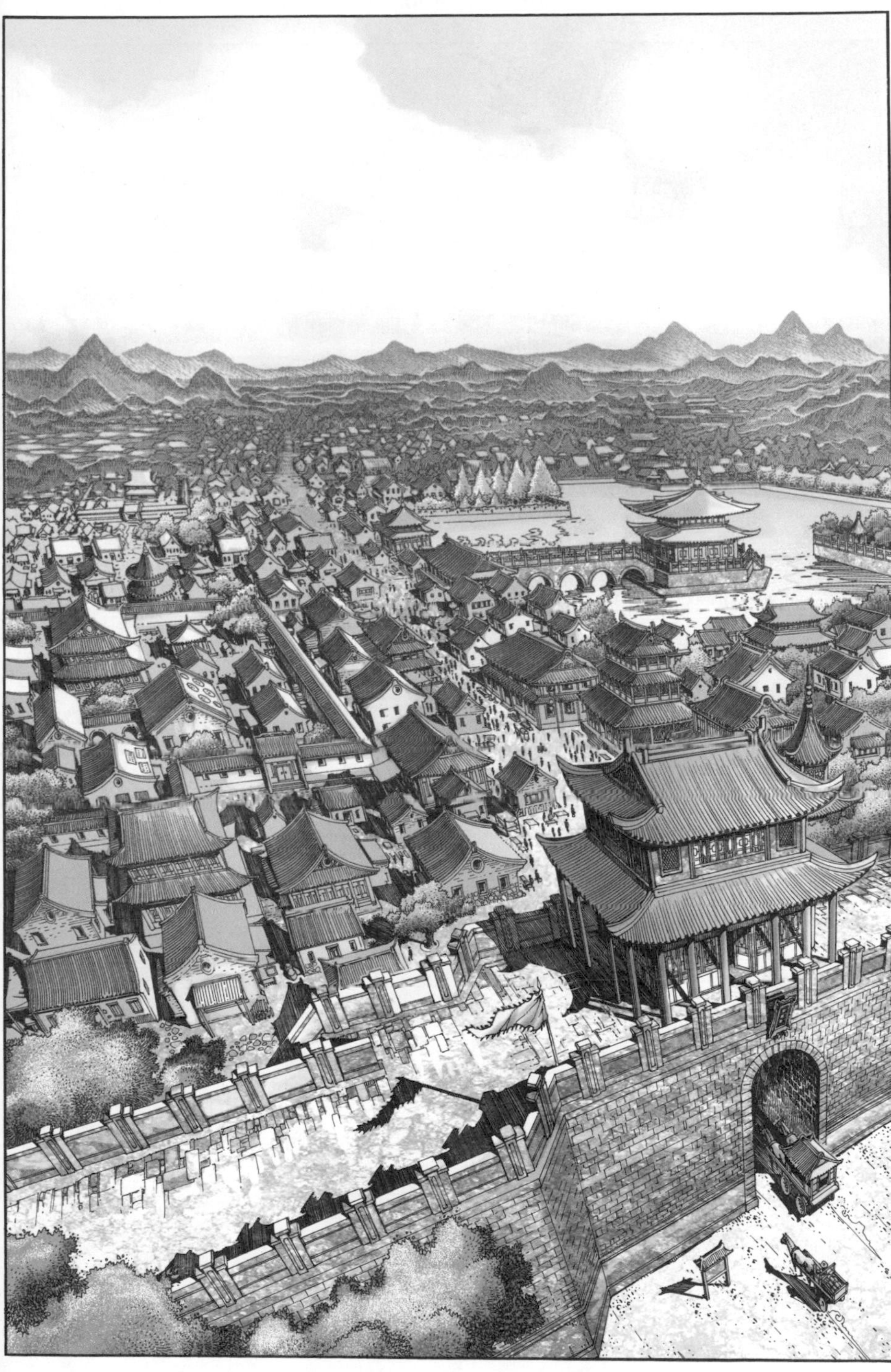

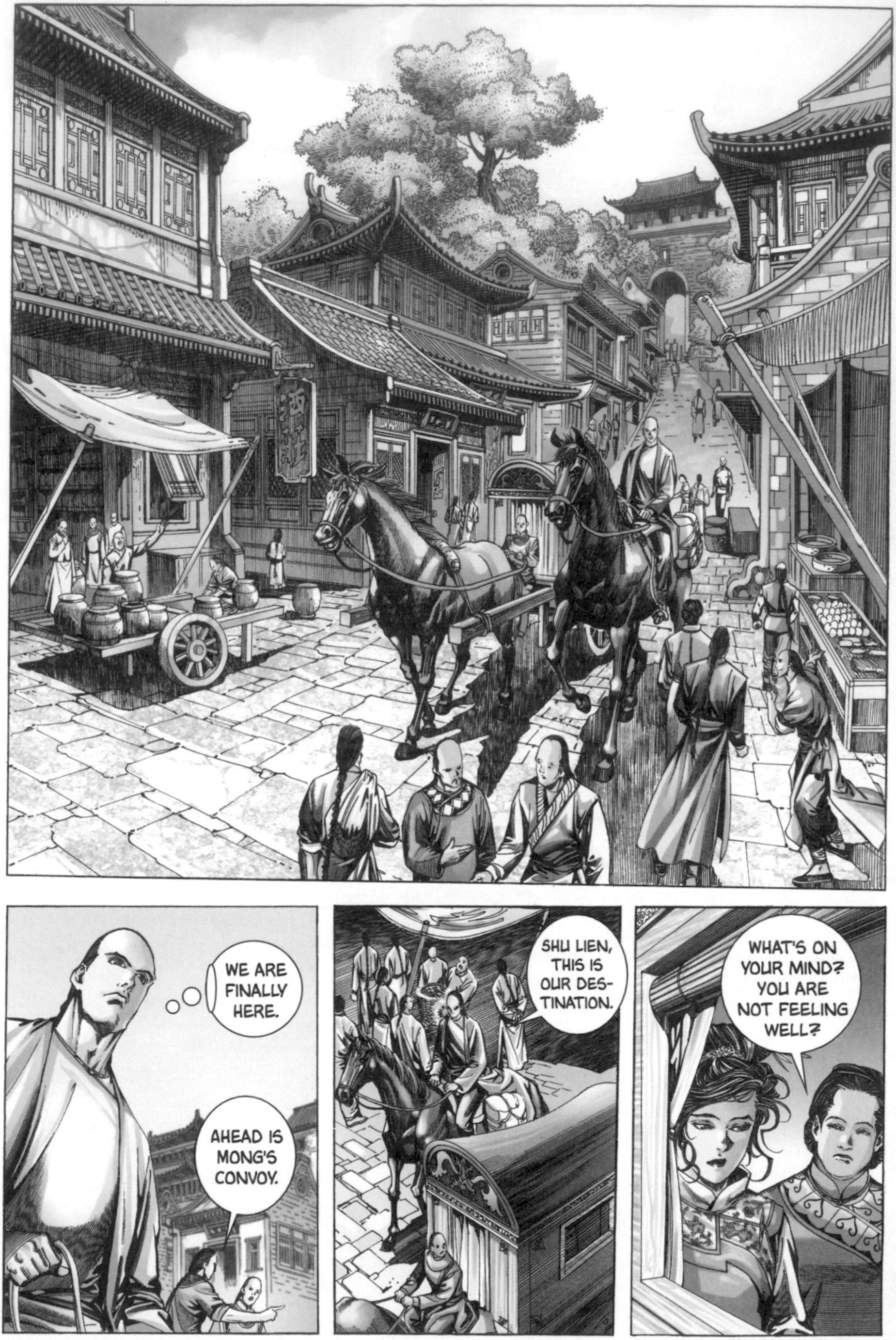
WE ARE FINALLY HERE.
AHEAD IS MONG'S CONVOY.
SHU LIEN, THIS IS OUR DESTINATION.
WHAT'S ON YOUR MIND? YOU ARE NOT FEELING WELL?

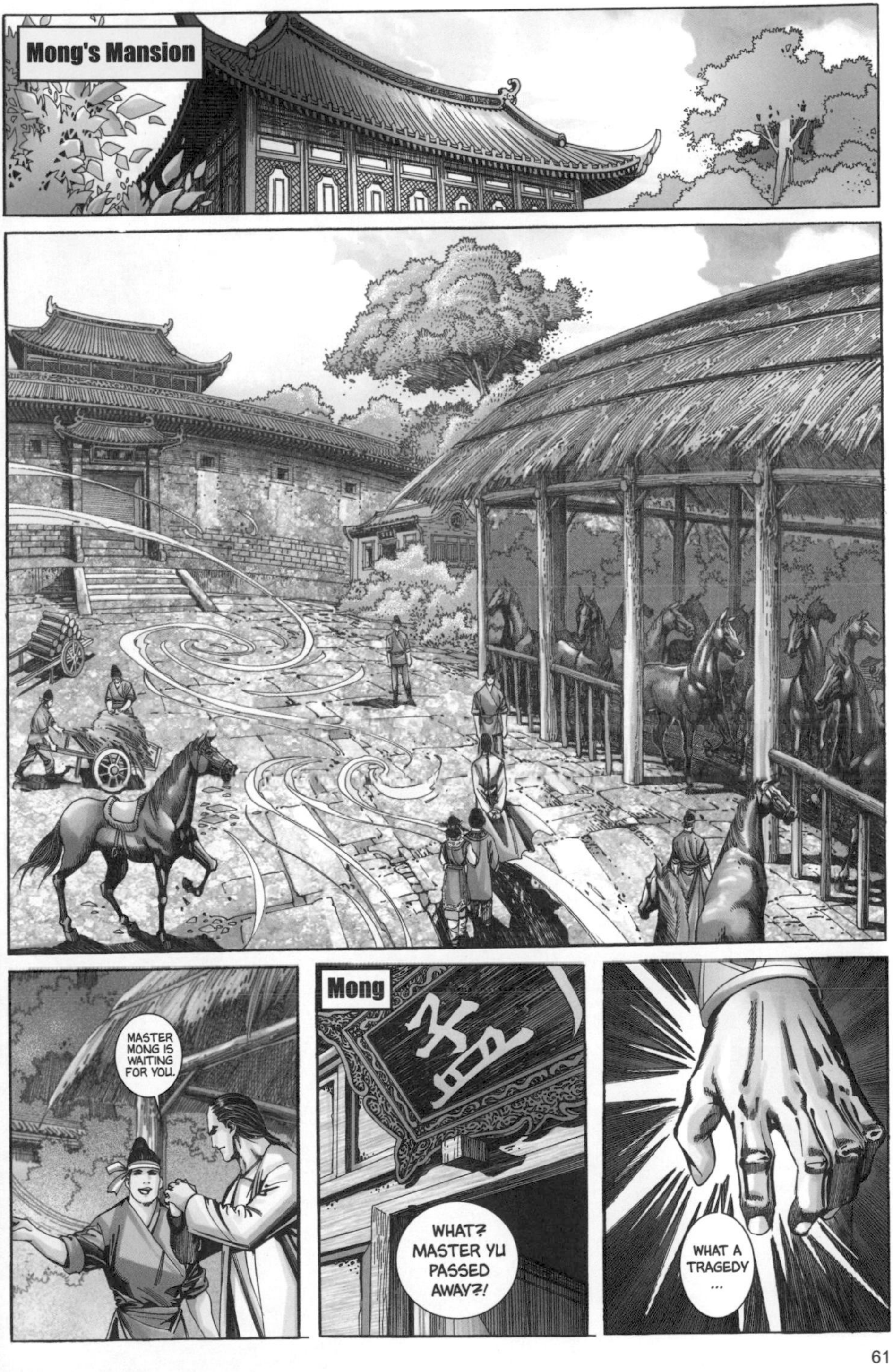
Mong's Mansion
MASTER MONG IS WAITING FOR YOU.
Mong
WHAT? MASTER YU PASSED AWAY?!
WHAT A TRAGEDY ...

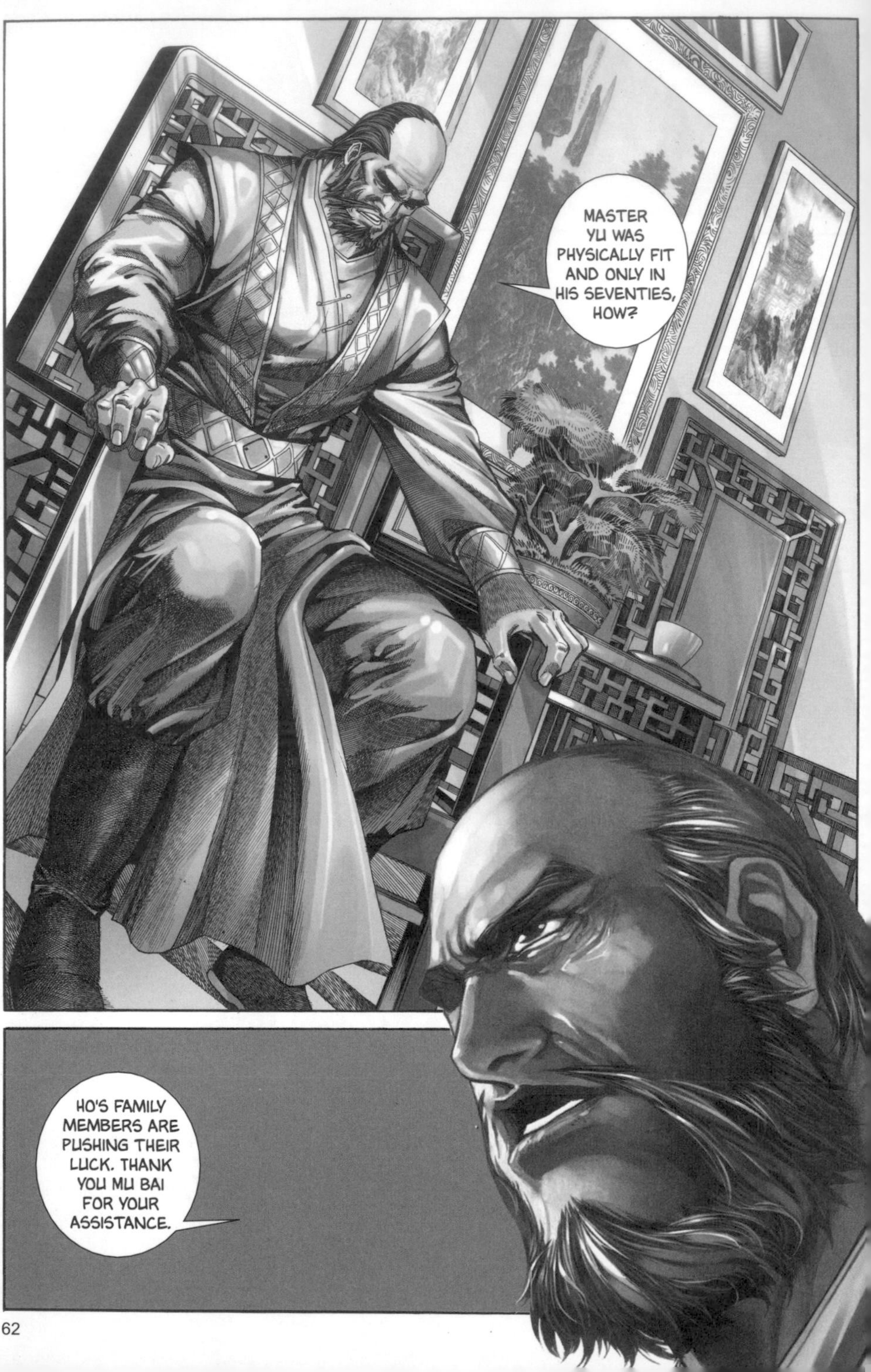
MASTER YU WAS PHYSICALLY FIT AND ONLY IN HIS SEVENTIES, HOW?
HO'S FAMILY MEMBERS ARE PUSHING THEIR LUCK. THANK YOU MU BAI FOR YOUR ASSISTANCE.

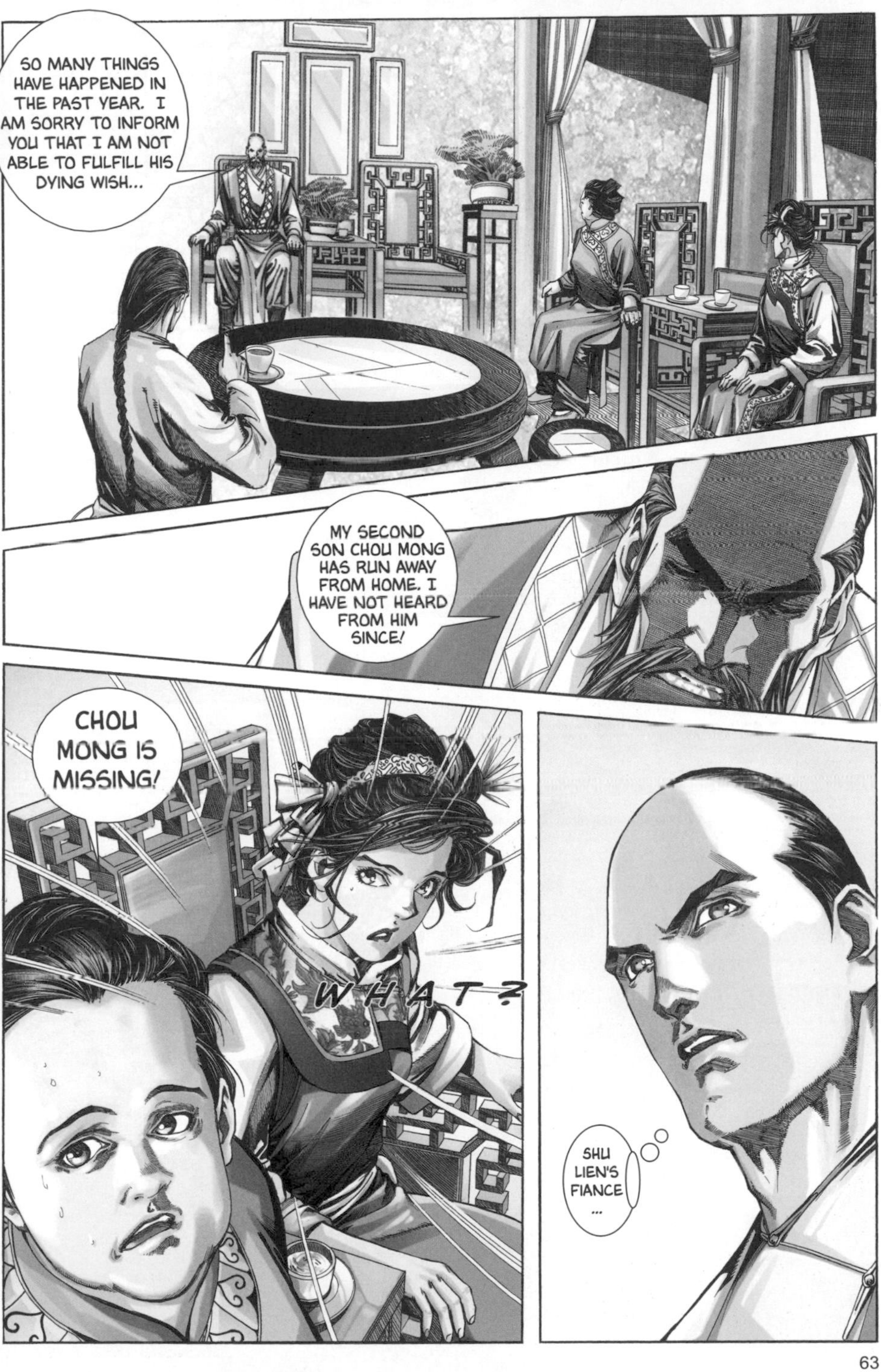
SO MANY THINGS HAVE HAPPENED IN THE PAST YEAR. I AM SORRY TO INFORM YOU THAT I AM NOT ABLE TO FULFILL HIS DYING WISH...
MY SECOND SON CHOU MONG HAS RUN AWAY FROM HOME. I HAVE NOT HEARD FROM HIM SINCE!
CHOU MONG IS MISSING!
WHAT?
SHU LIEN'S FIANCE ...

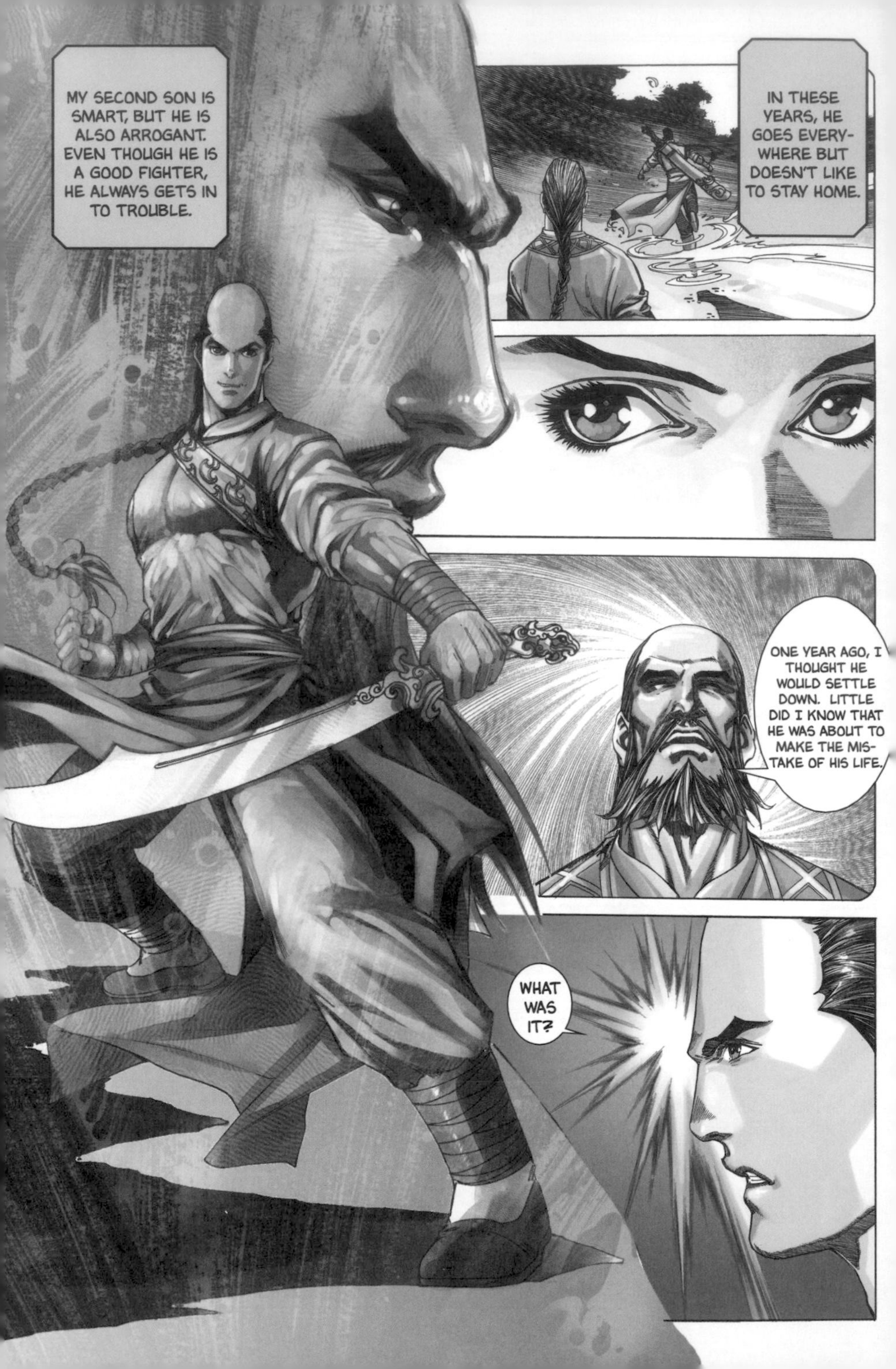
MY SECOND SON IS SMART, BUT HE IS ALSO ARROGANT. EVEN THOUGH HE IS A GOOD FIGHTER, HE ALWAYS GETS IN TO TROUBLE.
IN THESE YEARS, HE GOES EVERY-WHERE BUT DOESN'T LIKE TO STAY HOME.
ONE YEAR AGO, I THOUGHT HE WOULD SETTLE DOWN. LITTLE DID I KNOW THAT HE WAS ABOUT TO MAKE THE MIS-TAKE OF HIS LIFE.
WHAT WAS IT?

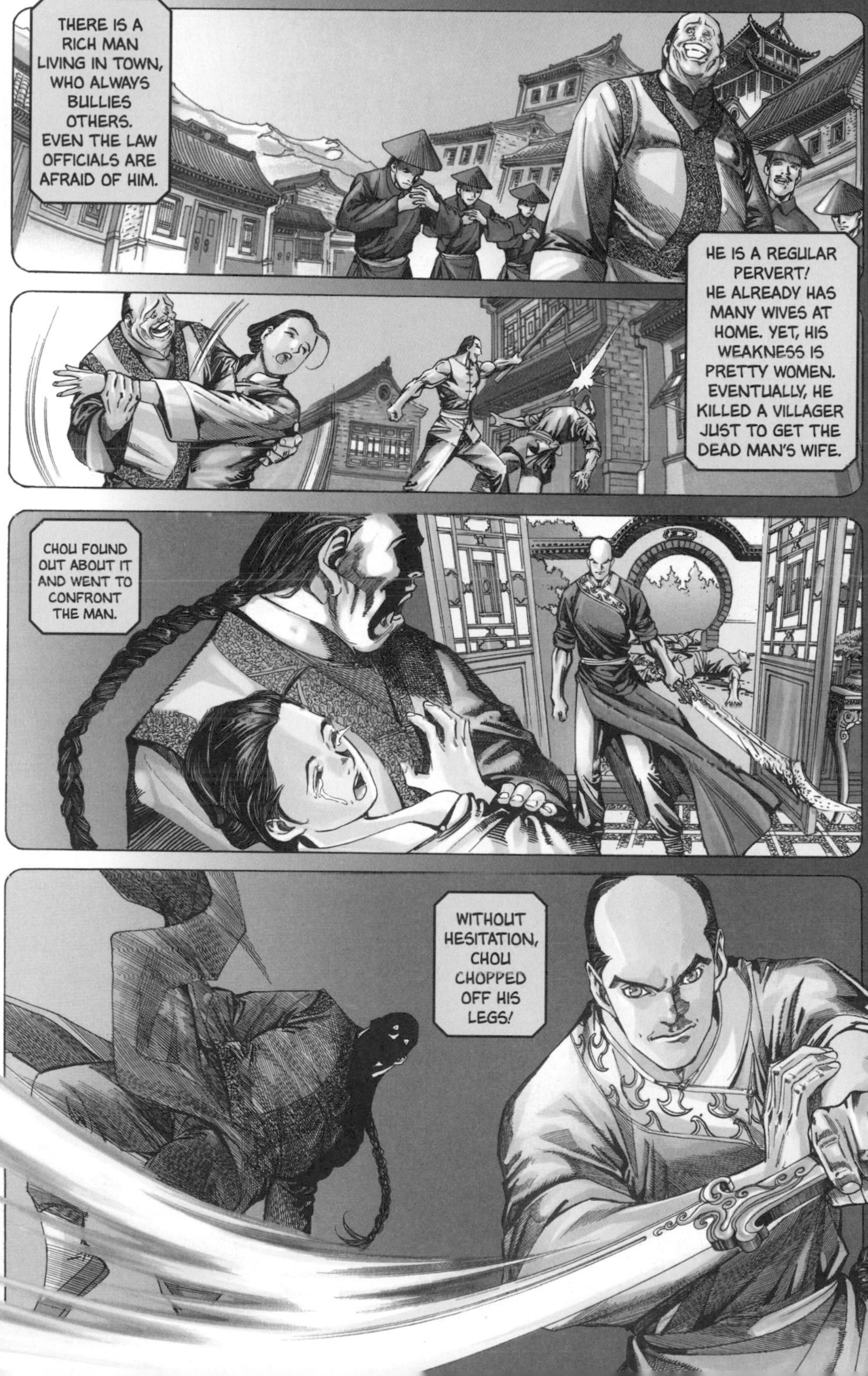
THERE IS A RICH MAN LIVING IN TOWN, WHO ALWAYS BULLIES OTHERS. EVEN THE LAW OFFICIALS ARE AFRAID OF HIM.
HE IS A REGULAR PERVERT! HE ALREADY HAS MANY WIVES AT HOME. YET, HIS WEAKNESS IS PRETTY WOMEN. EVENTUALLY, HE KILLED A VILLAGER JUST TO GET THE DEAD MAN'S WIFE.
CHOU FOUND OUT ABOUT IT AND WENT TO CONFRONT THE MAN.
WITHOUT HESITATION, CHOU CHOPPED OFF HIS LEGS!

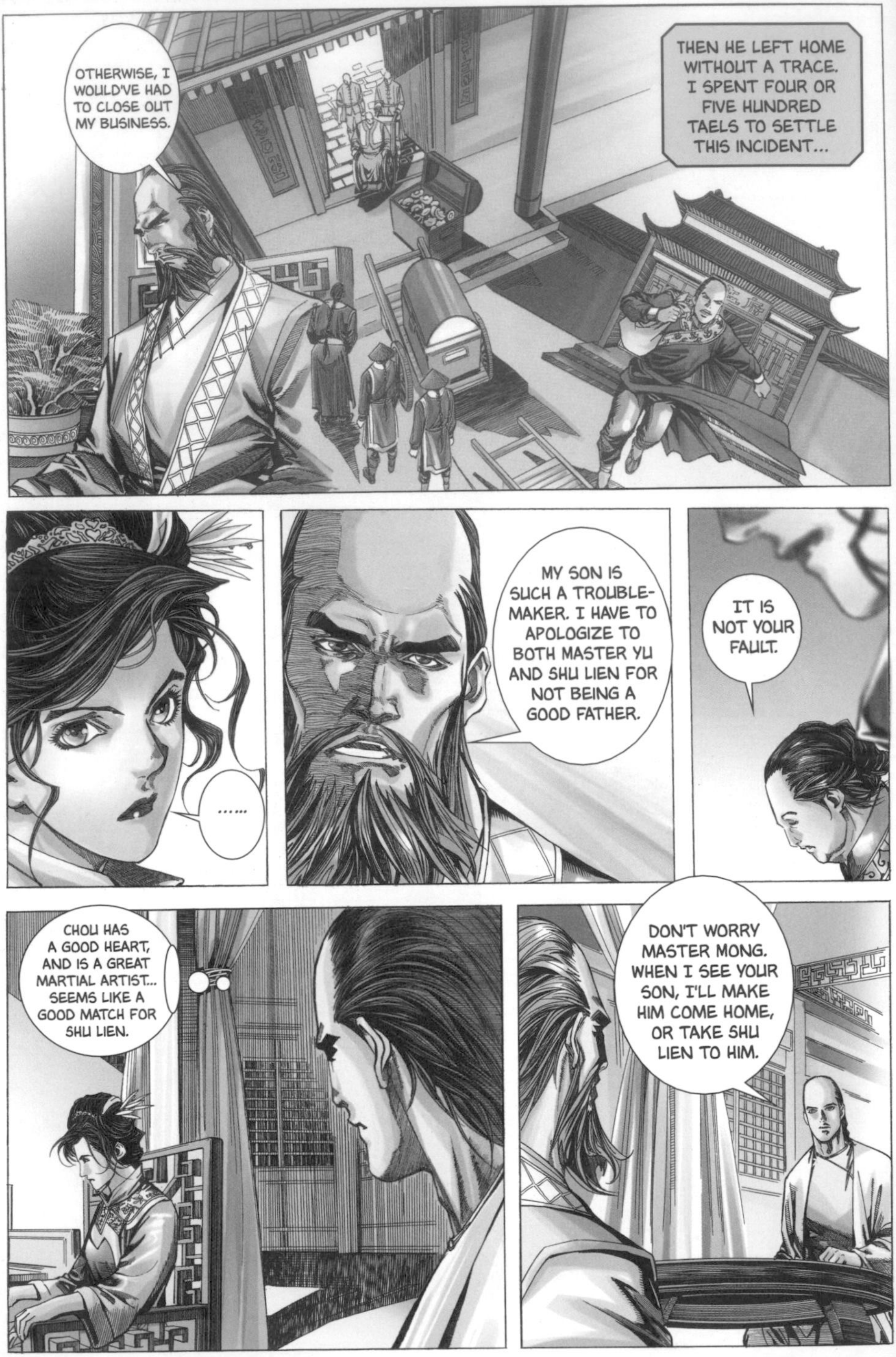

OTHERWISE, I WOULD'VE HAD TO CLOSE OUT MY BUSINESS.
THEN HE LEFT HOME WITHOUT A TRACE. I SPENT FOUR OR FIVE HUNDRED TAELS TO SETTLE THIS INCIDENT...
......
MY SON IS SUCH A TROUBLE-MAKER. I HAVE TO APOLOGIZE TO BOTH MASTER YU AND SHU LIEN FOR NOT BEING A GOOD FATHER.
IT IS NOT YOUR FAULT.
CHOU HAS A GOOD HEART, AND IS A GREAT MARTIAL ARTIST... SEEMS LIKE A GOOD MATCH FOR SHU LIEN.
DON'T WORRY MASTER MONG. WHEN I SEE YOUR SON, I'LL MAKE HIM COME HOME, OR TAKE SHU LIEN TO HIM.

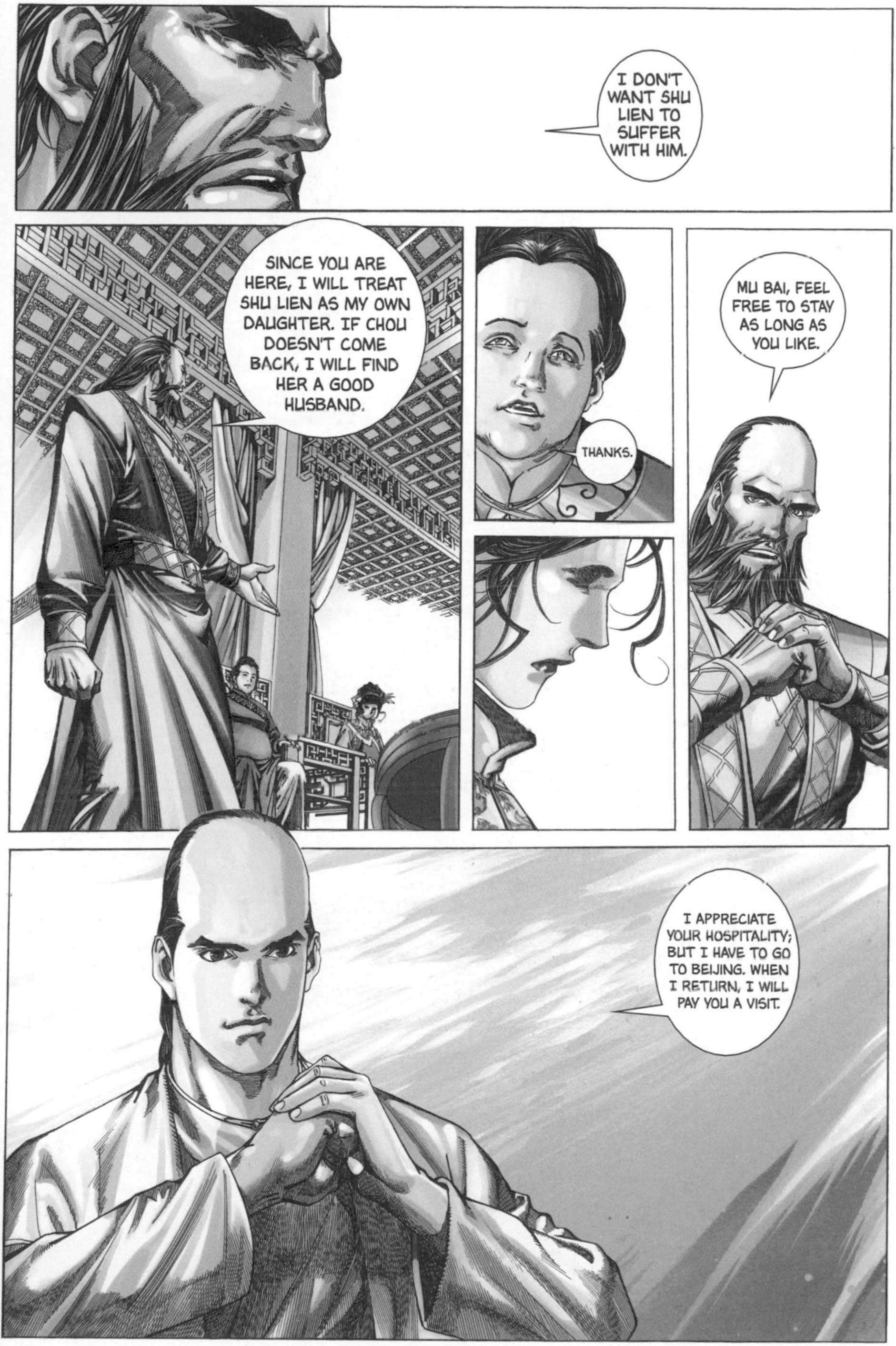
I DON'T WANT SHU LIEN TO SUFFER WITH HIM.
SINCE YOU ARE HERE, I WILL TREAT SHU LIEN AS MY OWN DAUGHTER. IF CHOU DOESN'T COME BACK, I WILL FIND HER A GOOD HUSBAND.
THANKS.
MU BAI, FEEL FREE TO STAY AS LONG AS YOU LIKE.
I APPRECIATE YOUR HOSPITALITY; BUT I HAVE TO GO TO BEIJING. WHEN I RETURN, I WILL PAY YOU A VISIT.

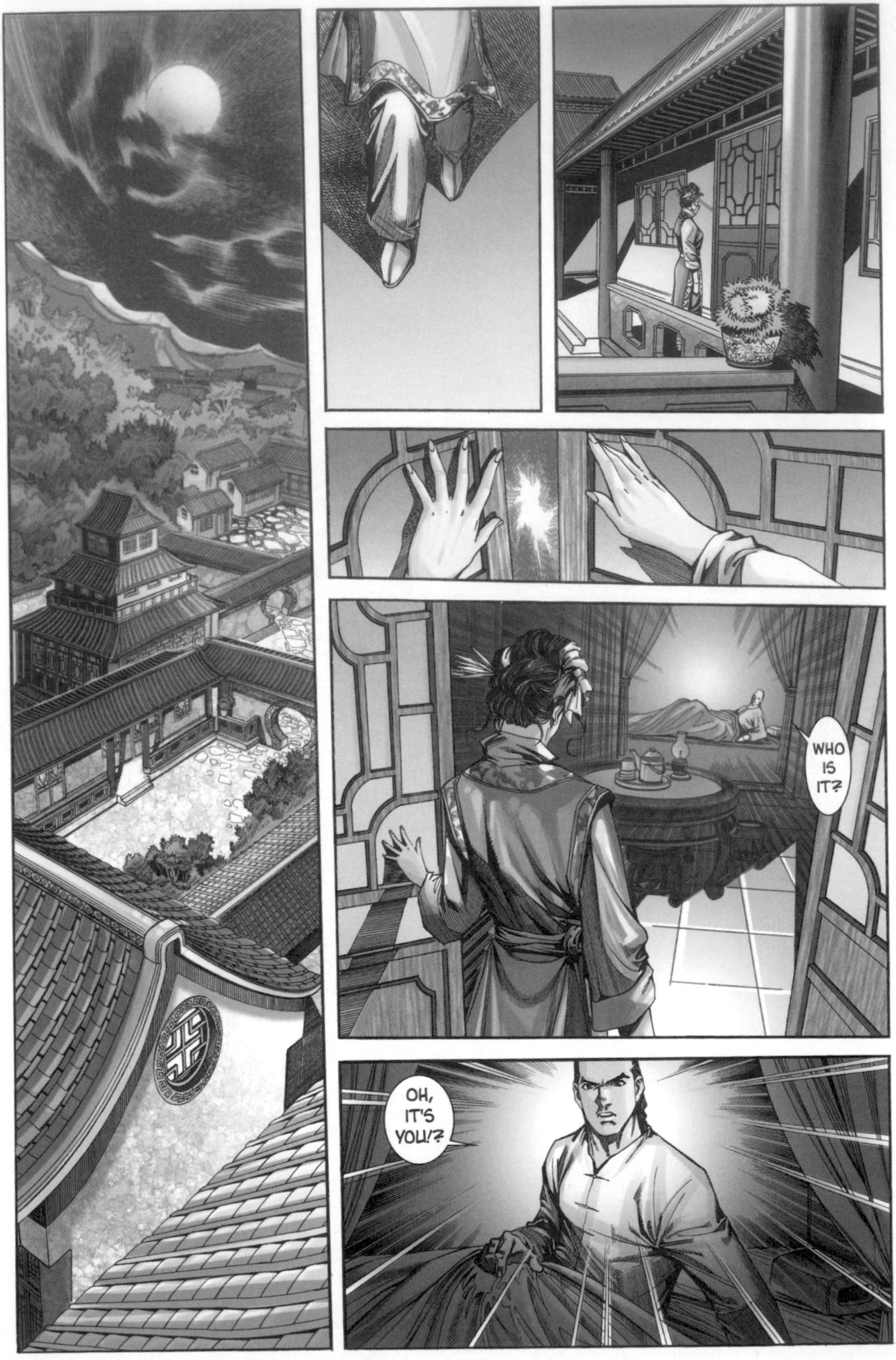
WHO IS IT?
OH, IT'S YOU!?

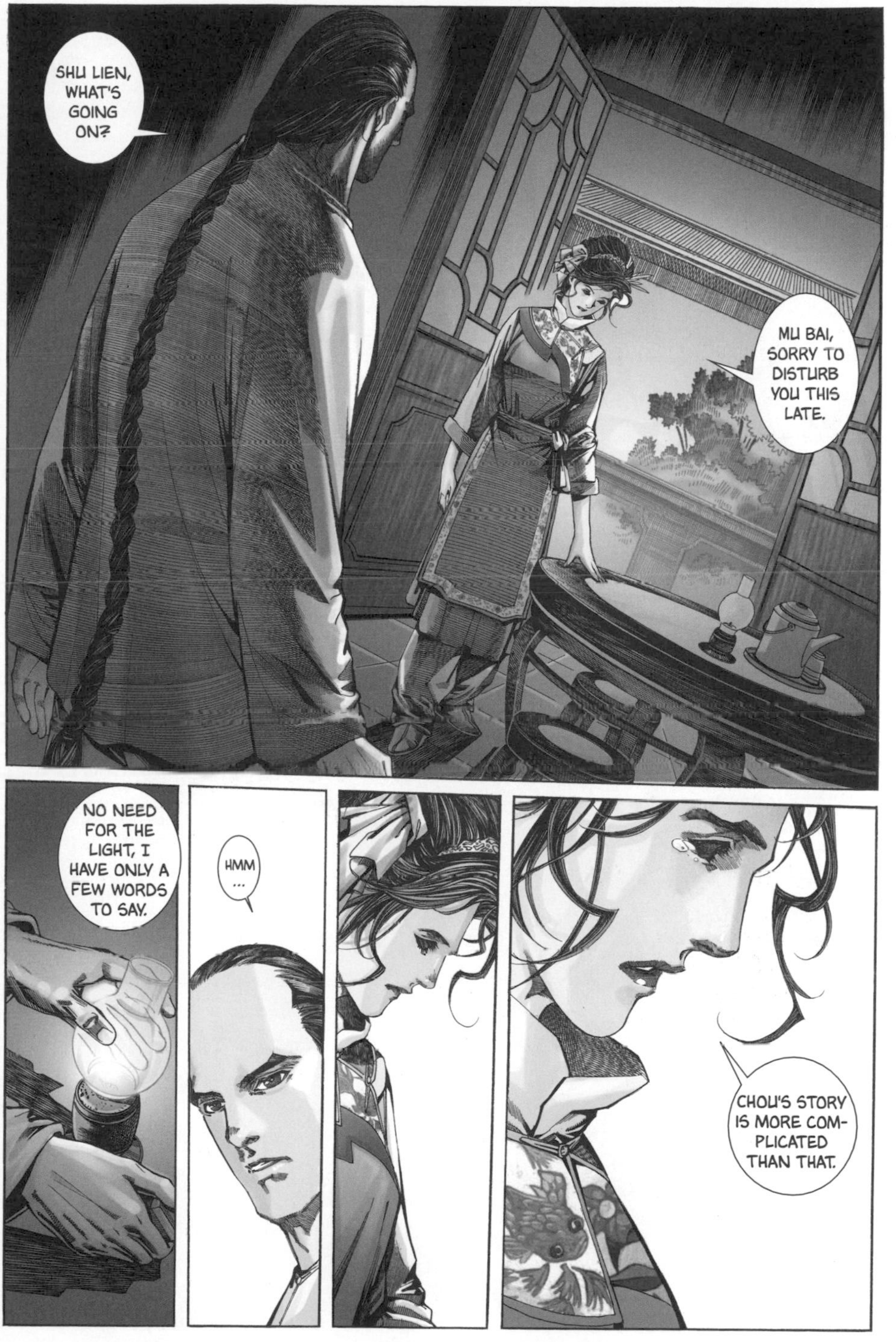
SHU LIEN, WHAT'S GOING ON?
MU BAI, SORRY TO DISTURB YOU THIS LATE.
NO NEED FOR THE LIGHT, I HAVE ONLY A FEW WORDS TO SAY.
HMM ...
CHOU'S STORY IS MORE COMPLICATED THAN THAT.

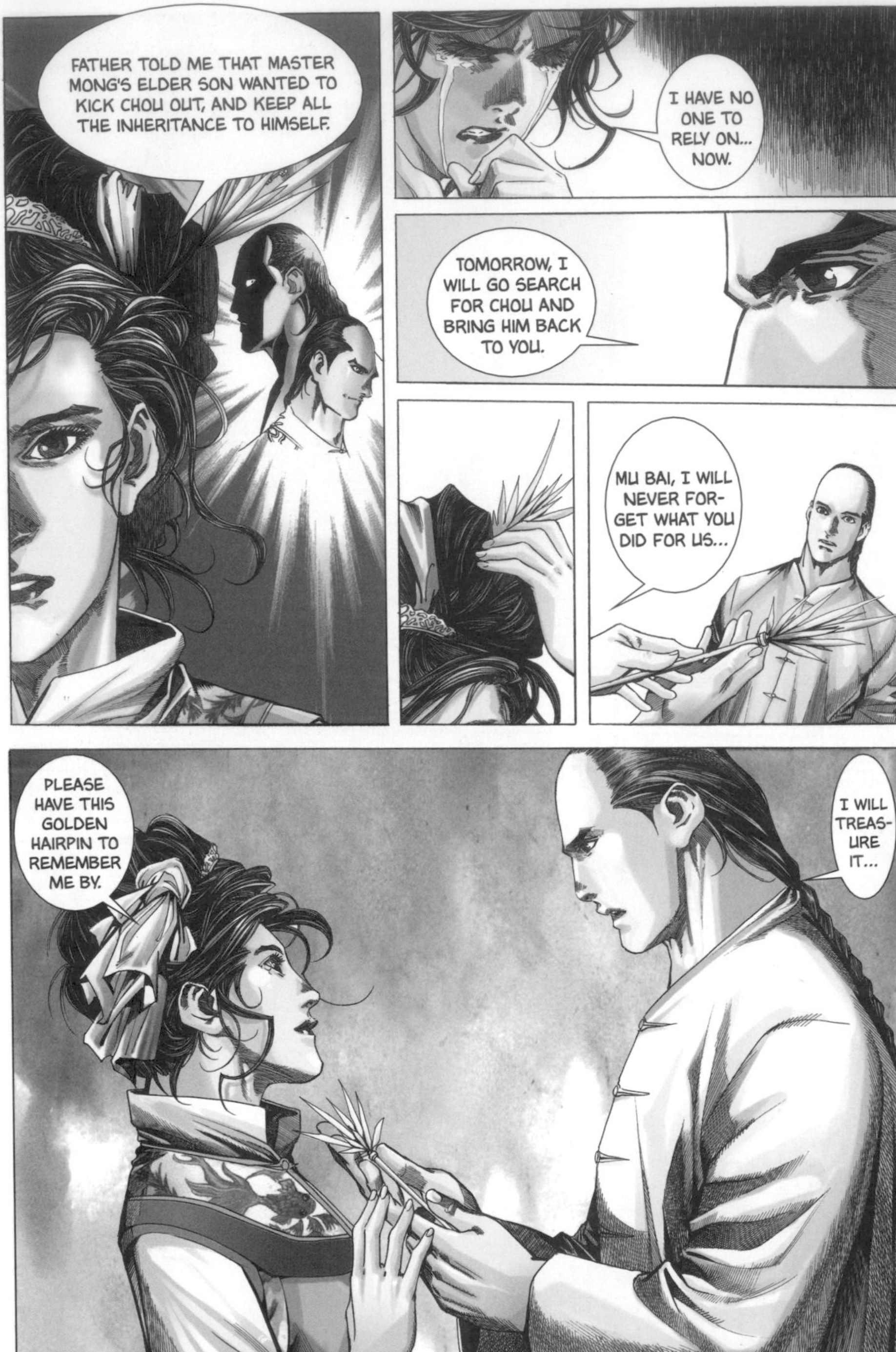
FATHER TOLD ME THAT MASTER MONG'S ELDER SON WANTED TO KICK CHOU OUT, AND KEEP ALL THE INHERITANCE TO HIMSELF.
I HAVE NO ONE TO RELY ON... NOW.
TOMORROW, I WILL GO SEARCH FOR CHOU AND BRING HIM BACK TO YOU.
MU BAI, I WILL NEVER FOR-GET WHAT YOU DID FOR US...
PLEASE HAVE THIS GOLDEN HAIRPIN TO REMEMBER ME BY.
I WILL TREAS-URE IT...

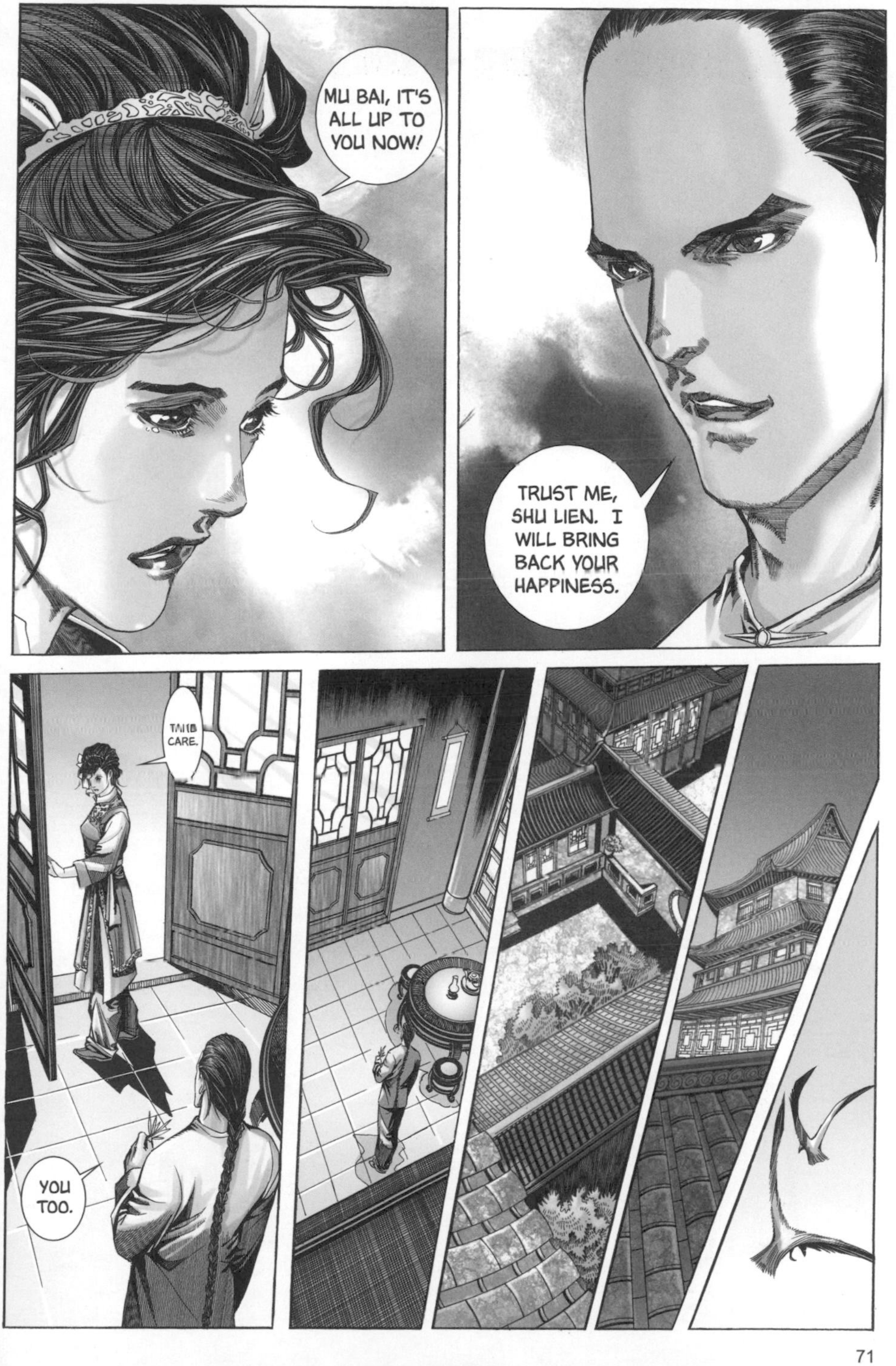
MU BAI, IT'S ALL UP TO YOU NOW!
TRUST ME, SHU LIEN. I WILL BRING BACK YOUR HAPPINESS.
CARE.
YOU TOO.

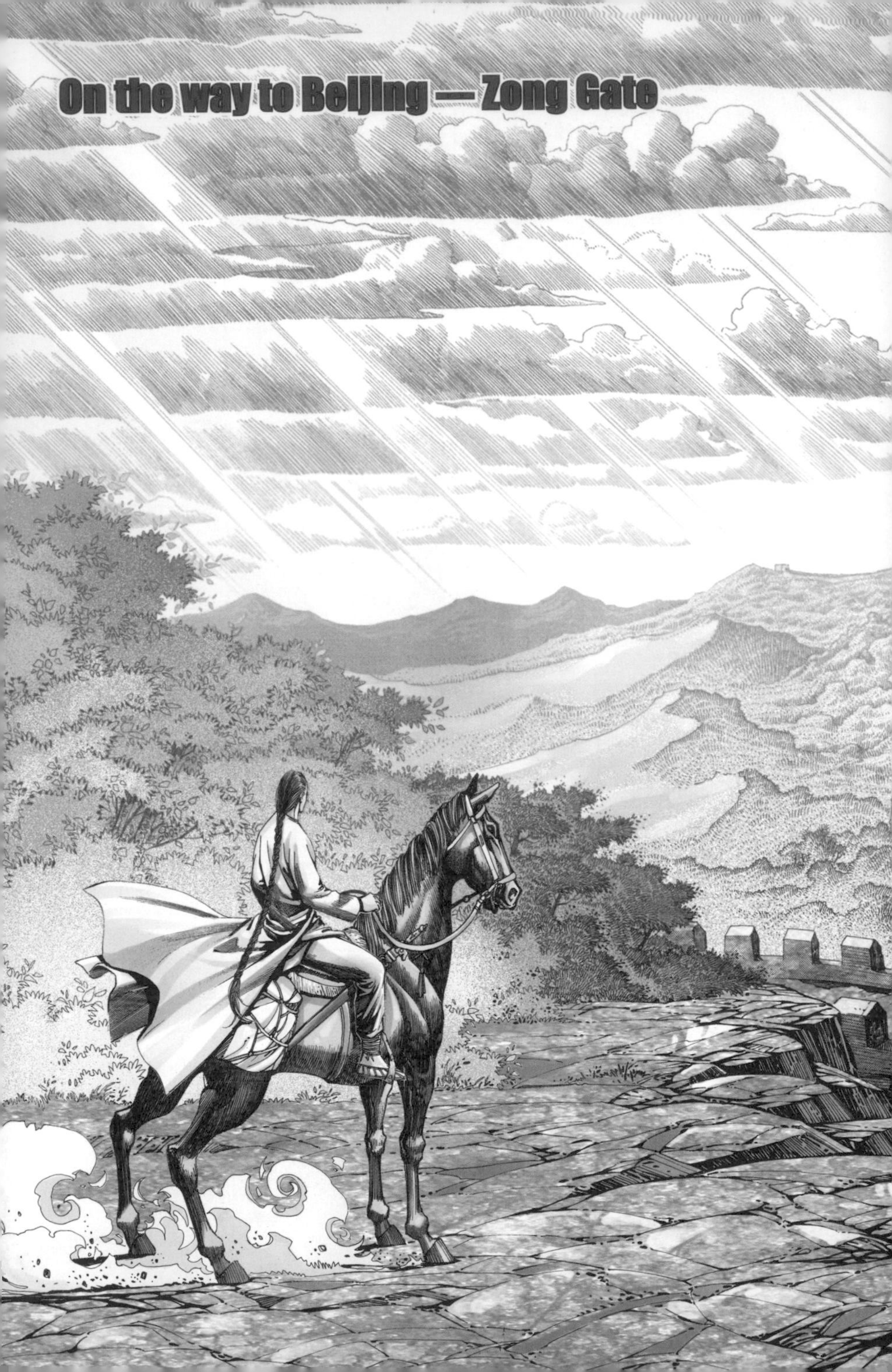
On the way to Beijing — Zong Gate

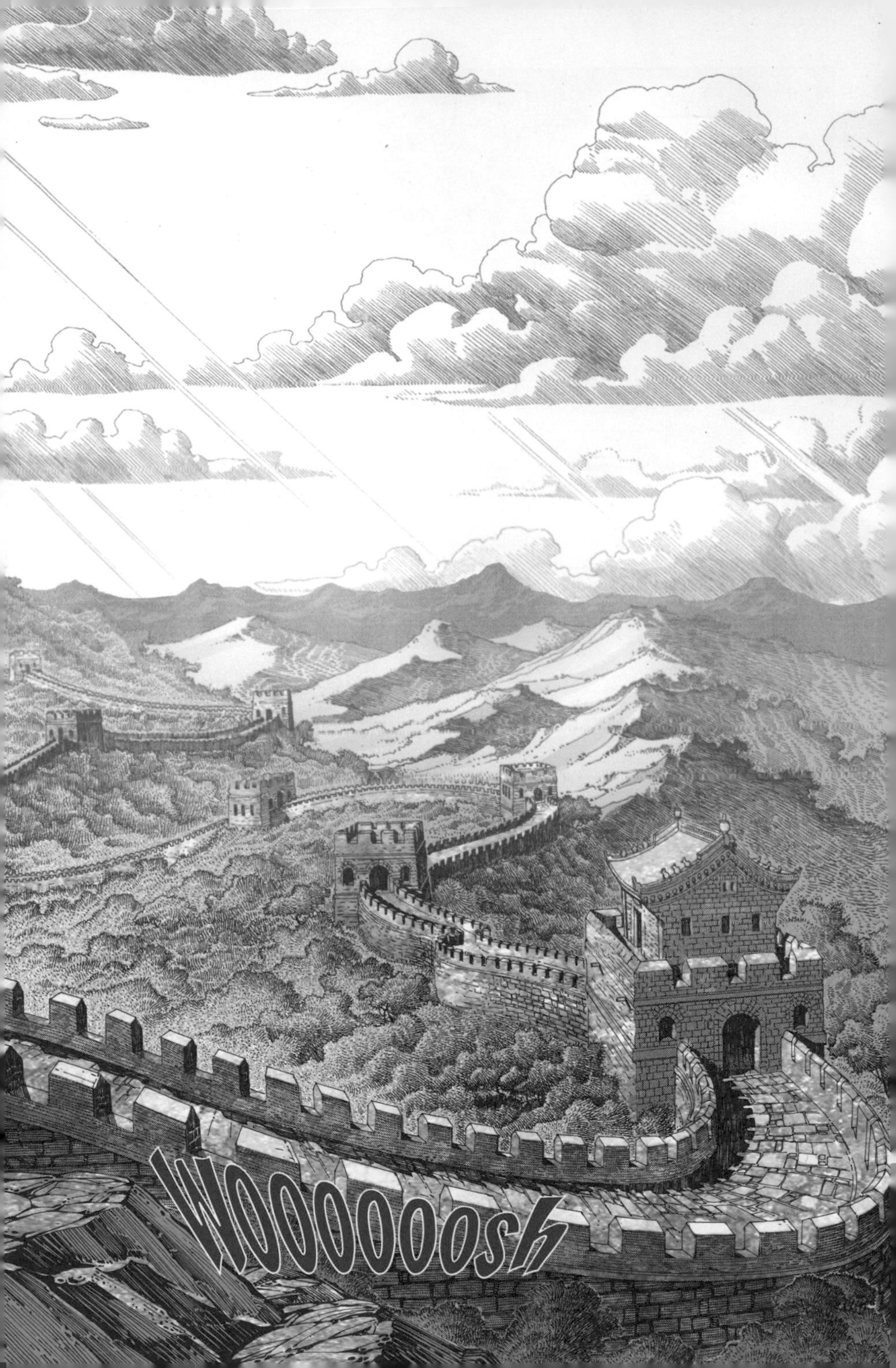
WOOOOOOsh

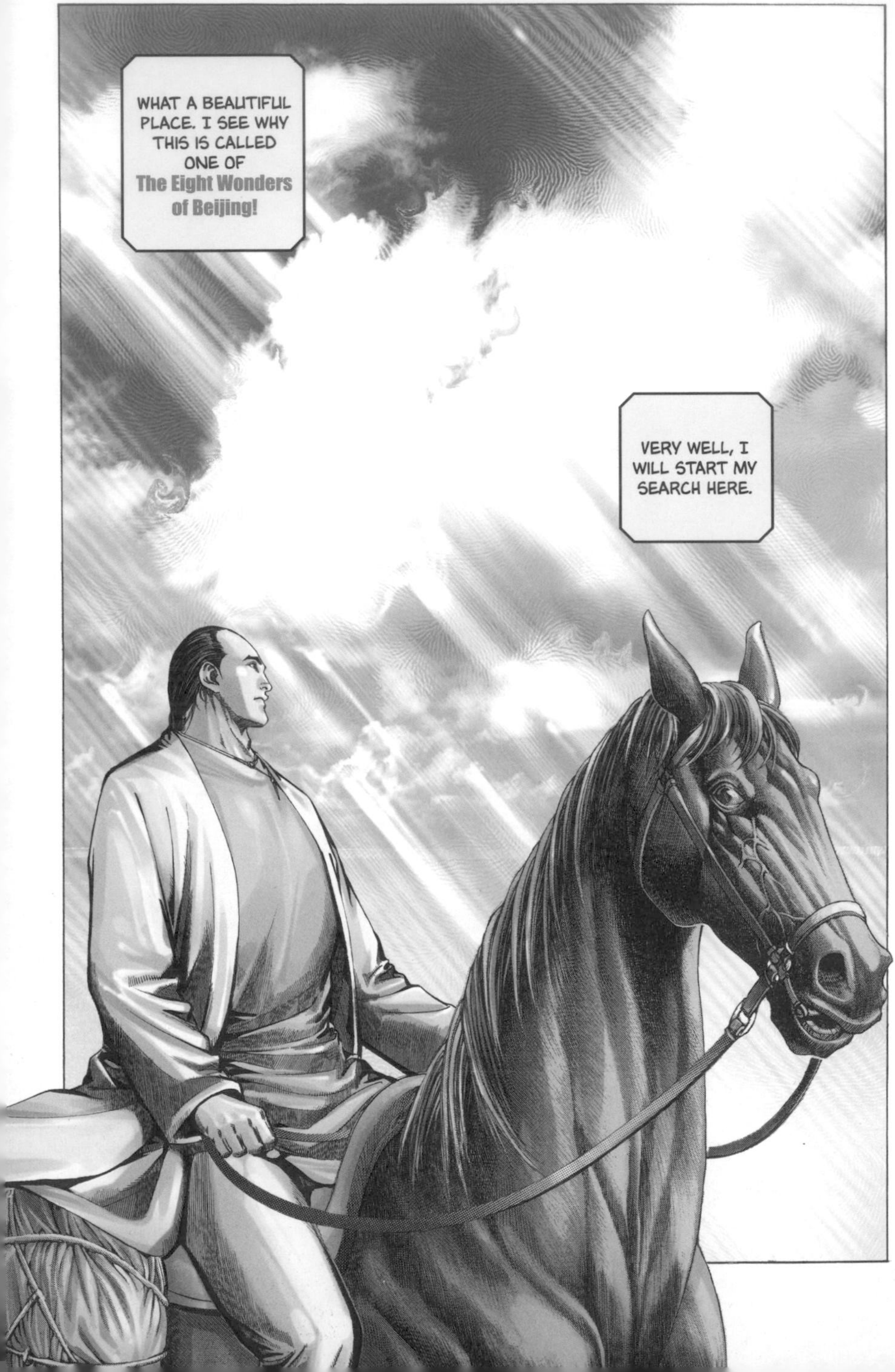
WHAT A BEAUTIFUL PLACE. I SEE WHY THIS IS CALLED ONE OF The Eight Wonders of Beijing!
VERY WELL, I WILL START MY SEARCH HERE.

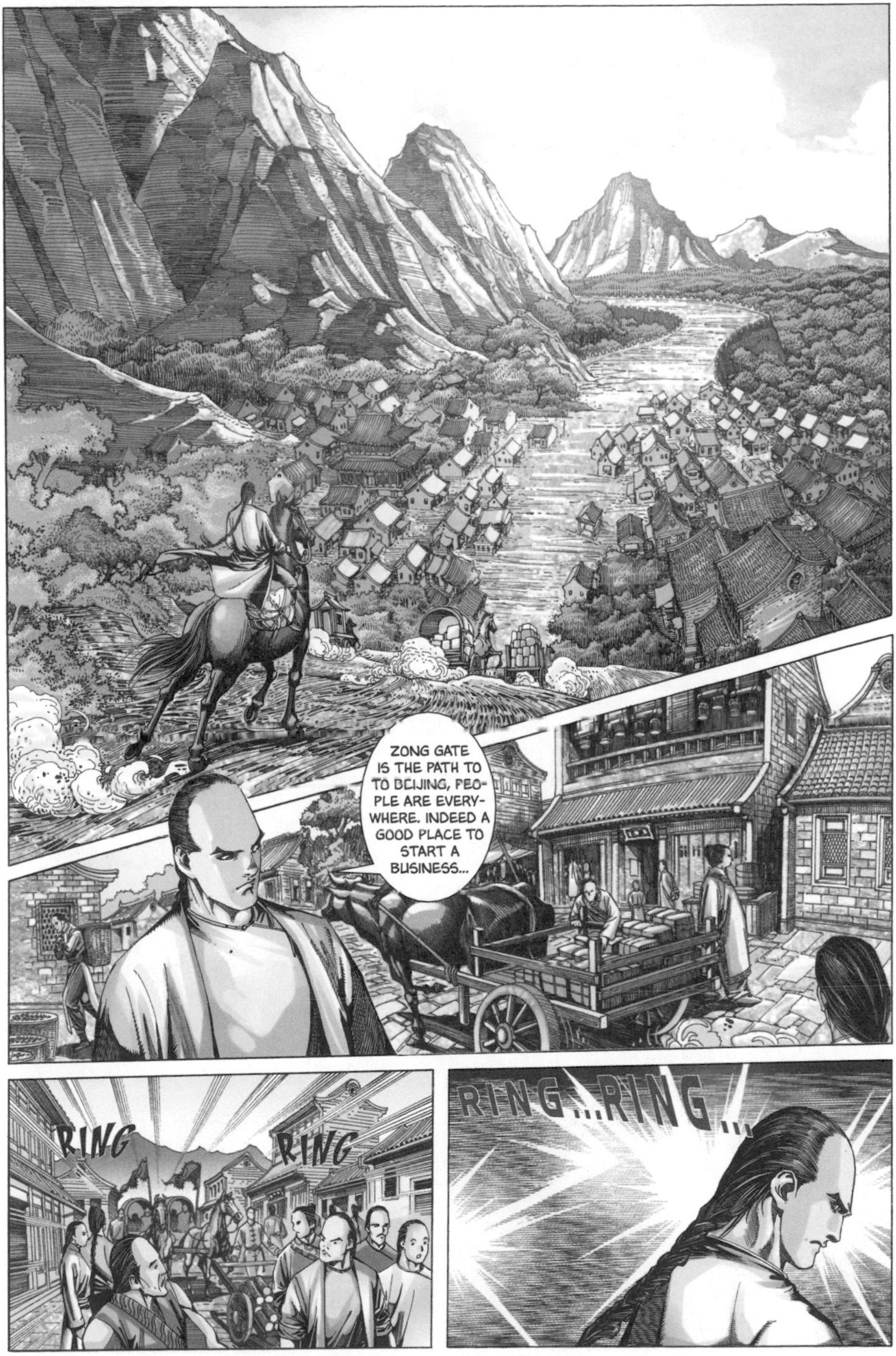
ZONG GATE IS THE PATH TO TO BEIJING, PEOPLE ARE EVERYWHERE. INDEED A GOOD PLACE TO START A BUSINESS...
RING
RING
RING...RING...

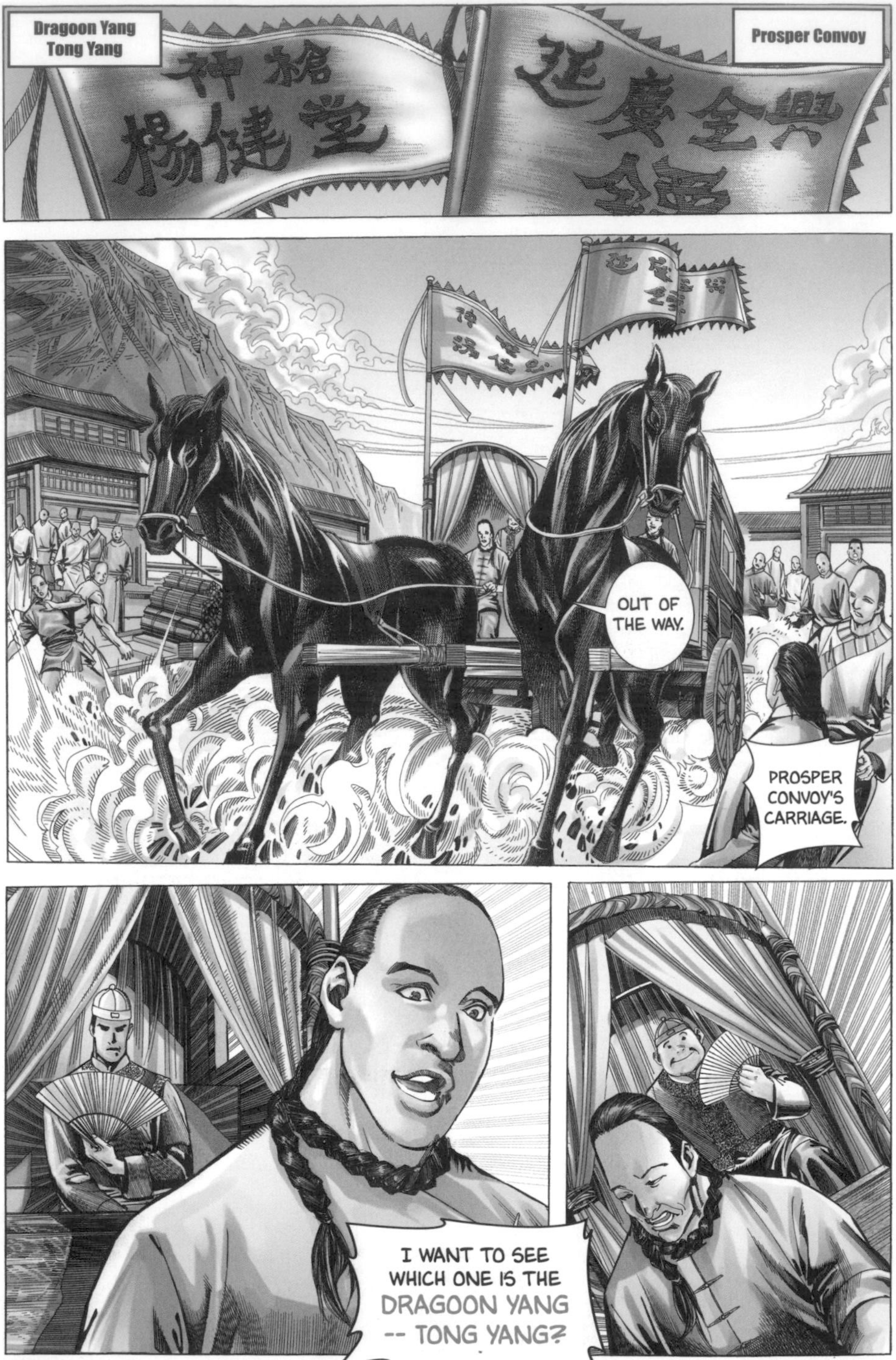
Dragoon Yang
Tong Yang
Prosper Convoy
OUT OF THE WAY.
PROSPER CONVOY'S CARRIAGE.
I WANT TO SEE WHICH ONE IS THE DRAGOON YANG -- TONG YANG?

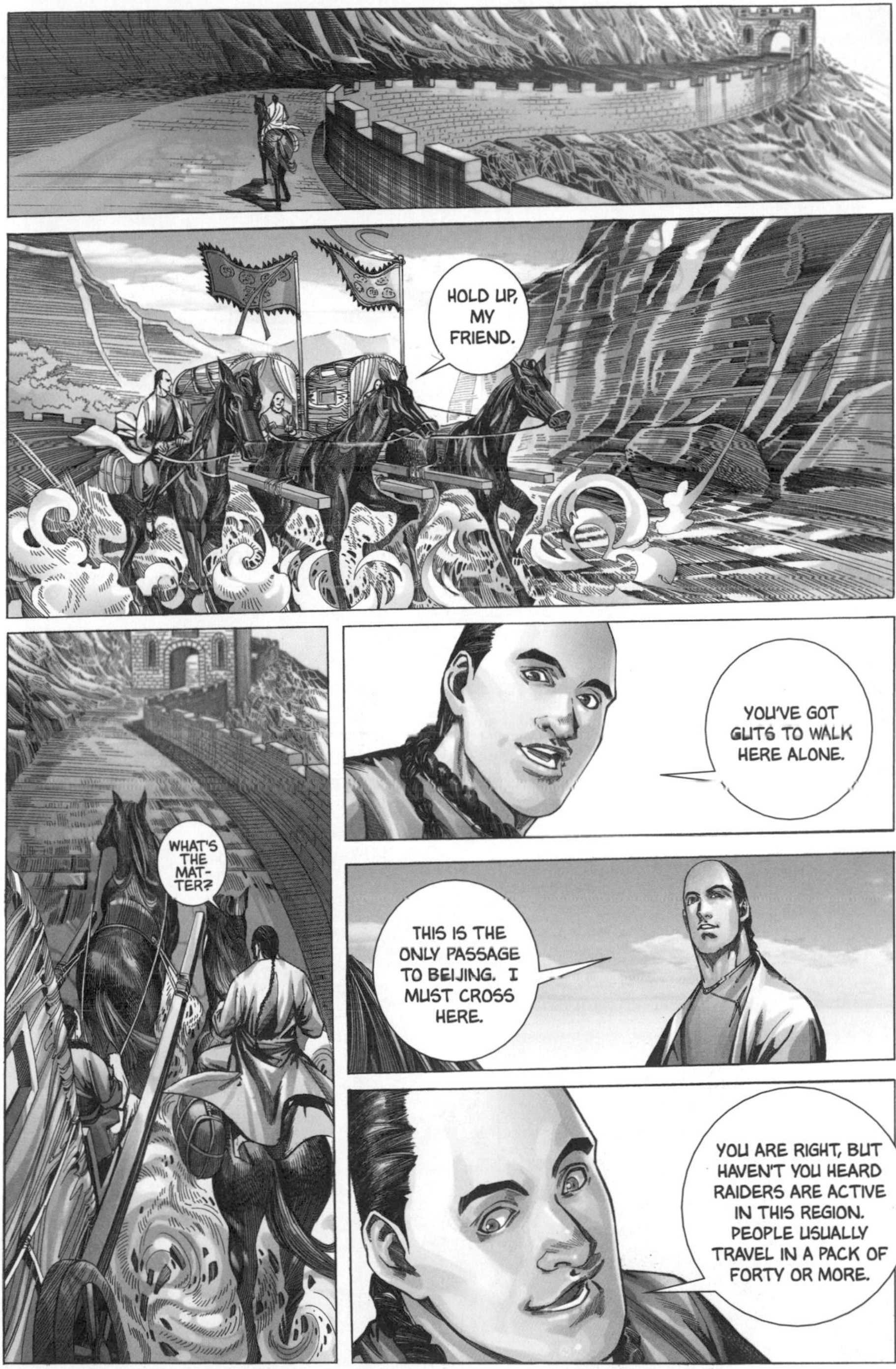
HOLD UP, MY FRIEND.
WHAT'S THE MATTER?
YOU'VE GOT GUTS TO WALK HERE ALONE.
THIS IS THE ONLY PASSAGE TO BEIJING. I MUST CROSS HERE.
YOU ARE RIGHT, BUT HAVEN'T YOU HEARD RAIDERS ARE ACTIVE IN THIS REGION. PEOPLE USUALLY TRAVEL IN A PACK OF FORTY OR MORE.

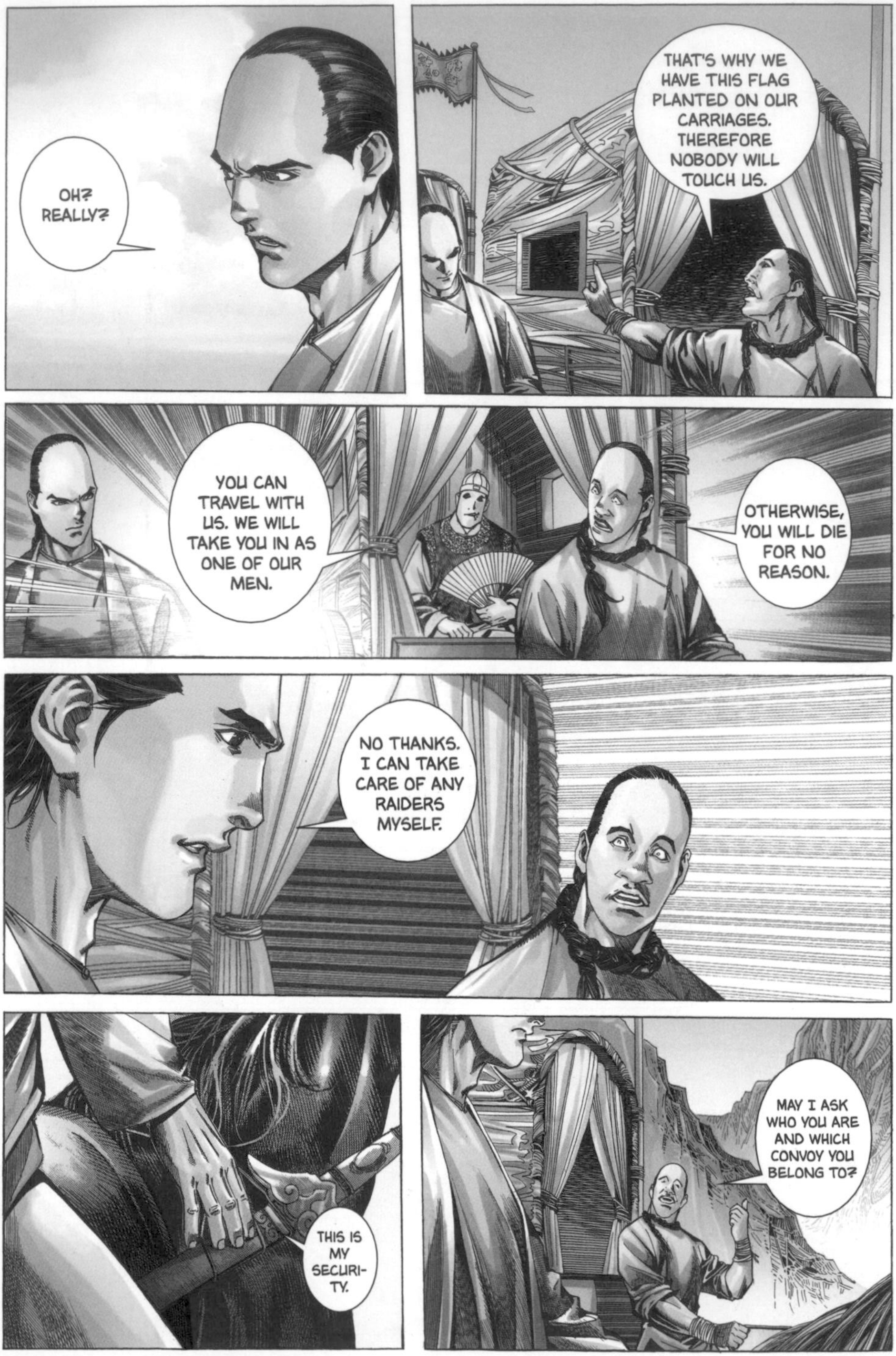
OH? REALLY?
THAT'S WHY WE HAVE THIS FLAG PLANTED ON OUR CARRIAGES. THEREFORE NOBODY WILL TOUCH US.
YOU CAN TRAVEL WITH US. WE WILL TAKE YOU IN AS ONE OF OUR MEN.
OTHERWISE, YOU WILL DIE FOR NO REASON.
NO THANKS. I CAN TAKE CARE OF ANY RAIDERS MYSELF.
THIS IS MY SECURI-TY.
MAY I ASK WHO YOU ARE AND WHICH CONVOY YOU BELONG TO?

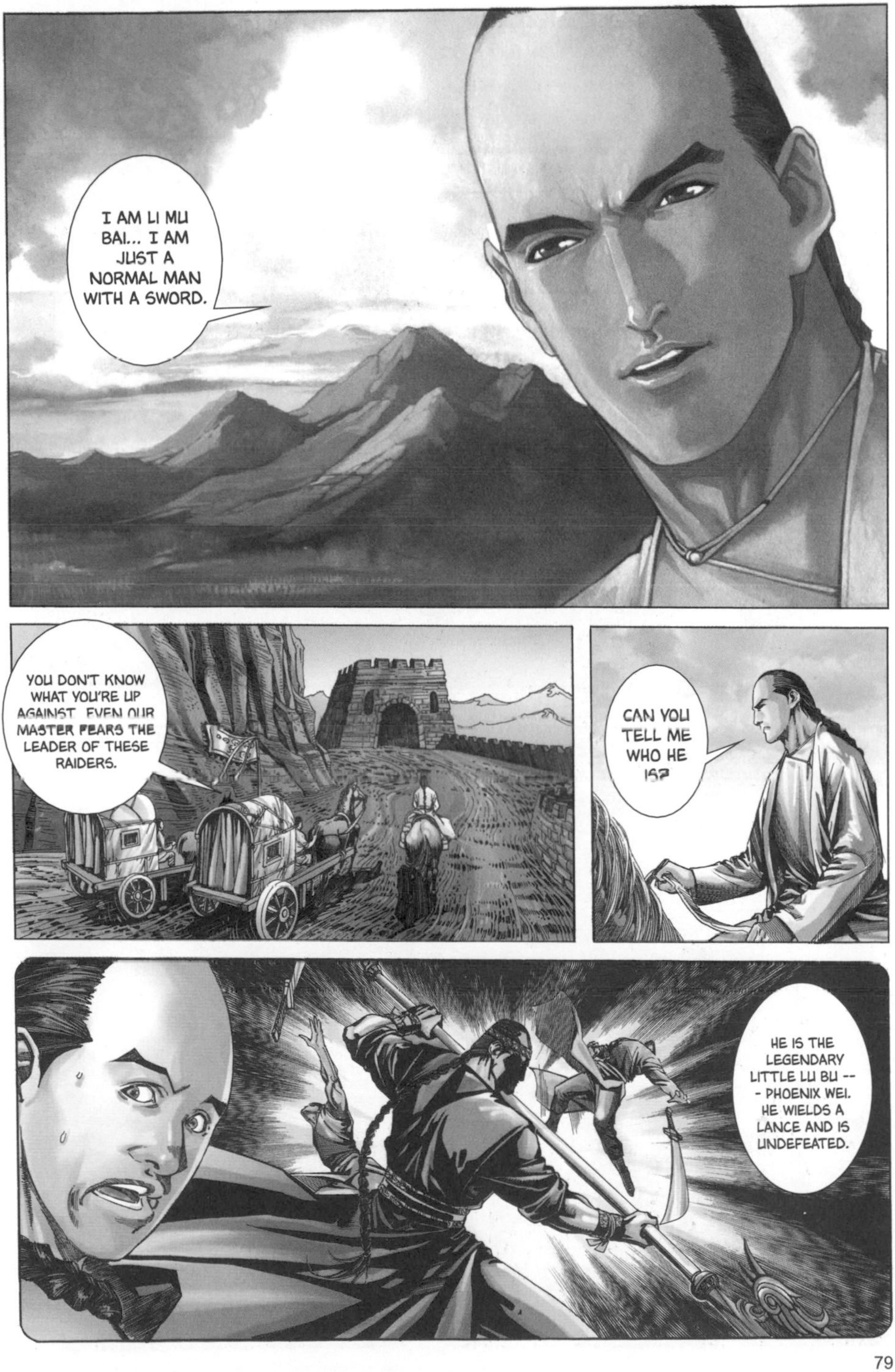
I AM LI MU BAI... I AM JUST A NORMAL MAN WITH A SWORD.
YOU DON'T KNOW WHAT YOU'RE UP AGAINST. EVEN OUR MASTER FEARS THE LEADER OF THESE RAIDERS.
CAN YOU TELL ME WHO HE IS?
HE IS THE LEGENDARY LITTLE LU BU --- PHOENIX WEI. HE WIELDS A LANCE AND IS UNDEFEATED.

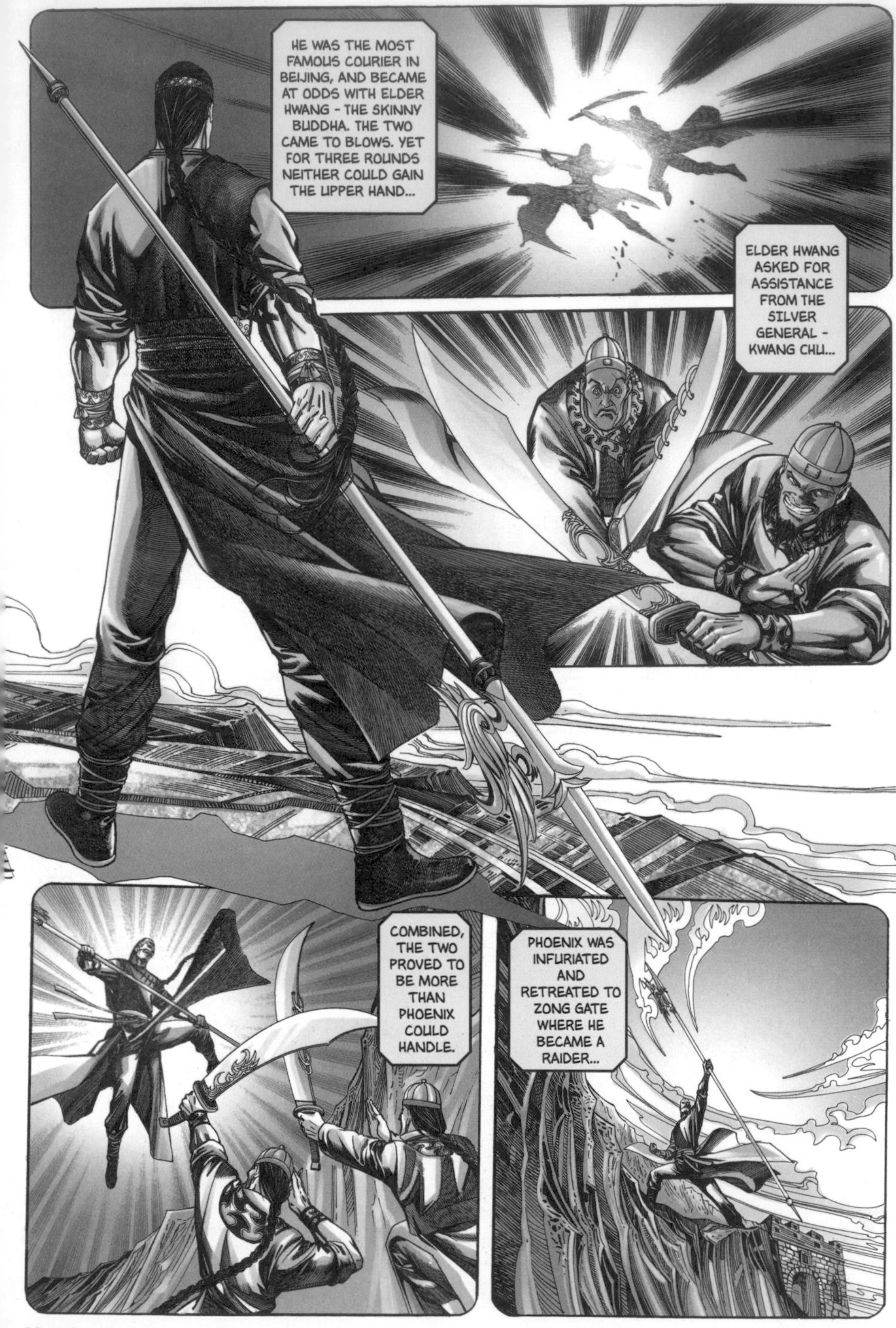
HE WAS THE MOST FAMOUS COURIER IN BEIJING, AND BECAME AT ODDS WITH ELDER HWANG - THE SKINNY BUDDHA. THE TWO CAME TO BLOWS. YET FOR THREE ROUNDS NEITHER COULD GAIN THE UPPER HAND...
ELDER HWANG ASKED FOR ASSISTANCE FROM THE SILVER GENERAL - KWANG CHU...
COMBINED, THE TWO PROVED TO BE MORE THAN PHOENIX COULD HANDLE.
PHOENIX WAS INFURIATED AND RETREATED TO ZONG GATE WHERE HE BECAME A RAIDER...

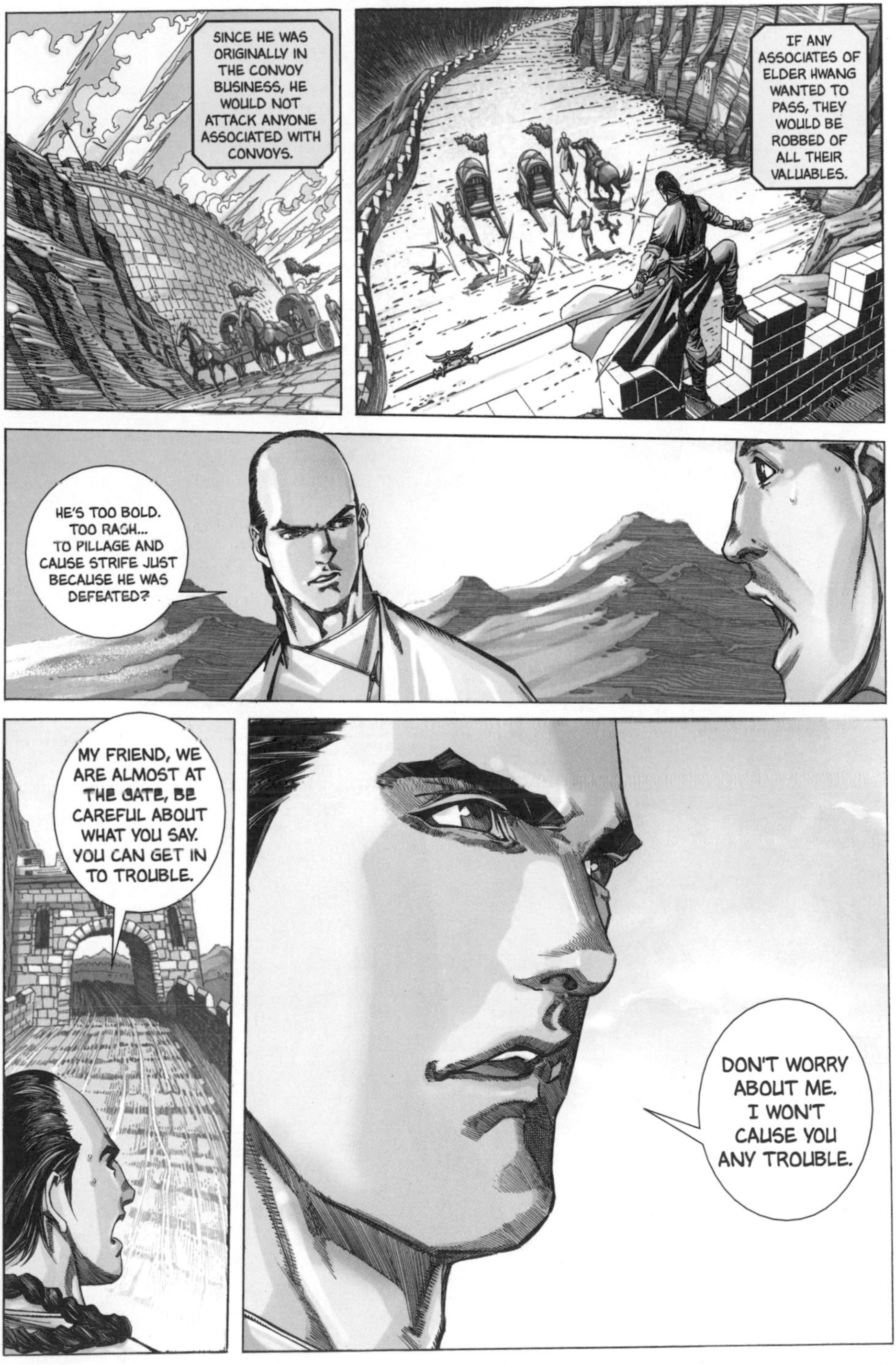
SINCE HE WAS ORIGINALLY IN THE CONVOY BUSINESS, HE WOULD NOT ATTACK ANYONE ASSOCIATED WITH CONVOYS.
IF ANY ASSOCIATES OF ELDER HWANG WANTED TO PASS, THEY WOULD BE ROBBED OF ALL THEIR VALUABLES.
HE'S TOO BOLD. TOO RASH... TO PILLAGE AND CAUSE STRIFE JUST BECAUSE HE WAS DEFEATED?
MY FRIEND, WE ARE ALMOST AT THE GATE, BE CAREFUL ABOUT WHAT YOU SAY. YOU CAN GET IN TO TROUBLE.
DON'T WORRY ABOUT ME. I WON'T CAUSE YOU ANY TROUBLE.

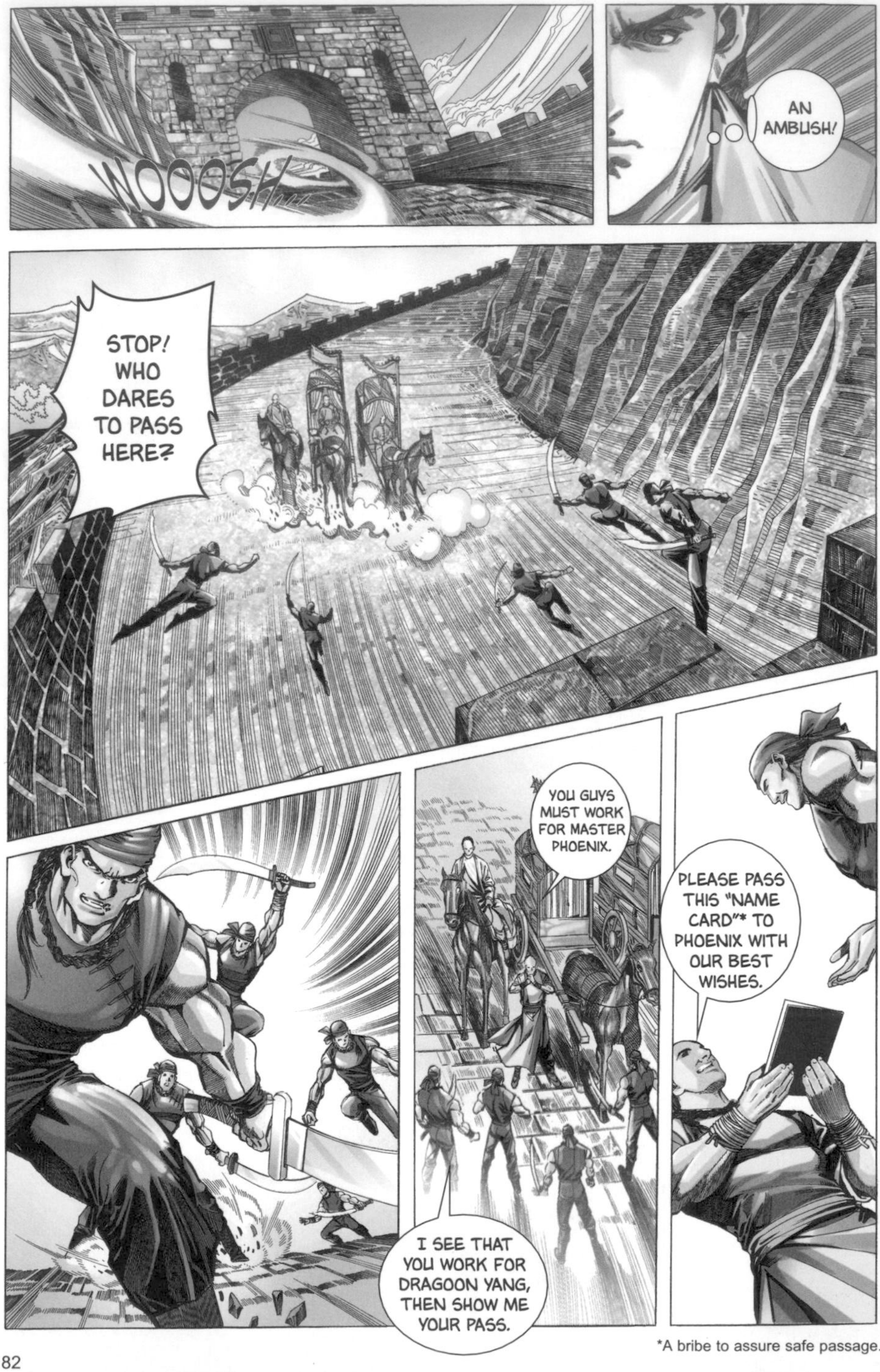
WOOSH...
AN AMBUSH!
STOP! WHO DARES TO PASS HERE?
YOU GUYS MUST WORK FOR MASTER PHOENIX.
I SEE THAT YOU WORK FOR DRAGOON YANG, THEN SHOW ME YOUR PASS.
PLEASE PASS THIS "NAME CARD"* TO PHOENIX WITH OUR BEST WISHES.

*A bribe to assure safe passage.

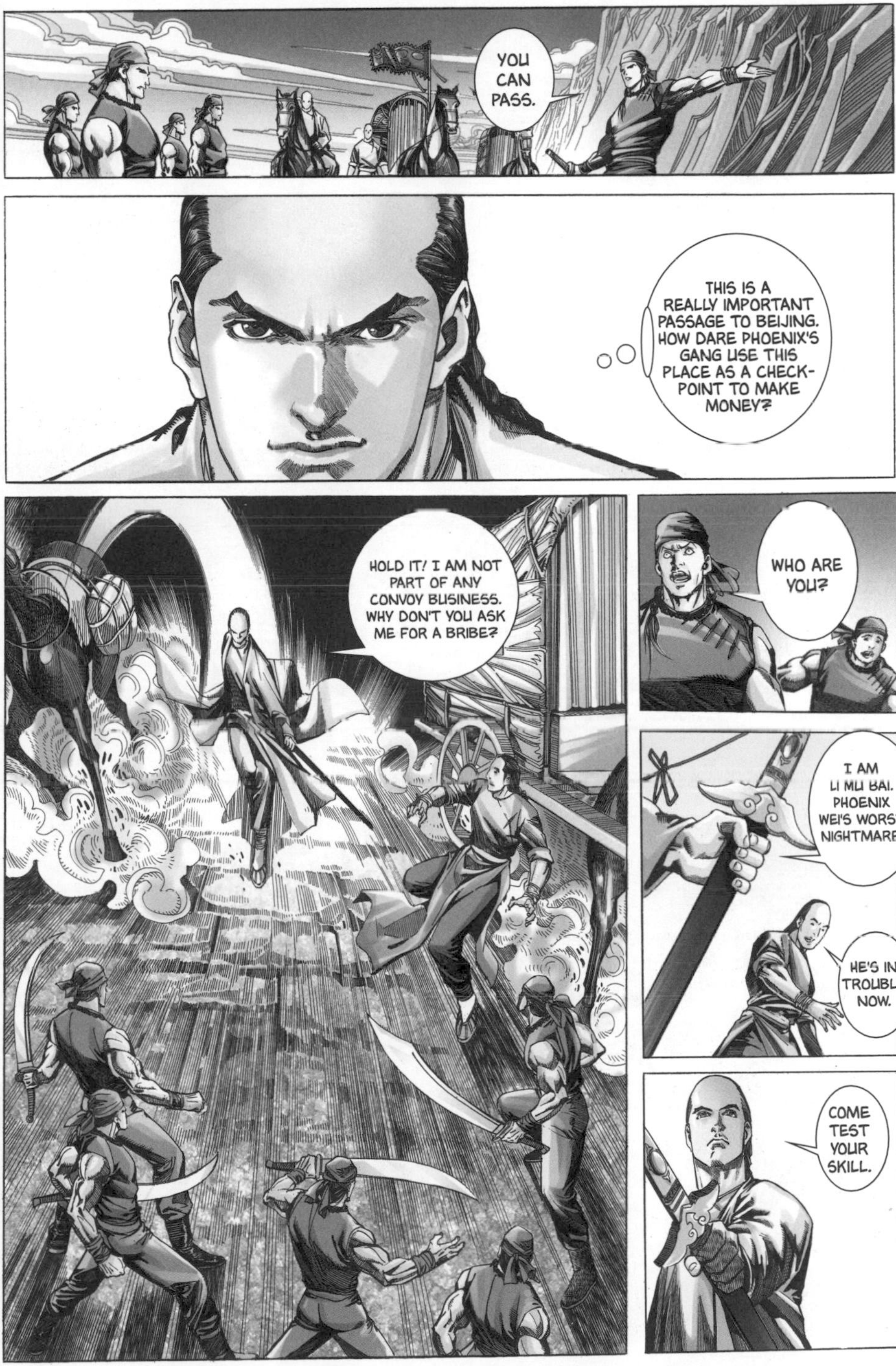
YOU CAN PASS.
THIS IS A REALLY IMPORTANT PASSAGE TO BEIJING. HOW DARE PHOENIX'S GANG USE THIS PLACE AS A CHECK-POINT TO MAKE MONEY?
HOLD IT! I AM NOT PART OF ANY CONVOY BUSINESS. WHY DON'T YOU ASK ME FOR A BRIBE?
WHO ARE YOU?
I AM LI MU BAI. PHOENIX WEI'S WORST NIGHTMARE.
HE'S IN TROUBLE NOW.
COME TEST YOUR SKILL.

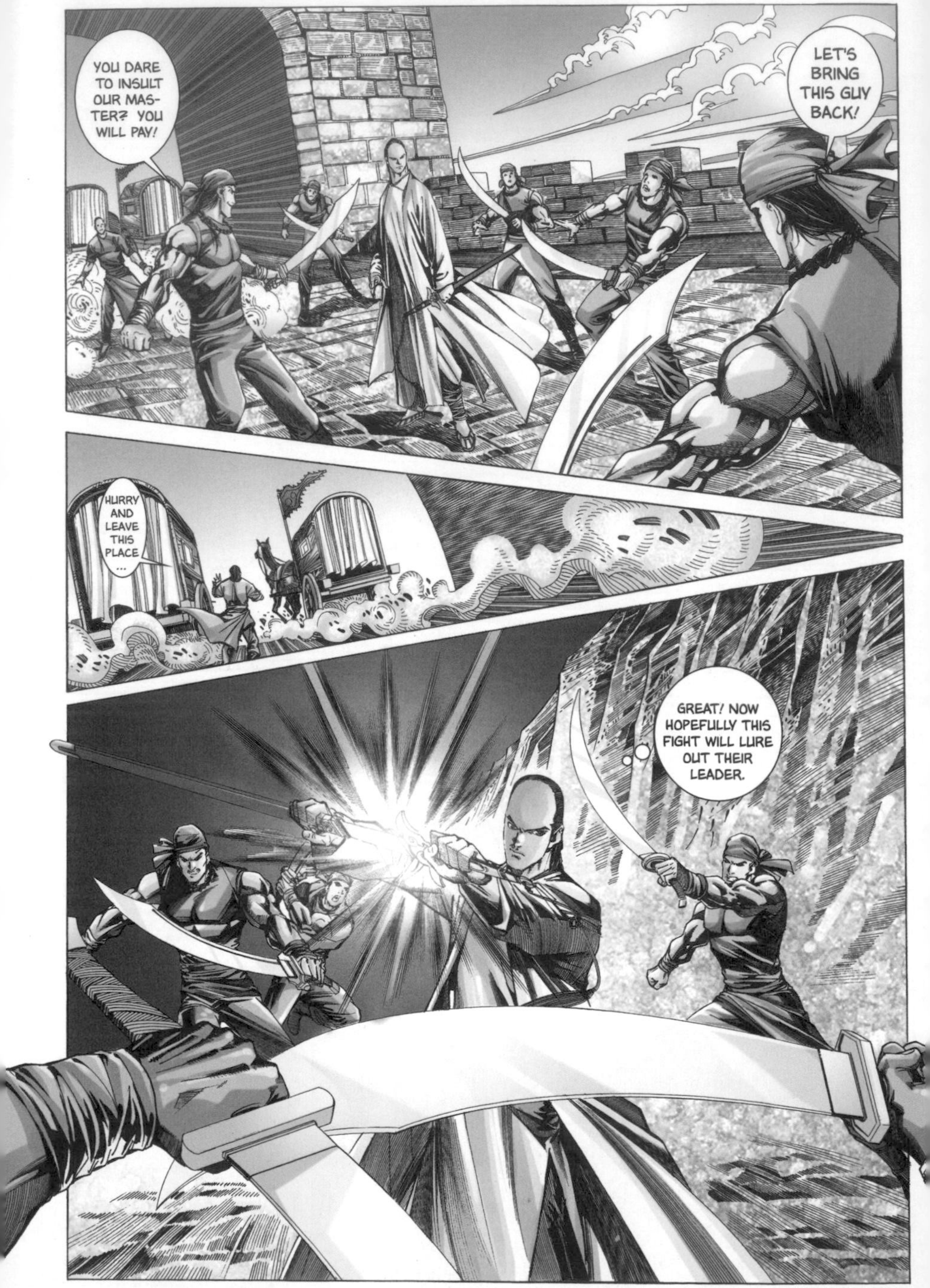
YOU DARE TO INSULT OUR MASTER? YOU WILL PAY!
LET'S BRING THIS GUY BACK!
HURRY AND LEAVE THIS PLACE ...
GREAT! NOW HOPEFULLY THIS FIGHT WILL LURE OUT THEIR LEADER.

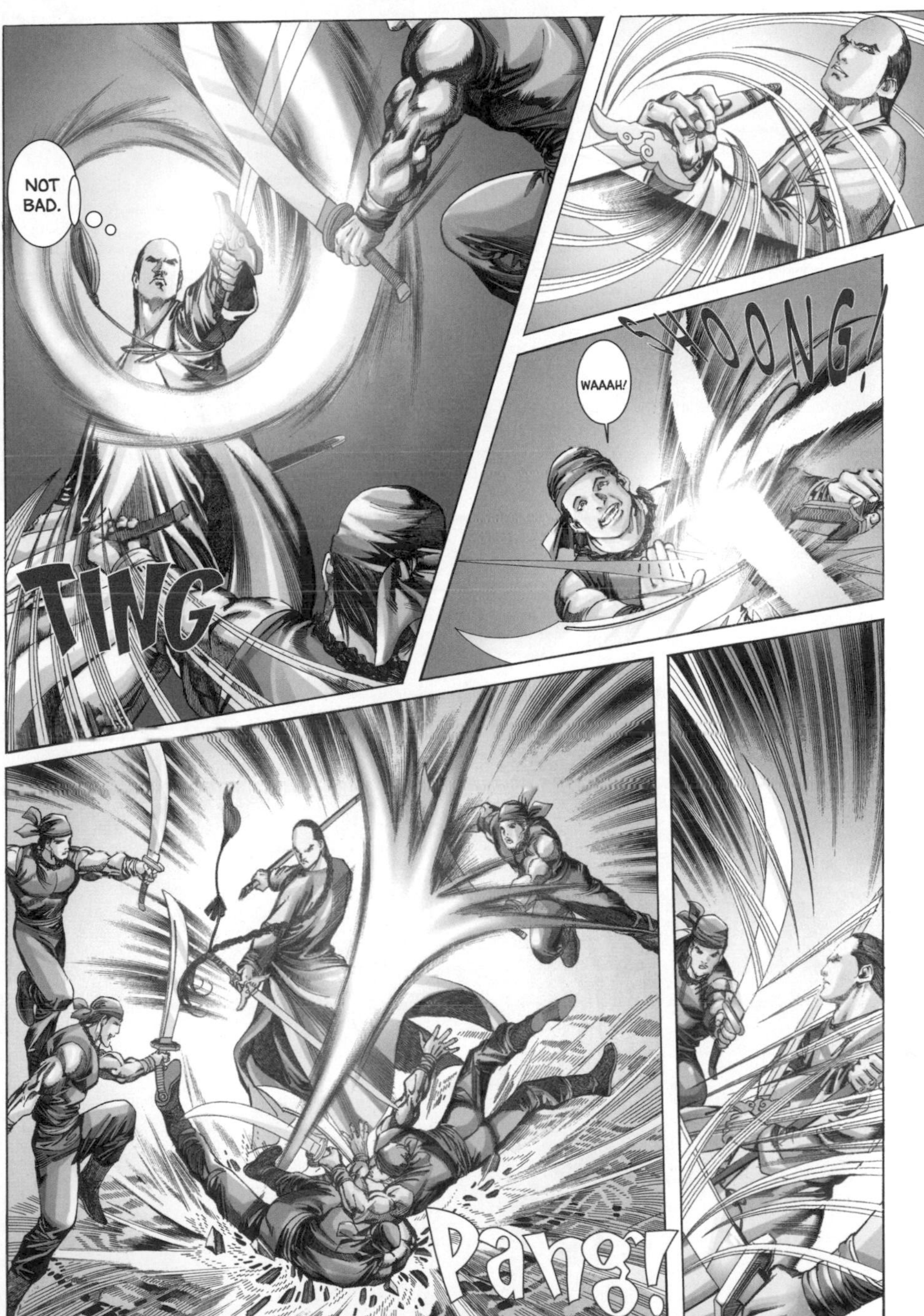
NOT BAD.
TING
SHOONG!
WAAAH!
Pang!

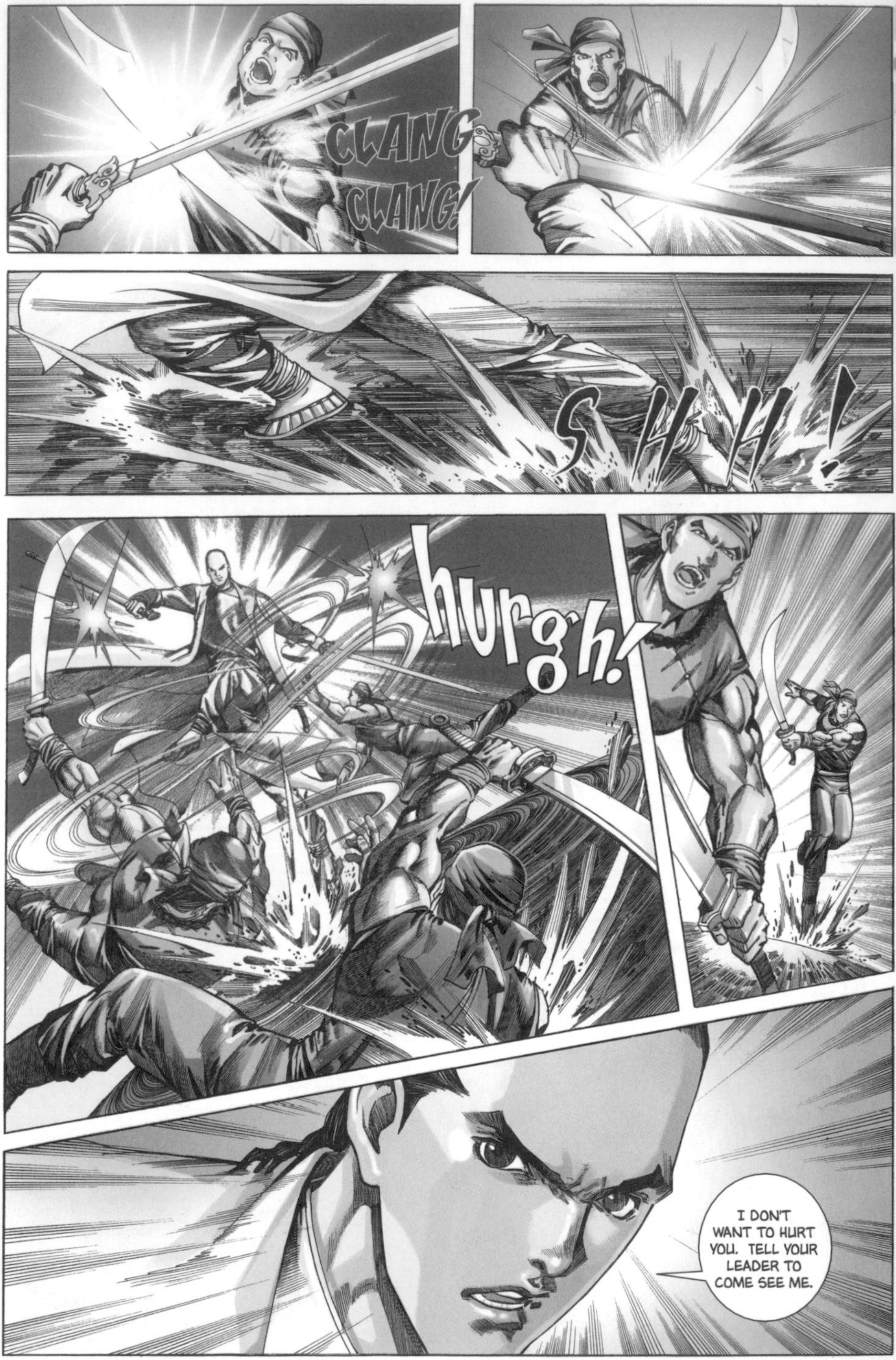
CLANG
CLANG!
SHH!
hurgh!
I DON'T WANT TO HURT YOU. TELL YOUR LEADER TO COME SEE ME.

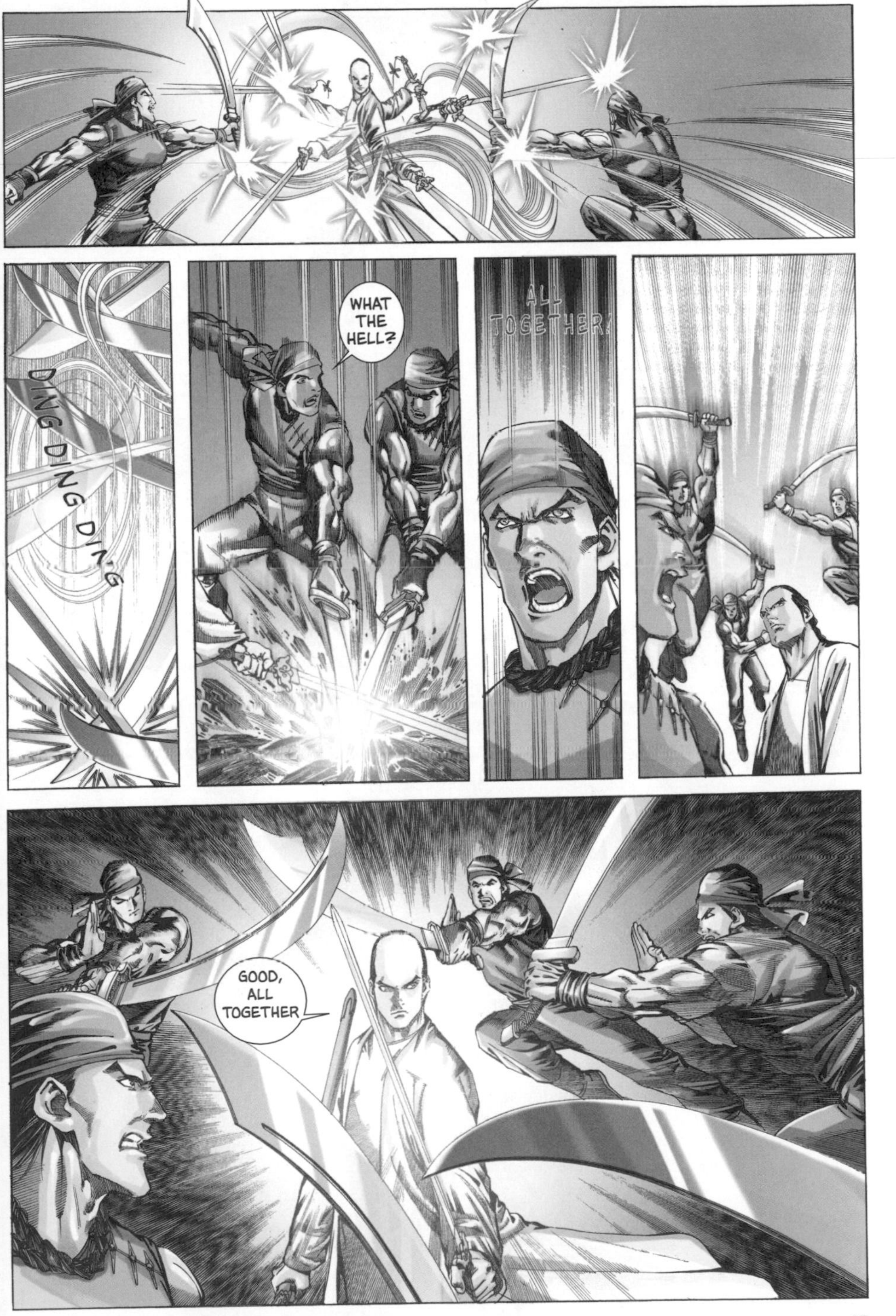
DING DING DING
WHAT THE HELL?
ALL TOGETHER!
GOOD, ALL TOGETHER

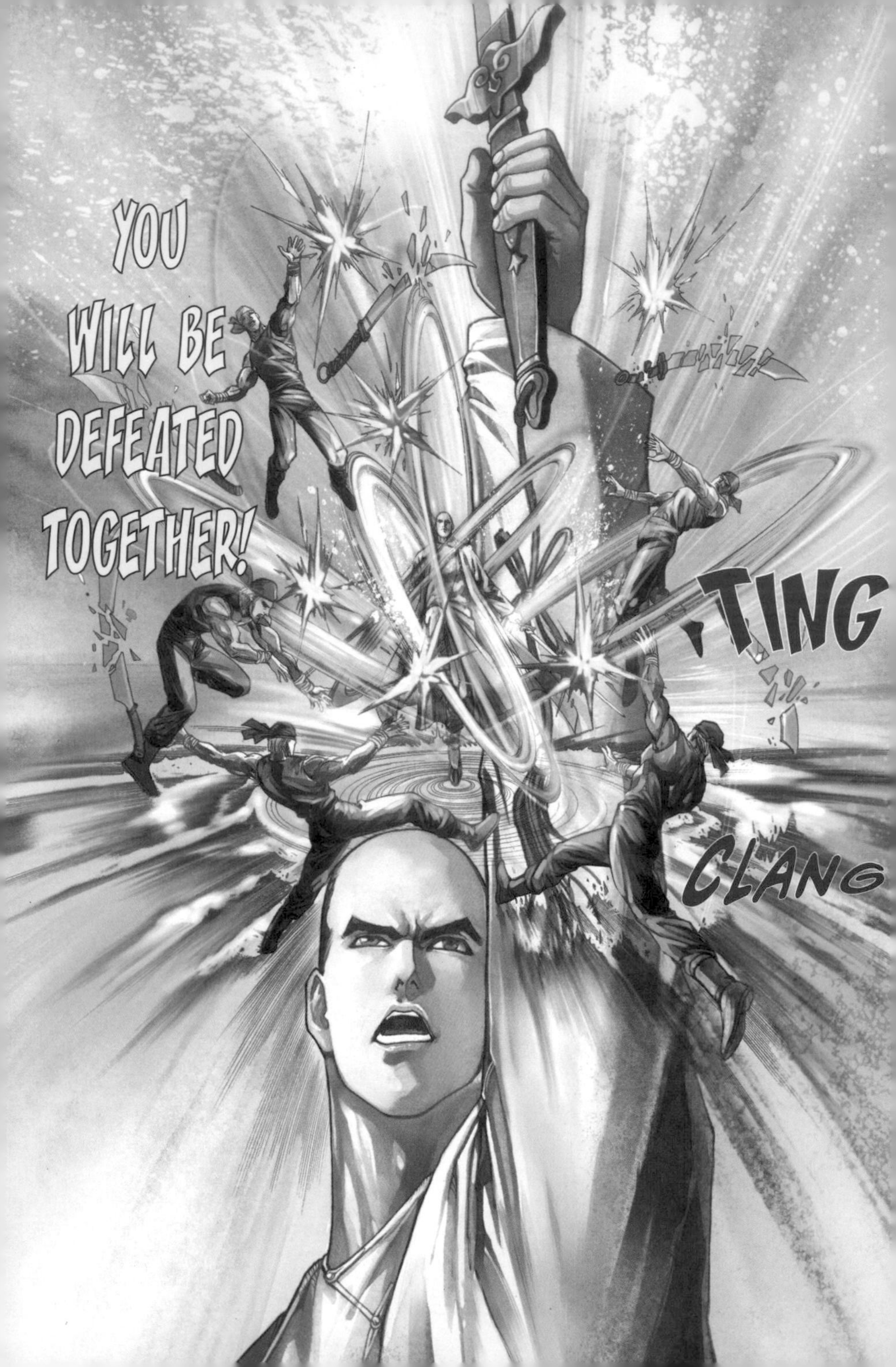
YOU WILL BE DEFEATED TOGETHER!
TING
CLANG

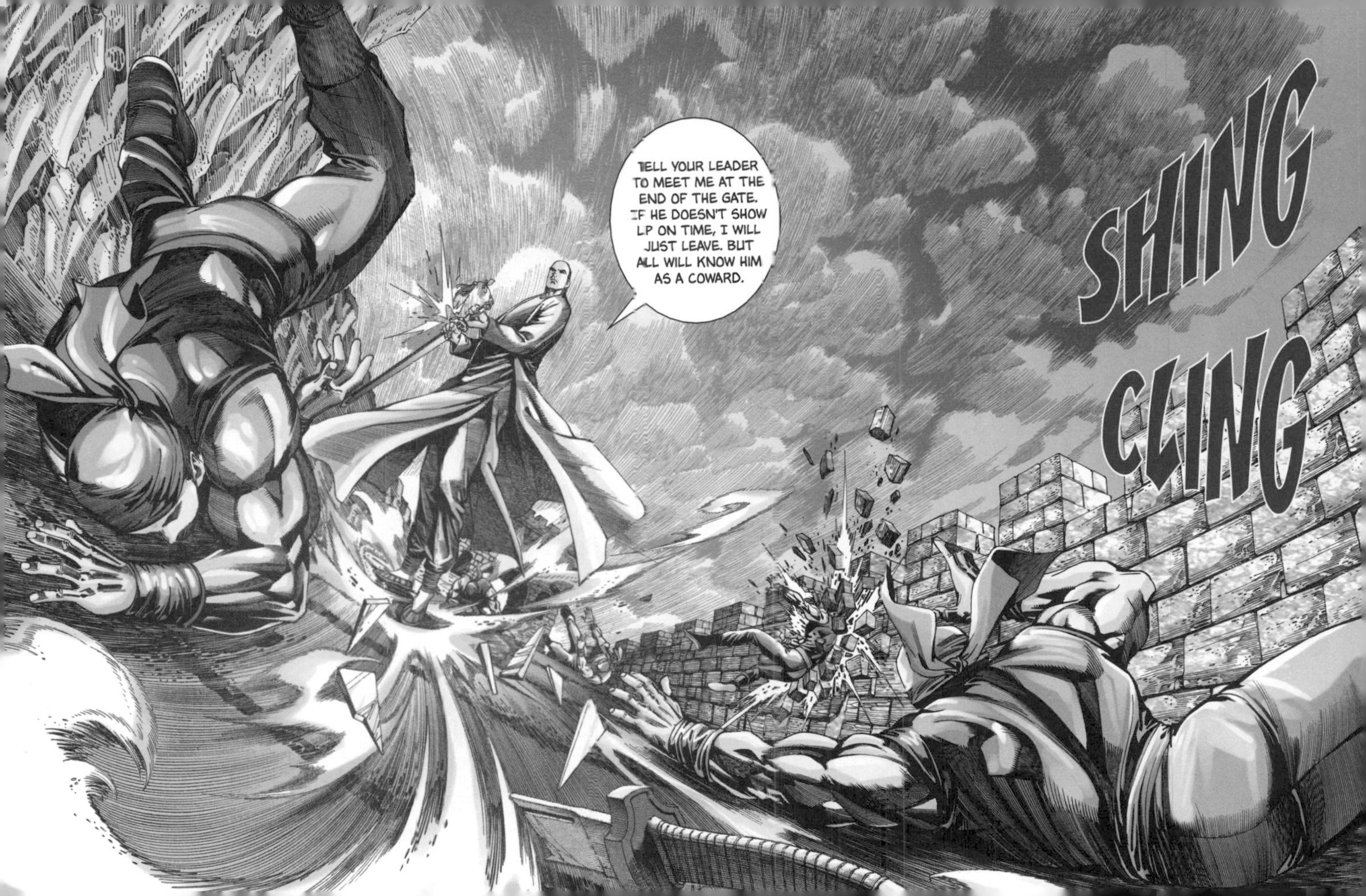
TELL YOUR LEADER TO MEET ME AT THE END OF THE GATE. IF HE DOESN'T SHOW UP ON TIME, I WILL JUST LEAVE. BUT ALL WILL KNOW HIM AS A COWARD.
SHING
CLING

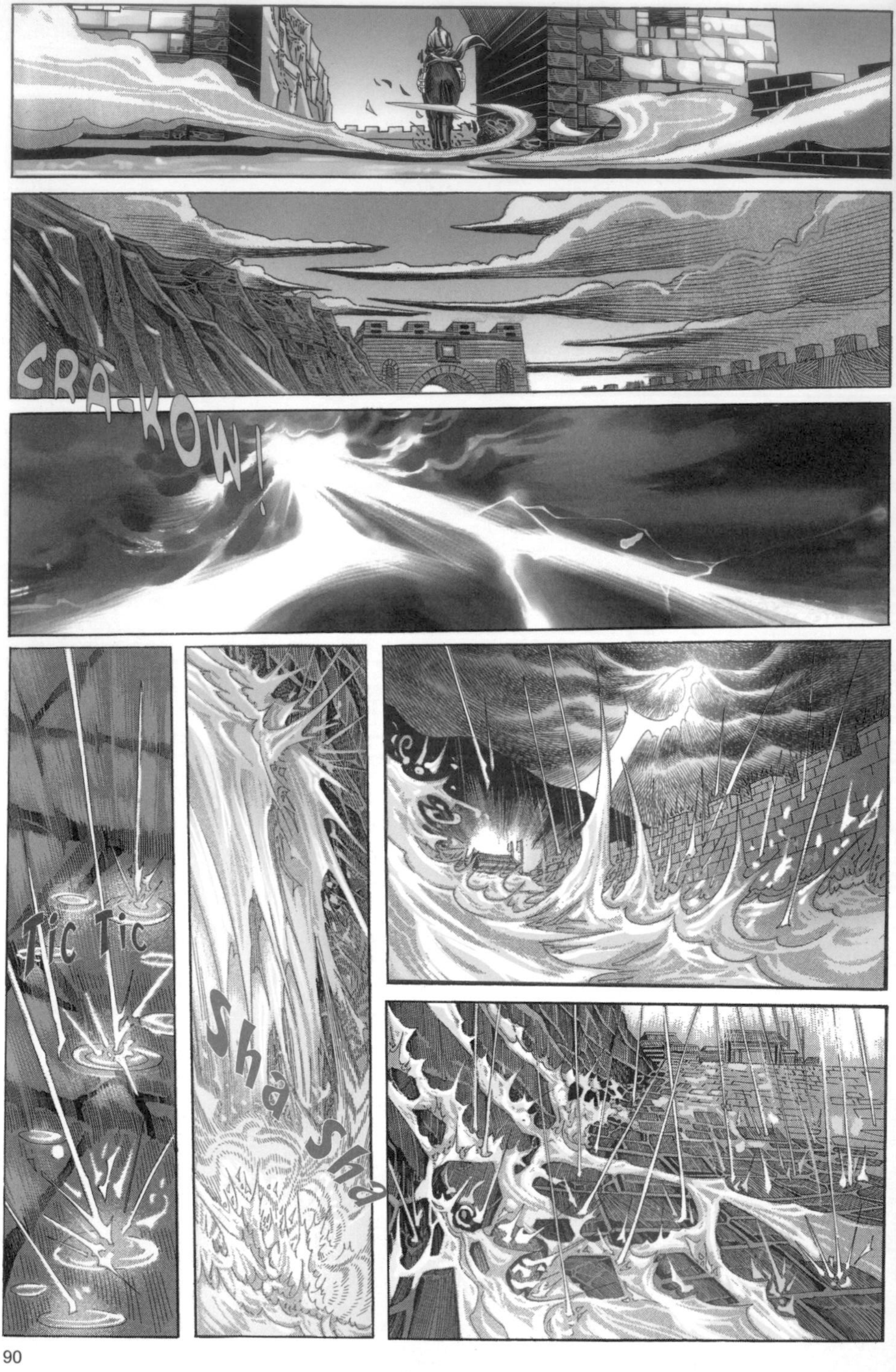
CRA-KOW!!
Tic Tic
Sha Sha

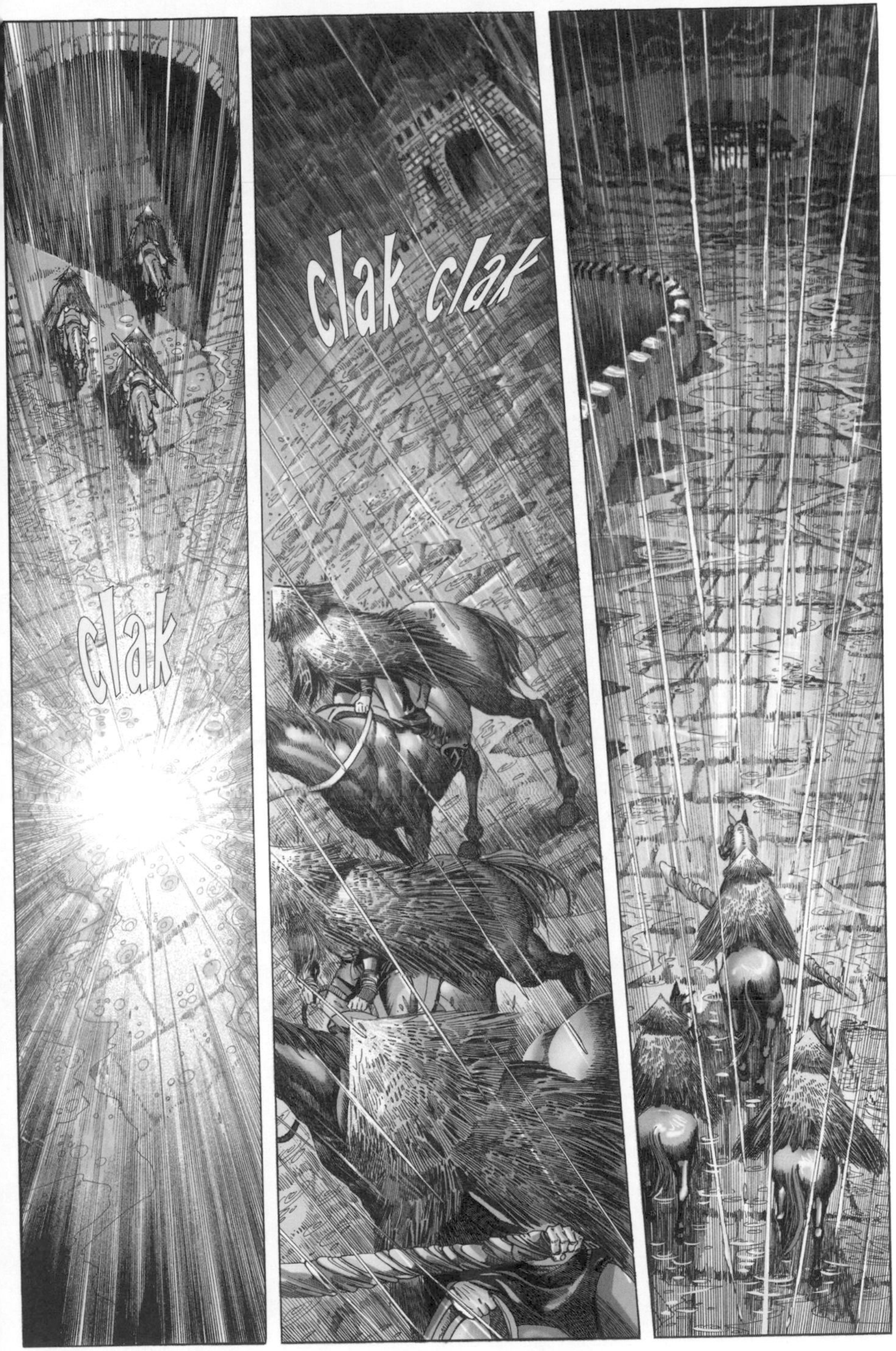
clak
clak clak

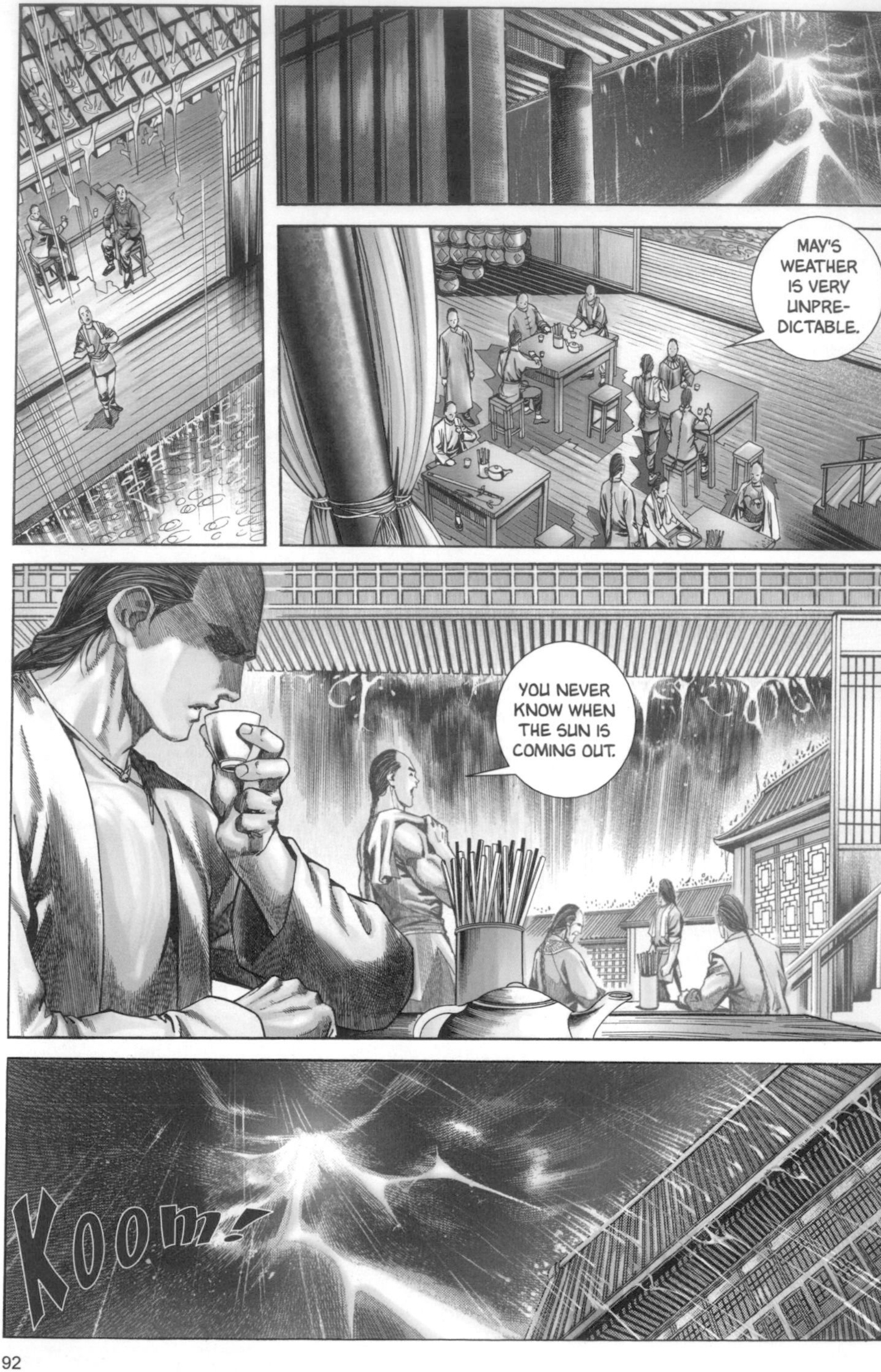
MAY'S WEATHER IS VERY UNPRE-DICTABLE.
YOU NEVER KNOW WHEN THE SUN IS COMING OUT.
Koom!

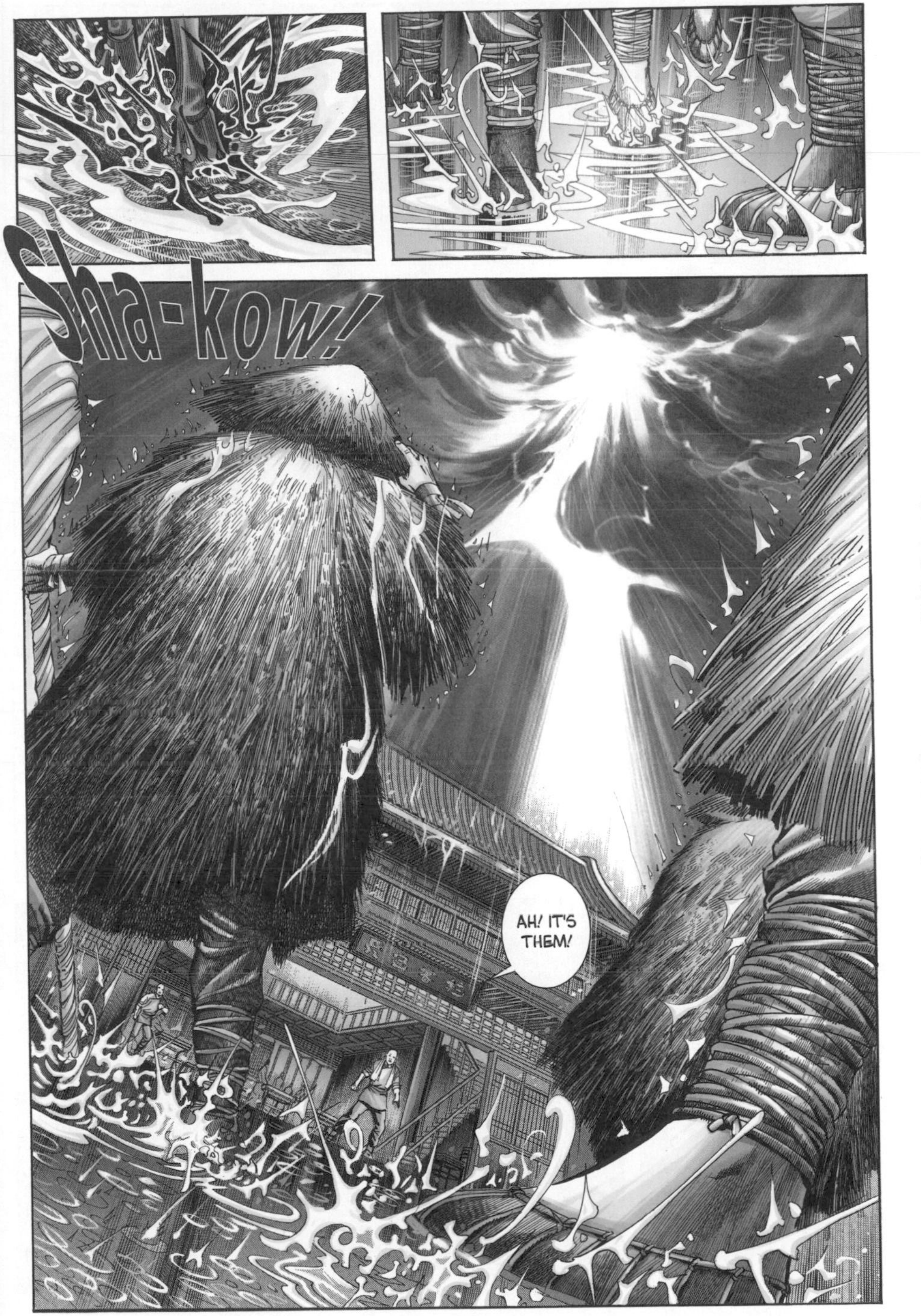
Sha-kow!
AH! IT'S THEM!

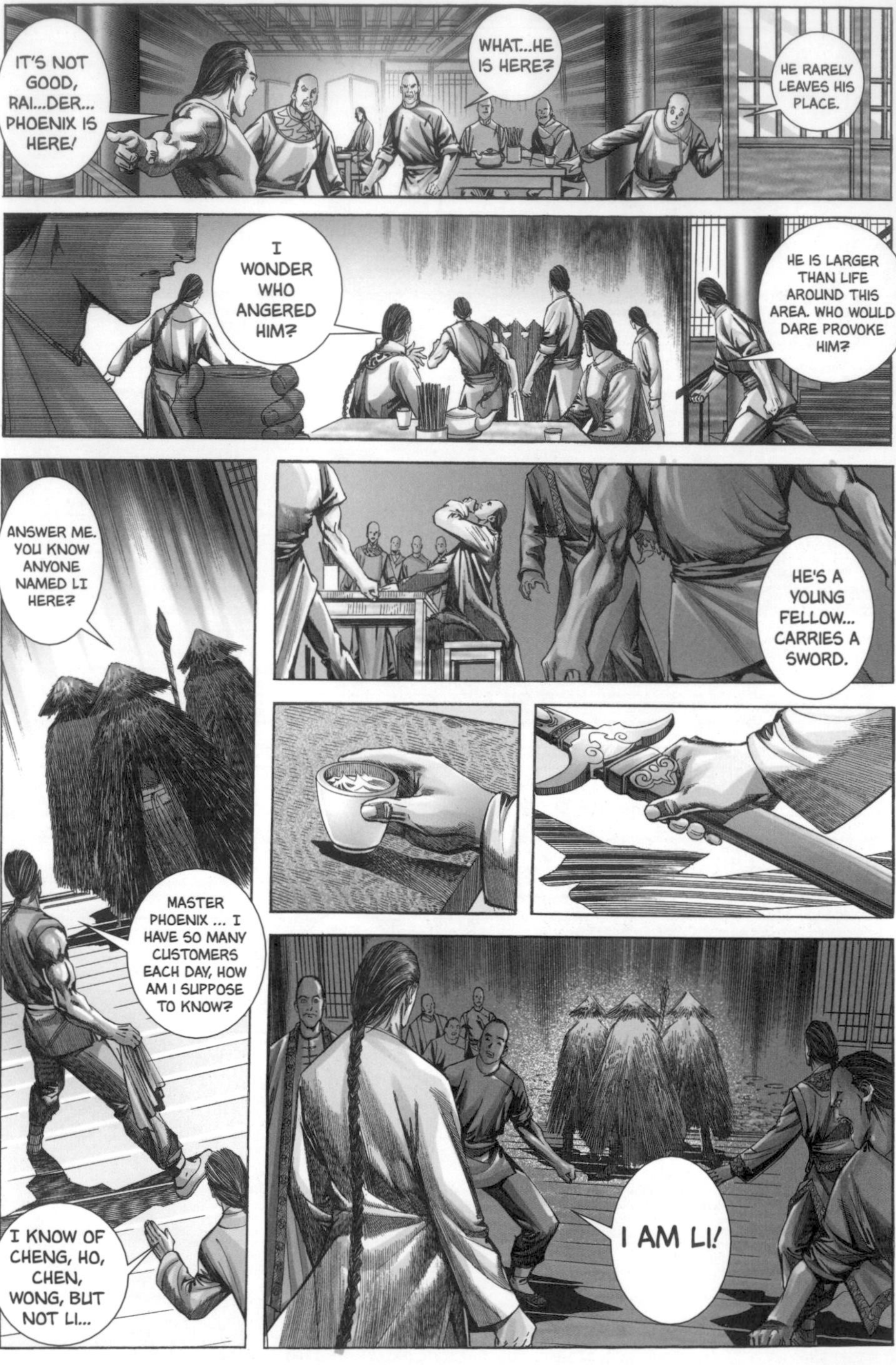
IT'S NOT GOOD, RAI...DER... PHOENIX IS HERE!
WHAT...HE IS HERE?
HE RARELY LEAVES HIS PLACE.
I WONDER WHO ANGERED HIM?
HE IS LARGER THAN LIFE AROUND THIS AREA. WHO WOULD DARE PROVOKE HIM?
ANSWER ME. YOU KNOW ANYONE NAMED LI HERE?
HE'S A YOUNG FELLOW... CARRIES A SWORD.
MASTER PHOENIX ... I HAVE SO MANY CUSTOMERS EACH DAY, HOW AM I SUPPOSE TO KNOW?
I KNOW OF CHENG, HO, CHEN, WONG, BUT NOT LI...
I AM LI!

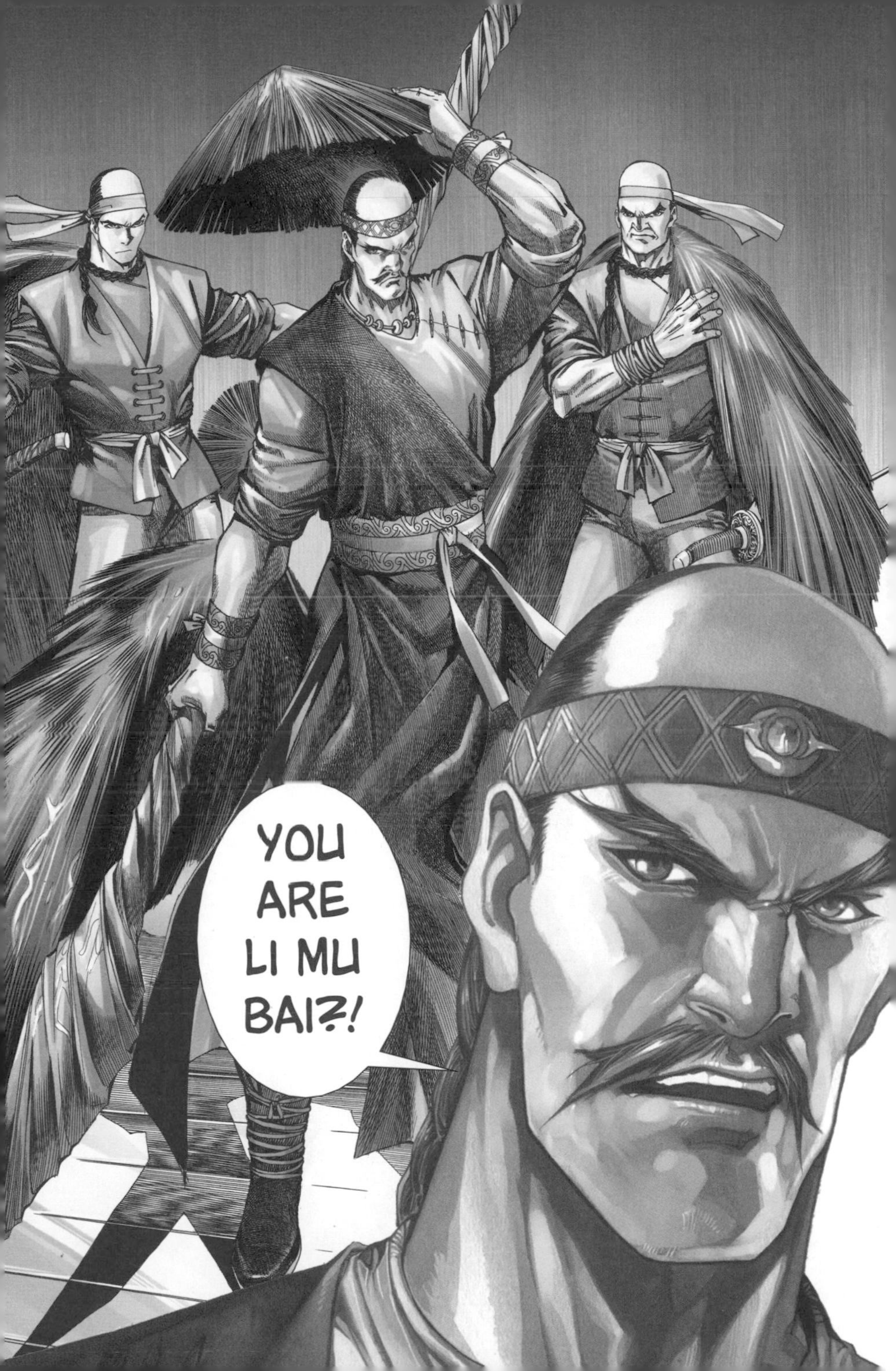
YOU
ARE
LI MU
BAI?!

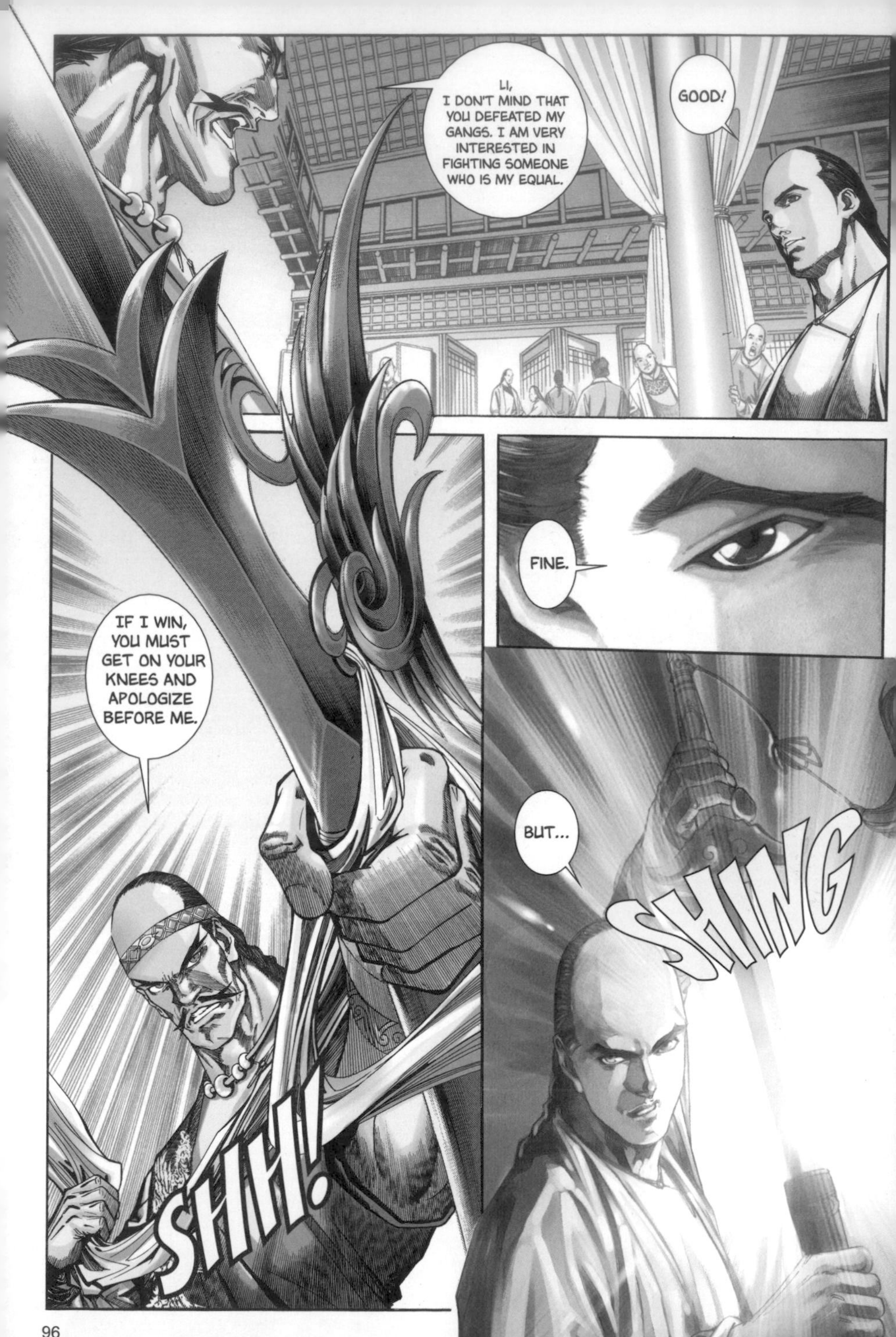
LI,
I DON'T MIND THAT YOU DEFEATED MY GANGS. I AM VERY INTERESTED IN FIGHTING SOMEONE WHO IS MY EQUAL.
GOOD!
IF I WIN, YOU MUST GET ON YOUR KNEES AND APOLOGIZE BEFORE ME.
SHH!
FINE.
BUT...
SHING

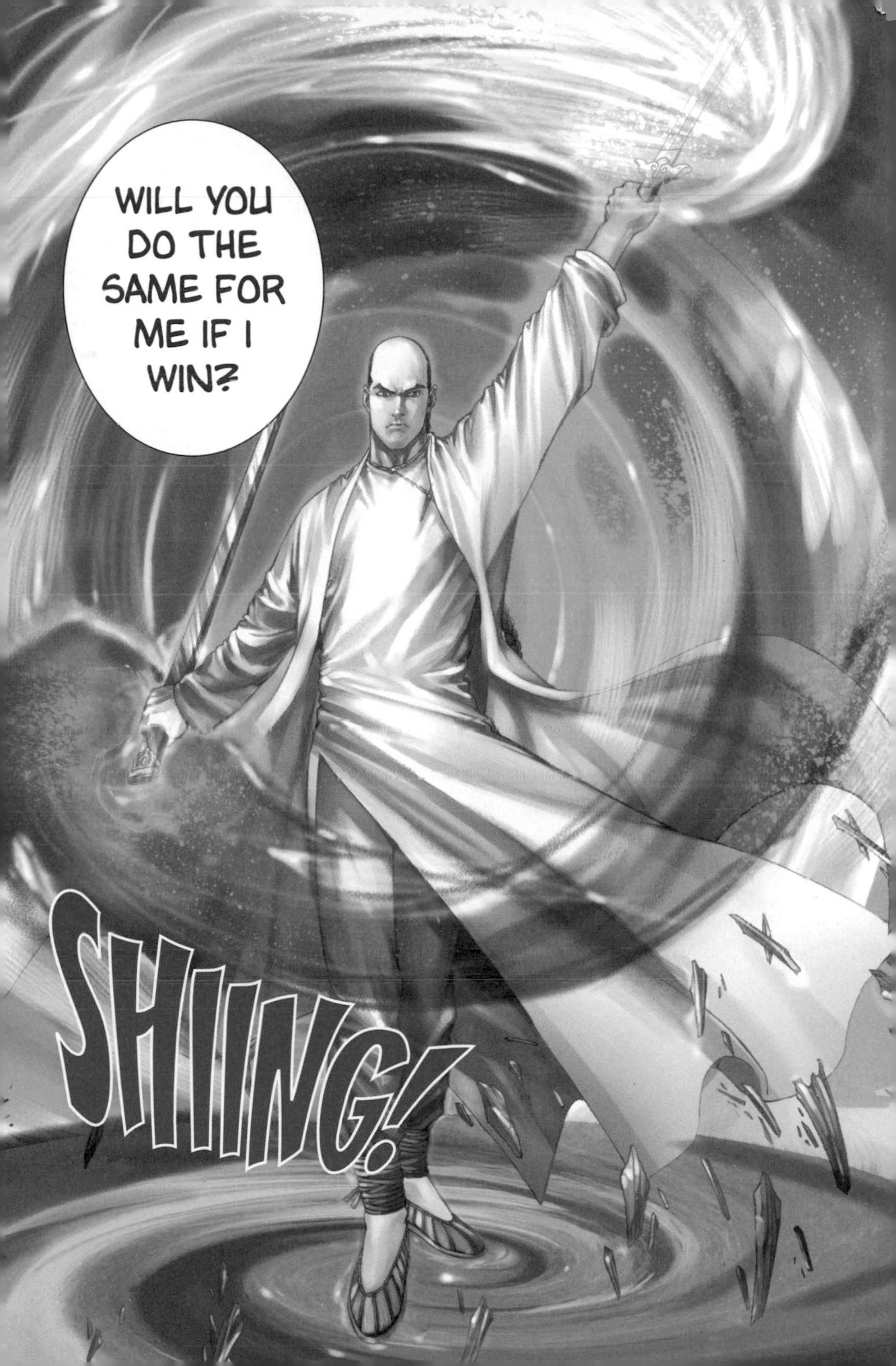
WILL YOU DO THE SAME FOR ME IF I WIN?
SHIING!

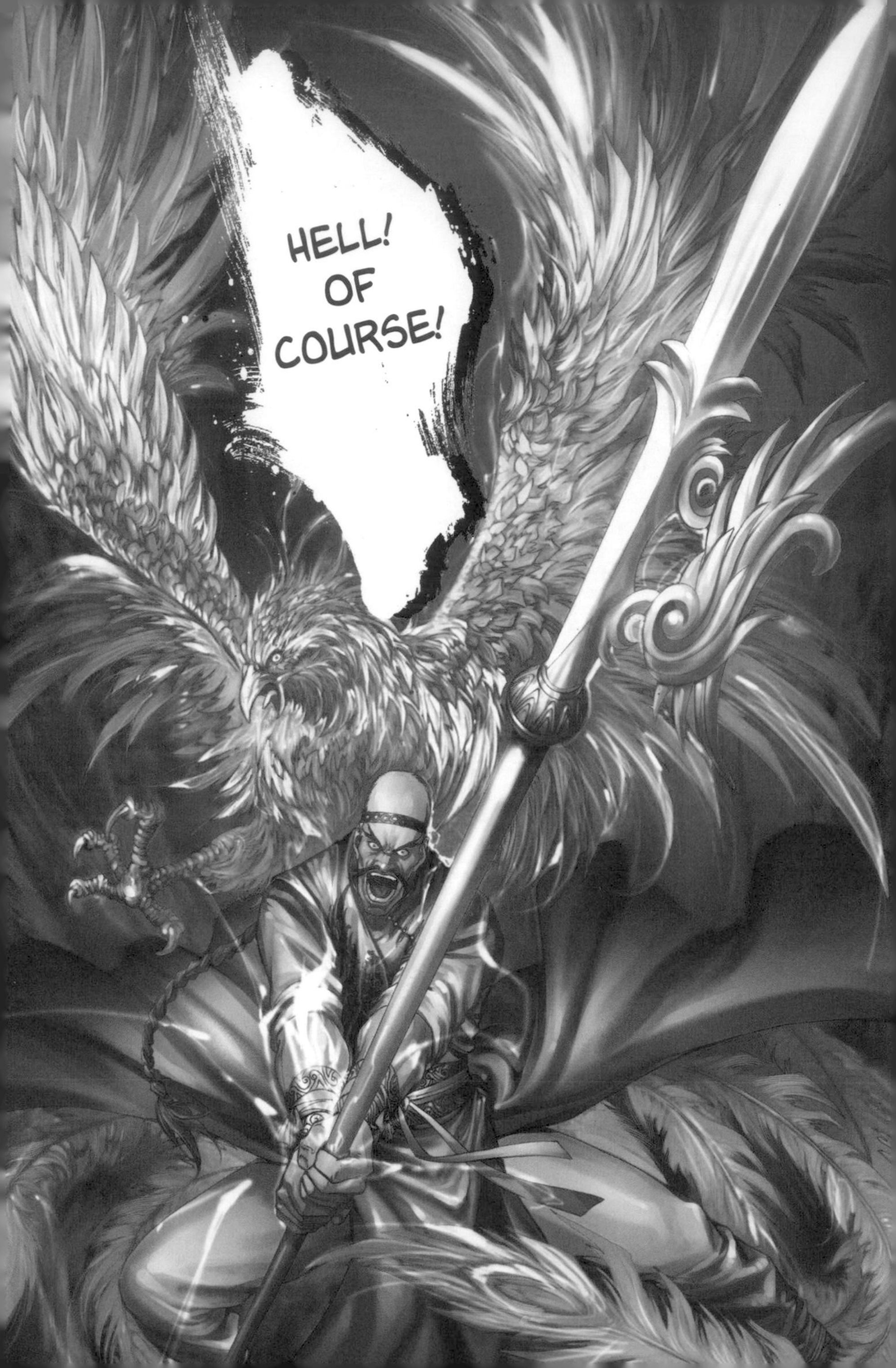
HELL! OF COURSE!

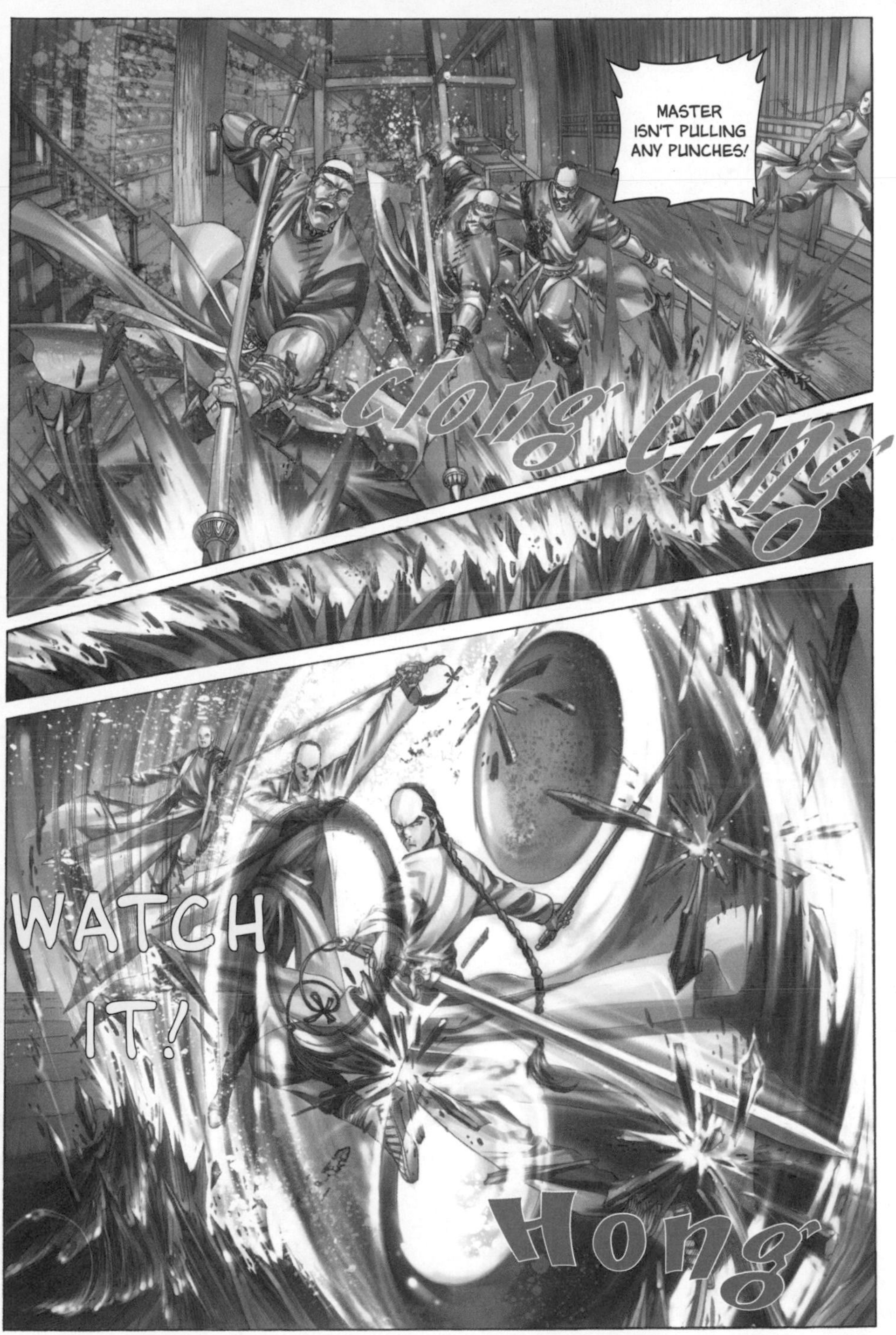
MASTER ISN'T PULLING ANY PUNCHES!
Clong Clong
WATCH IT!
Hong

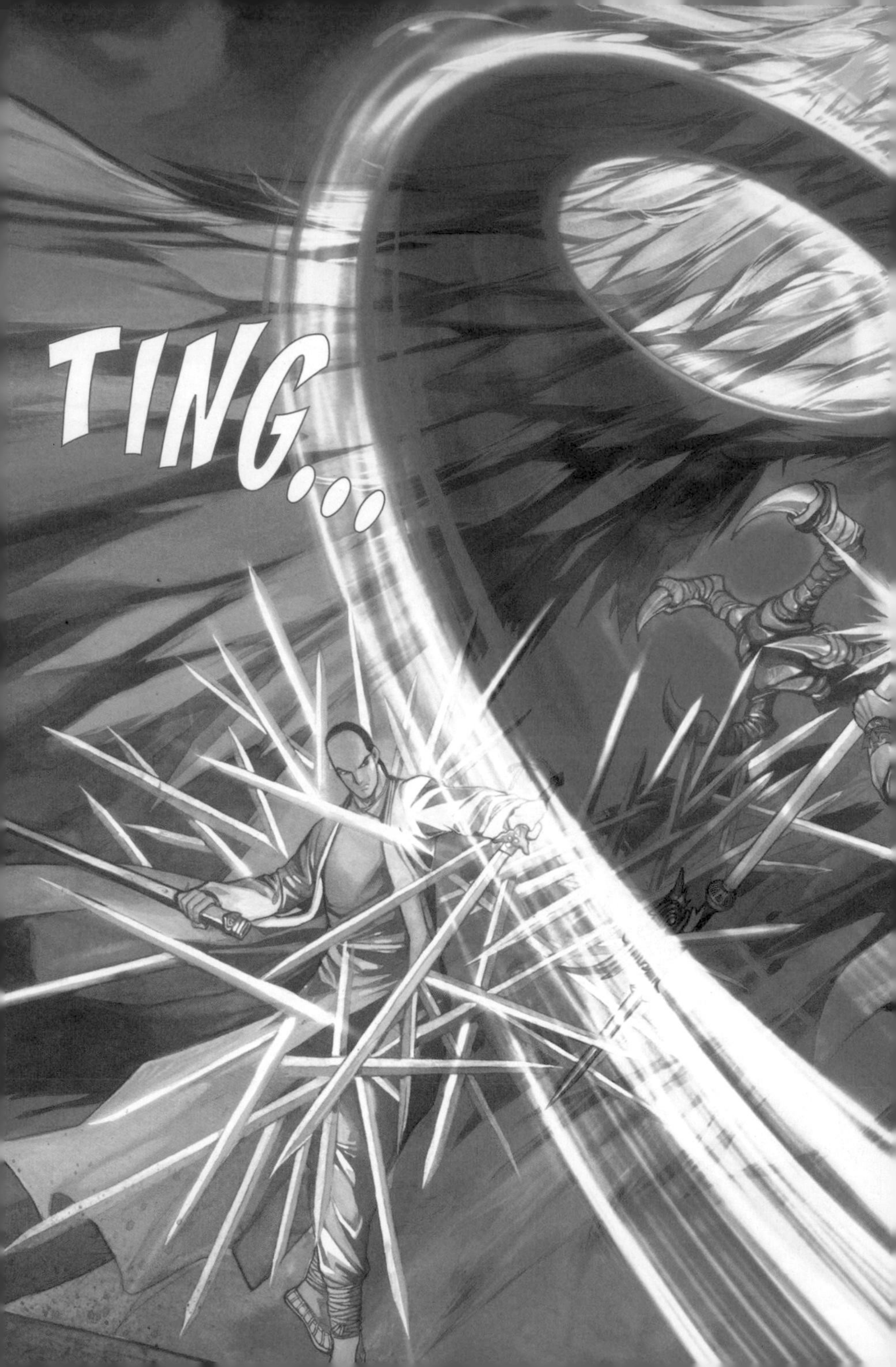
TING...

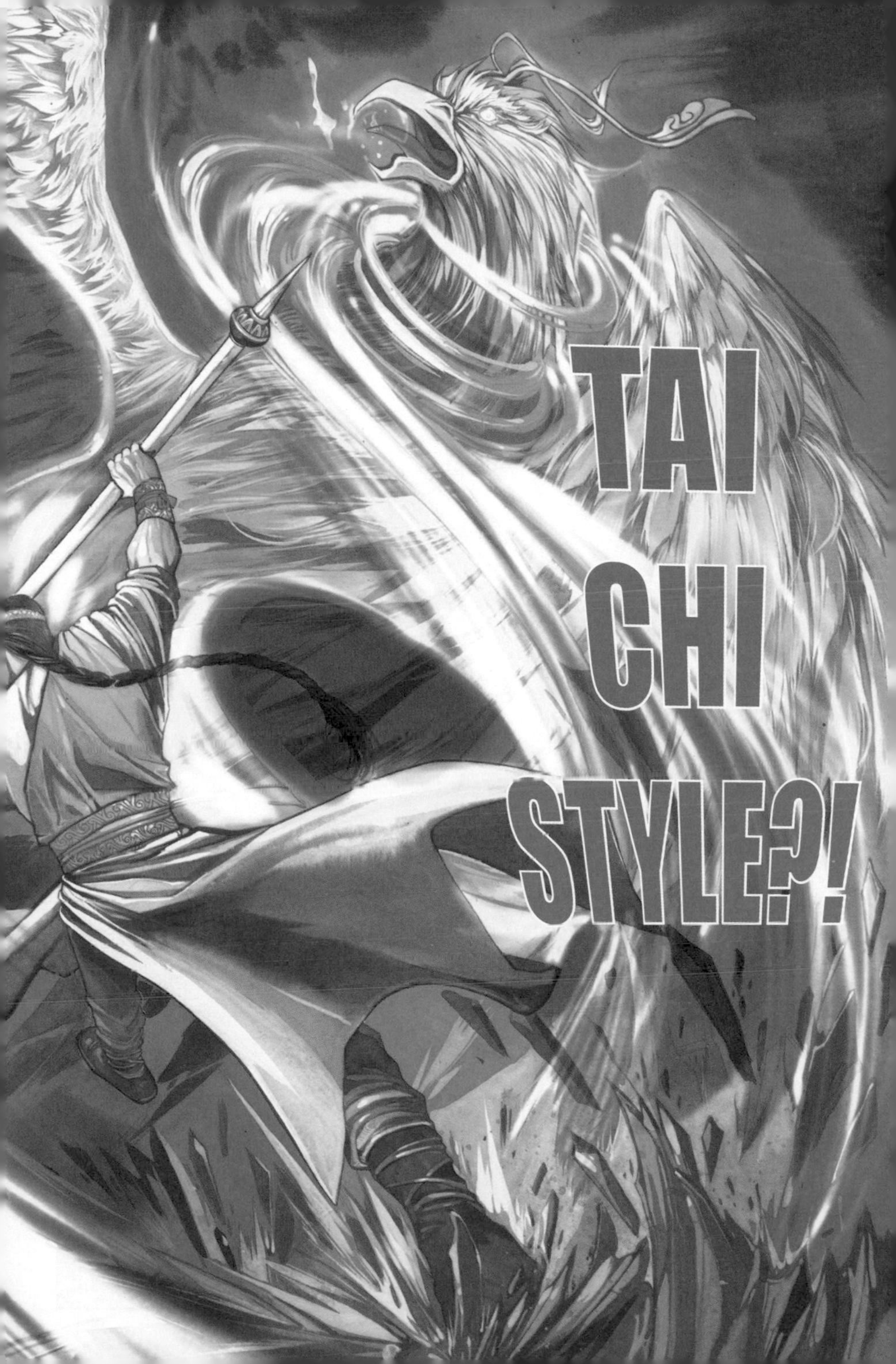
TAI CHI STYLE?!

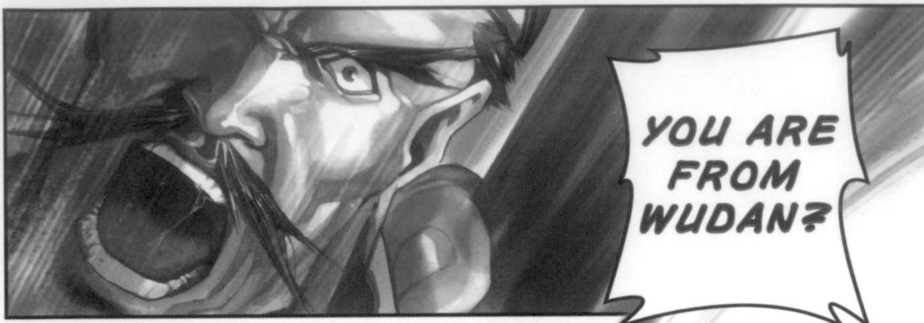
YOU ARE FROM WUDAN?

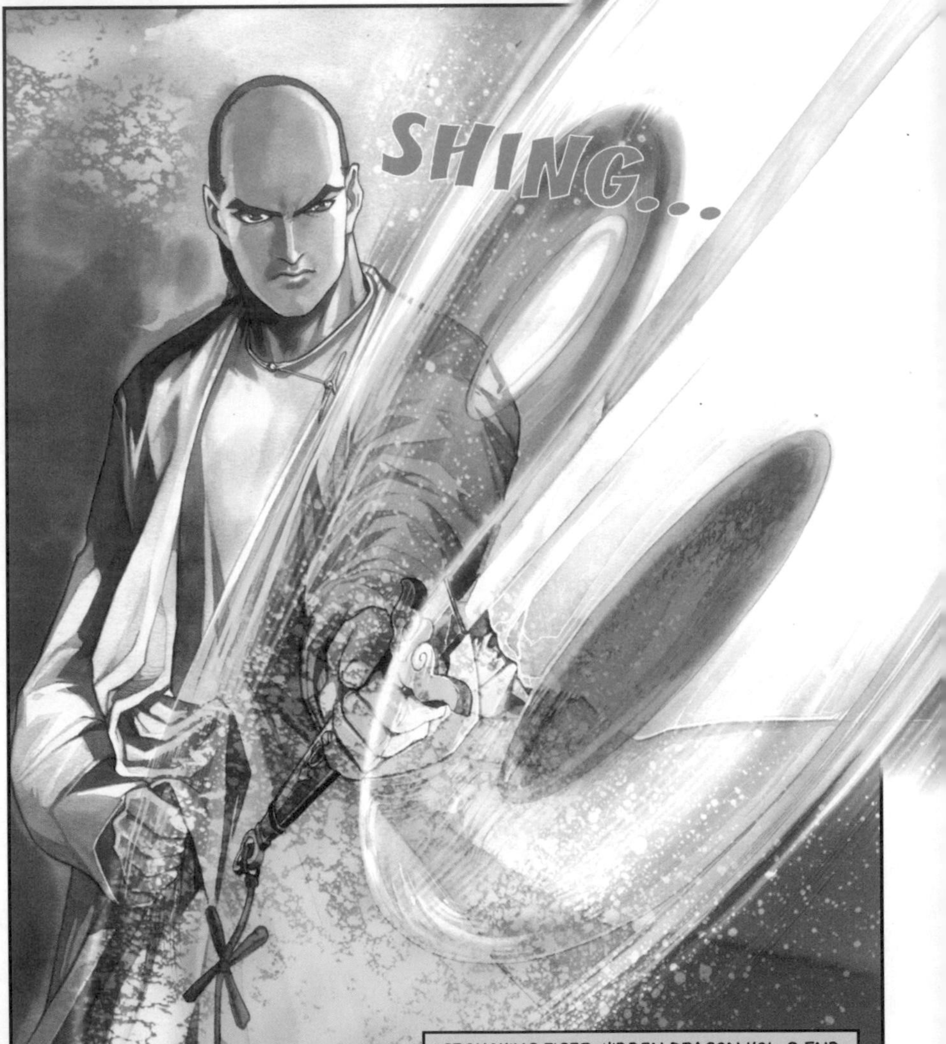
SHING...
CROUCHING TIGER, HIDDEN DRAGON VOL. 2 END

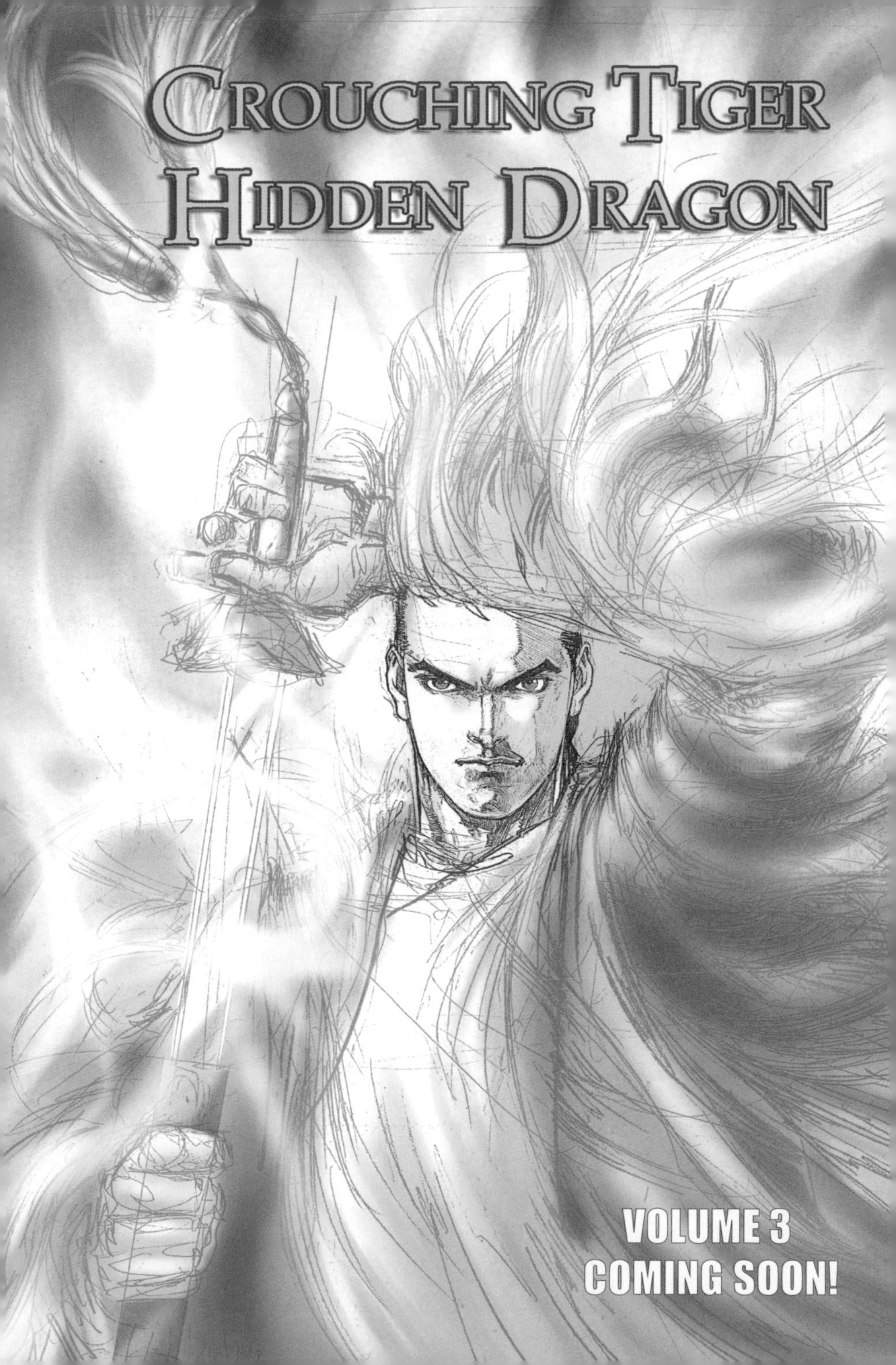
CROUCHING TIGER
HIDDEN DRAGON
VOLUME 3
COMING SOON!

Andy's Diary

LET'S TALK ABOUT THE CURRENT ISSUE OF *CROUCHING TIGER*. I OUT-DID MYSELF BY DRAWING 10 EXTRA PAGES. THEREFORE I HELD BACK THE RELEASE DATE BY A WHOLE WEEK. I HOPE IT'S WORTH THE WAIT. *CROUCHING TIGER* IS NOT YOUR TYPICAL KUNG FU COMIC. IT'S ONE OF A KIND ART PIECE, FOCUSES ON THE EMOTIONS OF EACH CHARACTER. THE THEME DOES NOT EMPHASIZE VIOLENCE OR RELIGION, SO THE READERS CAN CONCENTRATE ON THE CONTENT, MORE THAN THE UNIMPORTANT DETAILS.

THE PREMIER ISSUE OF *CROUCHING TIGER* WAS A BIG SUCCESS; I COULD FINALLY RELAX AFTER SO MUCH PRESSURE. OUR READERS ARE EXCITED ABOUT THIS KIND OF COMIC. THEREFORE I THANK YOU FOR ALL THE SUPPORT.

RECENTLY I ATTENDED THE HK UNIVERSITY COMICS' ART SHOW. I HAD A GREAT TIME SELLING MY COMICS AND TALKING WITH COMIC FANS.

A FRENCH COMPANY HAS INTEREST IN BUYING THE COPYRIGHT OF OUR "CROUCHING TIGER" COMIC. THEY INVITED ME TO THEIR NOVEMBER COMIC SHOW. I HAD REJECTED ALL THE RECENT INVITATIONS. HOWEVER I CAN'T REFUSE THIS OFFER. WITH THE COMPLETION OF EPISODE ONE, I FINALLY HAVE SOME FREE TIME, AND I AM LOOKING FORWARD TO THIS TRIP. I AM SO EXCITED!

THIS ISSUE OF *CROUCHING TIGER* HAS A LOT OF DIALOGUE. HOWEVER, NEXT ISSUE WILL BE THE OPPOSITE. BESIDE THE BATTLE OF LI VS WEI, THERE ARE 2 MORE MAJOR BATTLES. IT WILL ALSO FEATURE ANOTHER ULTIMATE FIGHTER. WHO IS HE/SHE? TAKE A GUESS... ALL I CAN SAY IS MU-BAI IS IN BIG TROUBLE. SEE YOU NEXT TIME!

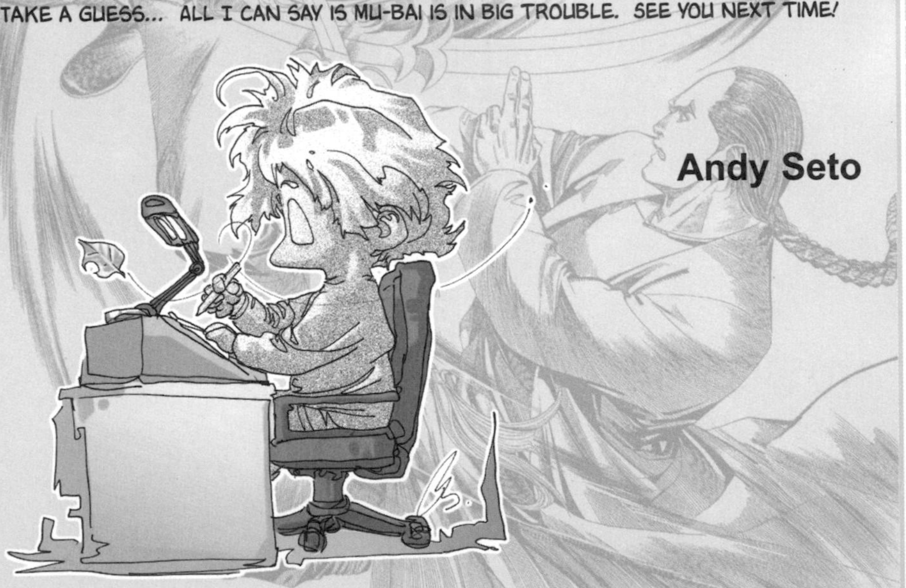

Andy Seto

CROUCHING TIGER
HIDDEN DRAGON

Fantasy, Realism & Martial Arts

by So Man Sing

Wang Du Lu

I have a friend, who is an ABC (American born Chinese). He likes to listen to Chinese music and watch Chinese movies; however, he cannot stand our kung fu movies. He feels that our movies are too exaggerated, and pointless. So imagine how a westerner feels about these kinds of movies.

How can we design the martial art scenes so they will be accepted by both the eastern and western readers?

I think "realism" is very important. By using "believable" fighting styles in real life, we can create a more acceptable story. The battle scenes may seem very simple, but if we pay more attention to the details, we can see that every move contains some style of ancient Chinese martial arts. On the other hand, it also shows that the highest form of Chinese martial arts emphasizes chi --- the inner strength.

Let's look at the end of the movie version. It showed that Jen is jumping down the cliff, and the movie ended right there. However, the novel went beyond that. After Jen jumped down and disappeared, nobody could find her body. Some may say, "She can't die from that, with her kung fu skills, she can almost fly!" The fact is, she is really alive. She faked her own death. She later shows up in the fifth episode of the original series.

Crouching Tiger is just so unique. Regarding "realism" it seems so true to life. Regarding "fantasy", it is truly fantastic! This is what we need: An amazing fantasy story that is believable to our readers, and at the same time, shows the potential of Chinese kung fu.

A current picture of
Mrs. Wang

WEAPONS

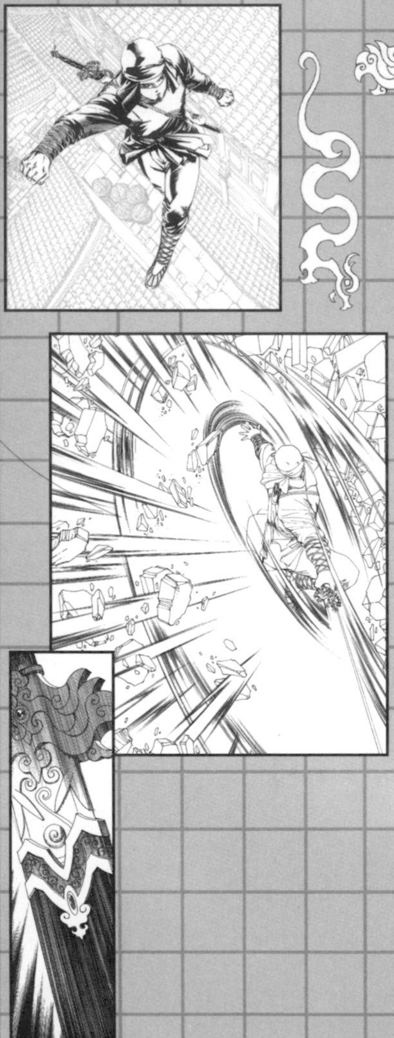

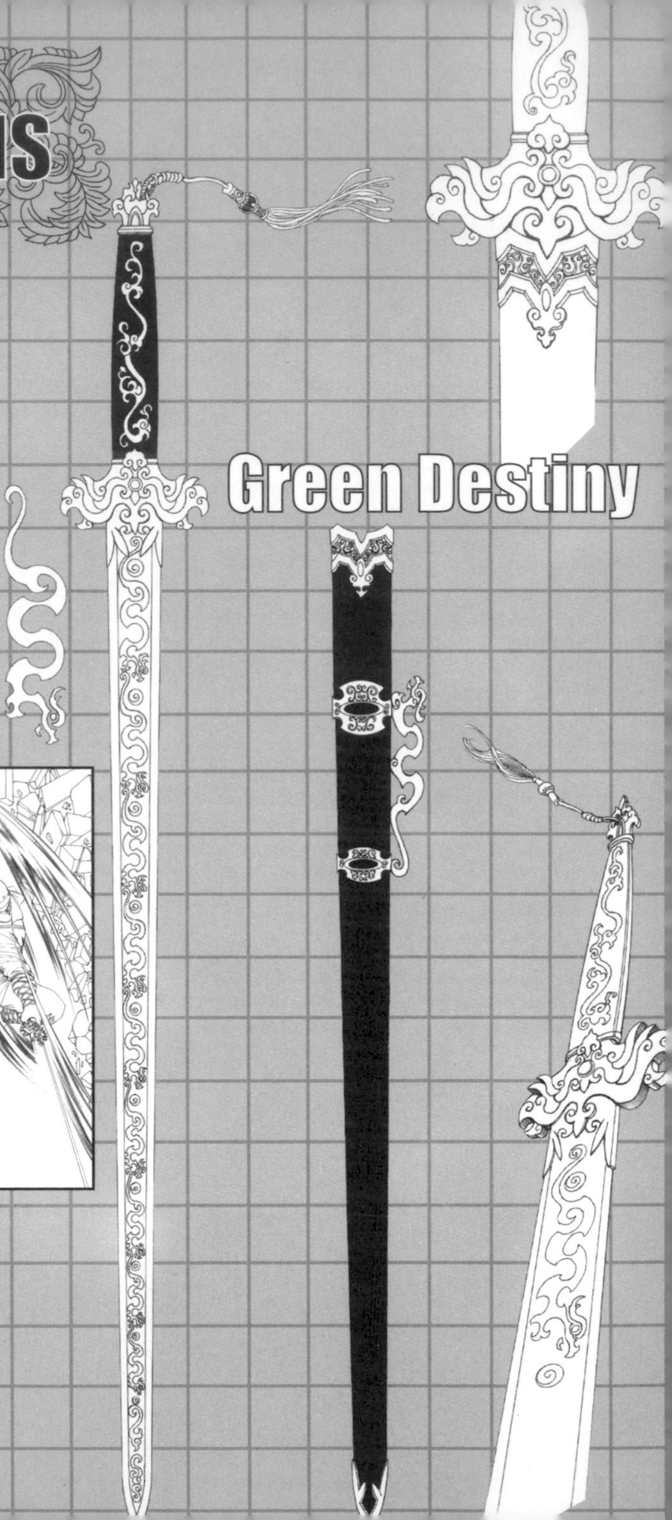
Green Destiny

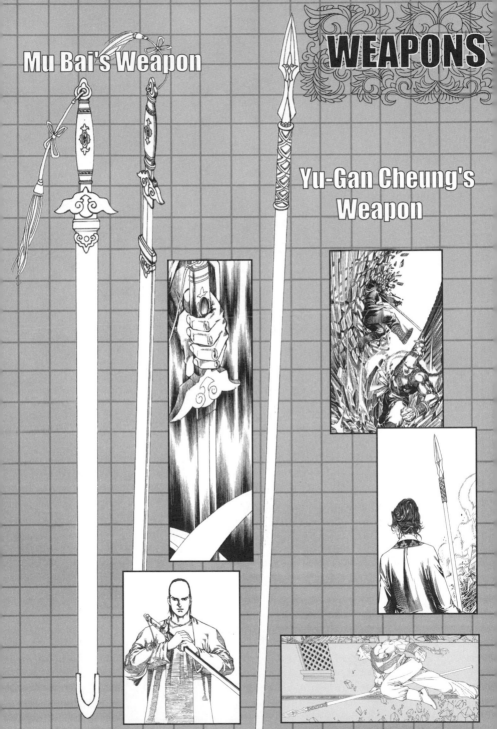

WEAPONS

Mu Bai's Weapon

Yu-Gan Cheung's Weapon

W[illegible]APONS

Shu Lien's Weapon

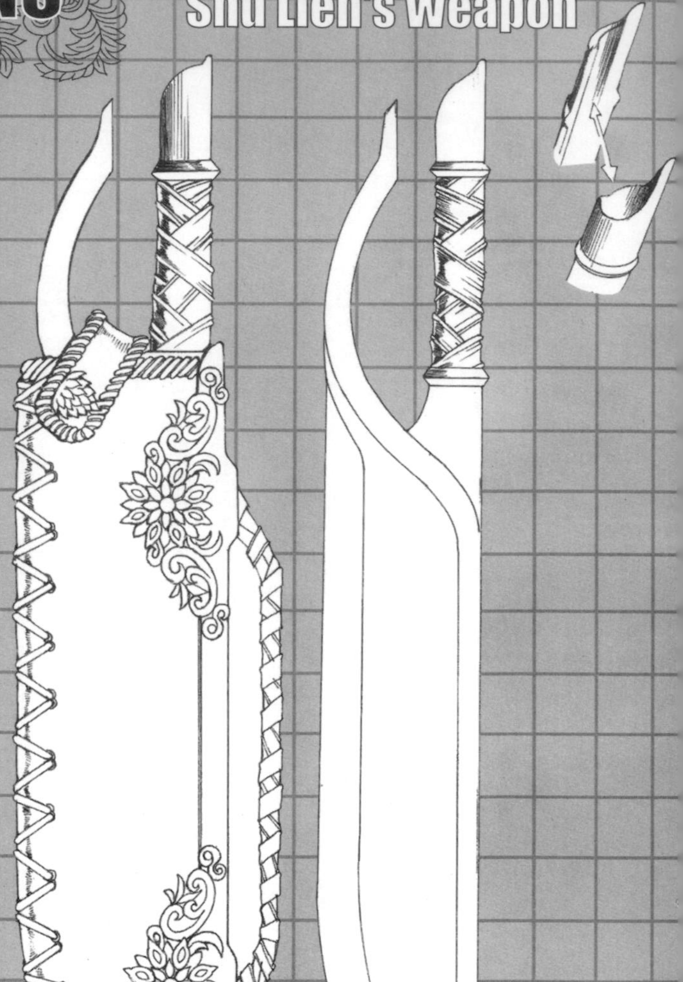

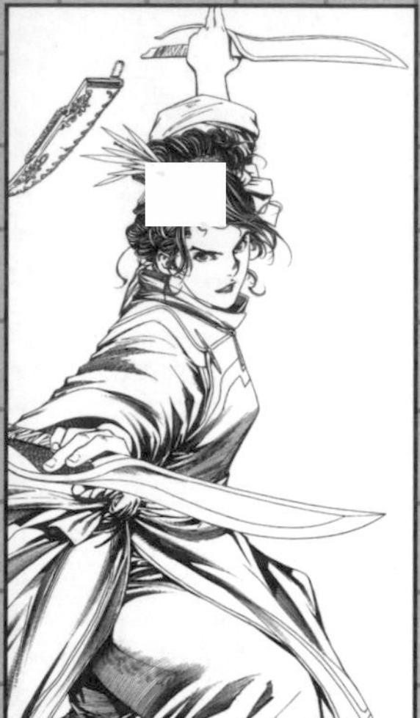

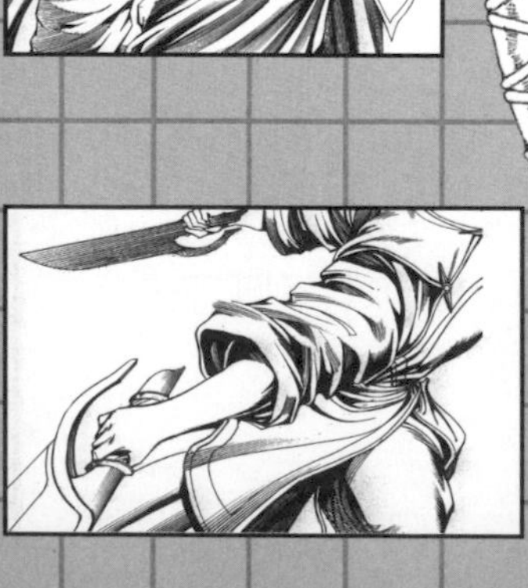

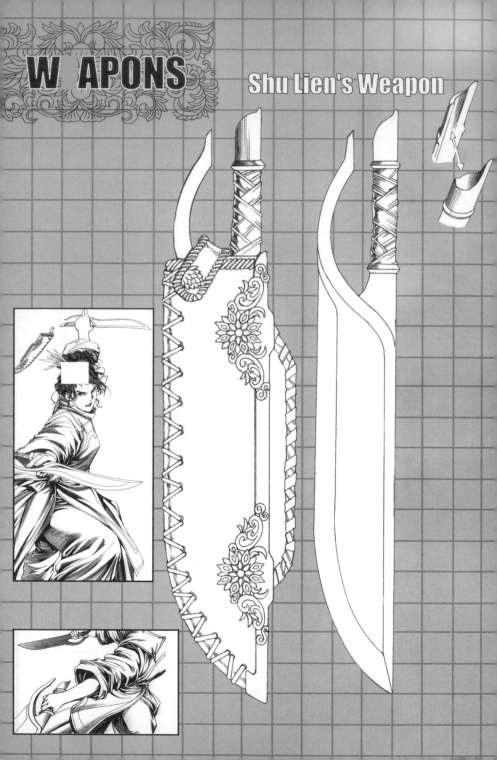

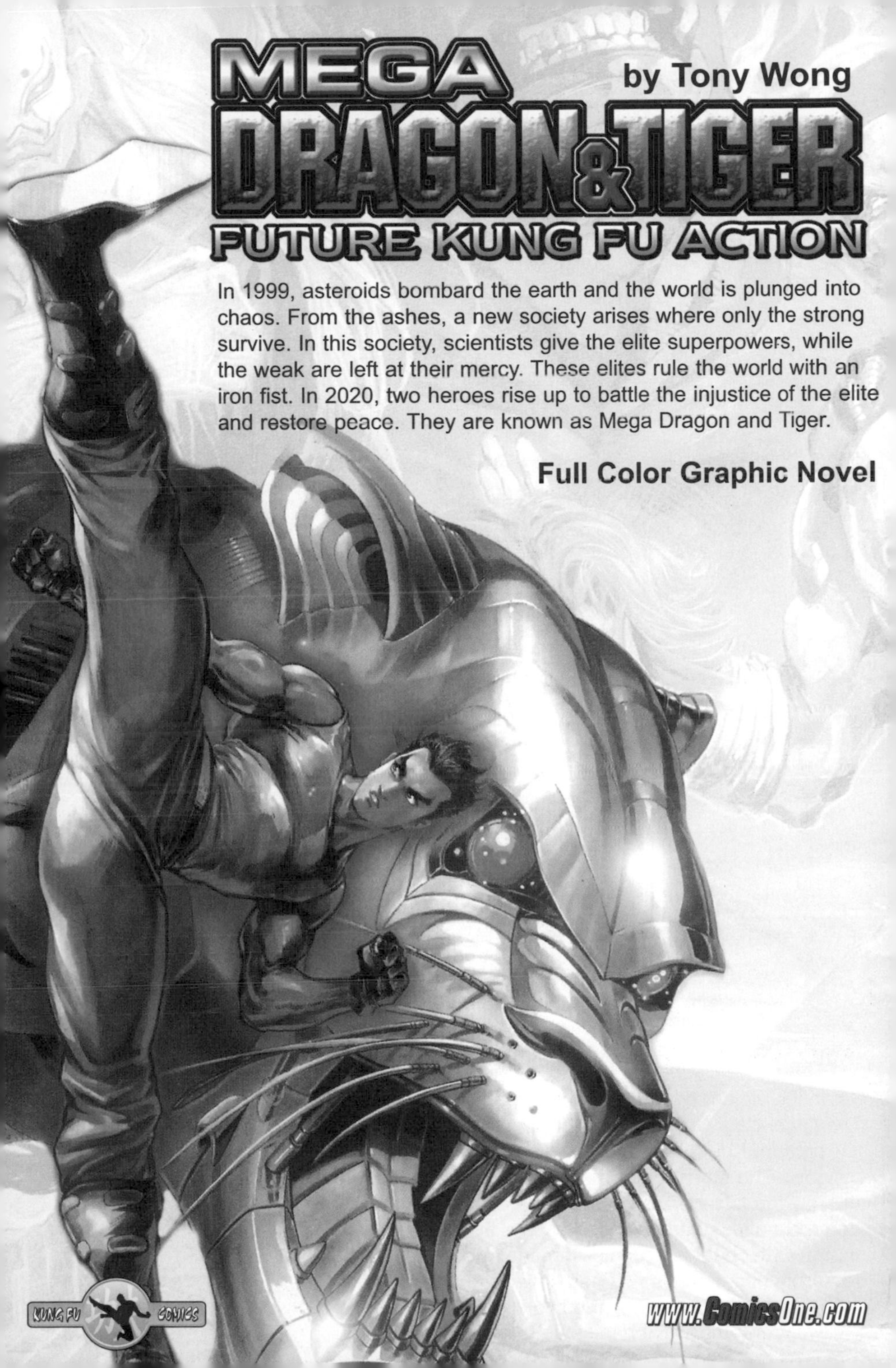
MEGA
DRAGON & TIGER
by Tony Wong
FUTURE KUNG FU ACTION
In 1999, asteroids bombard the earth and the world is plunged into chaos. From the ashes, a new society arises where only the strong survive. In this society, scientists give the elite superpowers, while the weak are left at their mercy. These elites rule the world with an iron fist. In 2020, two heroes rise up to battle the injustice of the elite and restore peace. They are known as Mega Dragon and Tiger.
Full Color Graphic Novel
KUNG FU COMICS
www.ComicsOne.com

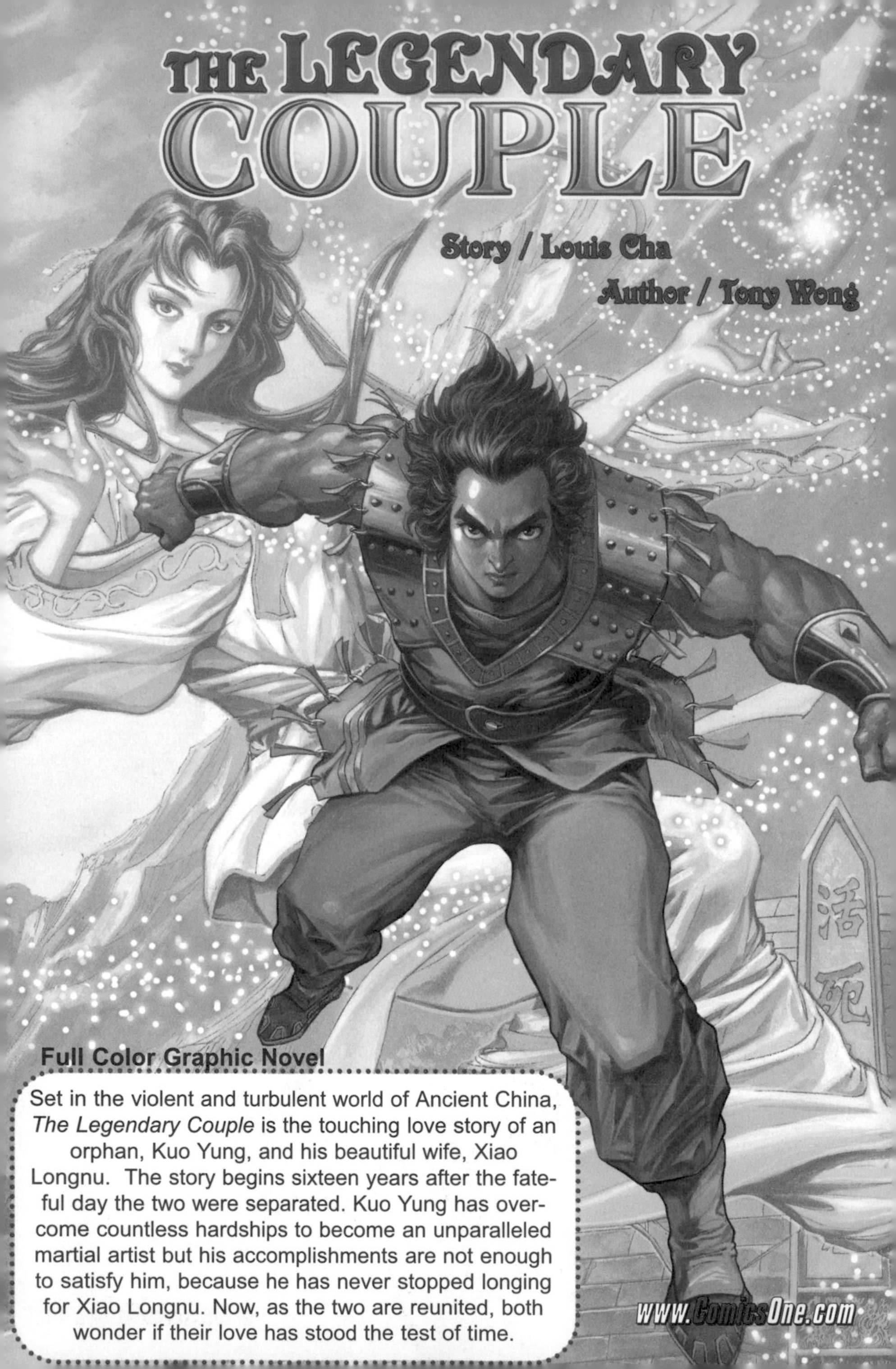
THE LEGENDARY COUPLE
Story / Louis Cha
Author / Tony Wong
活
死
Full Color Graphic Novel
Set in the violent and turbulent world of Ancient China, *The Legendary Couple* is the touching love story of an orphan, Kuo Yung, and his beautiful wife, Xiao Longnu. The story begins sixteen years after the fateful day the two were separated. Kuo Yung has overcome countless hardships to become an unparalleled martial artist but his accomplishments are not enough to satisfy him, because he has never stopped longing for Xiao Longnu. Now, as the two are reunited, both wonder if their love has stood the test of time.
www.ComicsOne.com

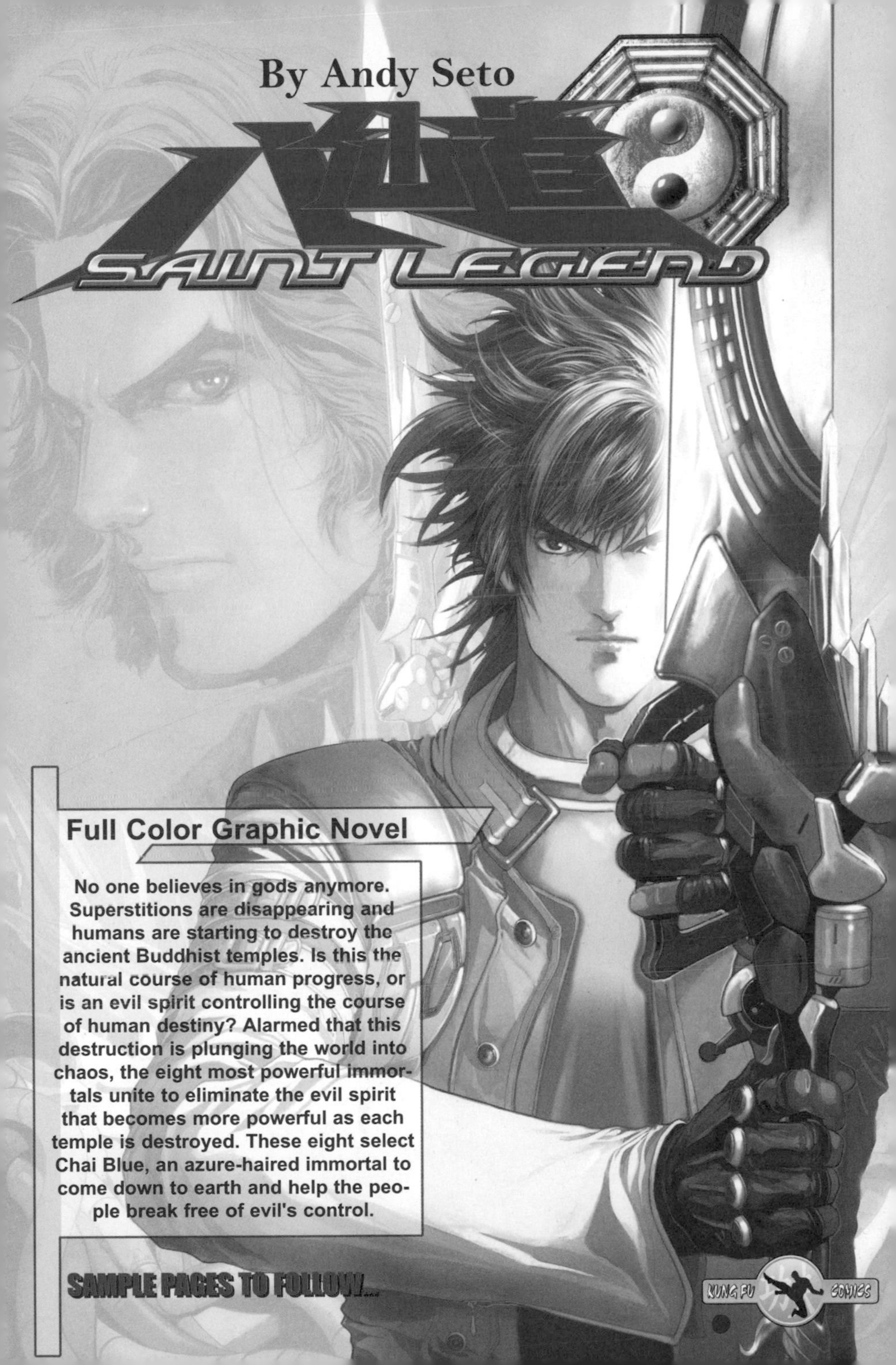
By Andy Seto
SAINT LEGEND
Full Color Graphic Novel
No one believes in gods anymore. Superstitions are disappearing and humans are starting to destroy the ancient Buddhist temples. Is this the natural course of human progress, or is an evil spirit controlling the course of human destiny? Alarmed that this destruction is plunging the world into chaos, the eight most powerful immortals unite to eliminate the evil spirit that becomes more powerful as each temple is destroyed. These eight select Chai Blue, an azure-haired immortal to come down to earth and help the people break free of evil's control.
SAMPLE PAGES TO FOLLOW...
KUNG FU COMICS

SAINT LEGEND SAMPLE PAGE

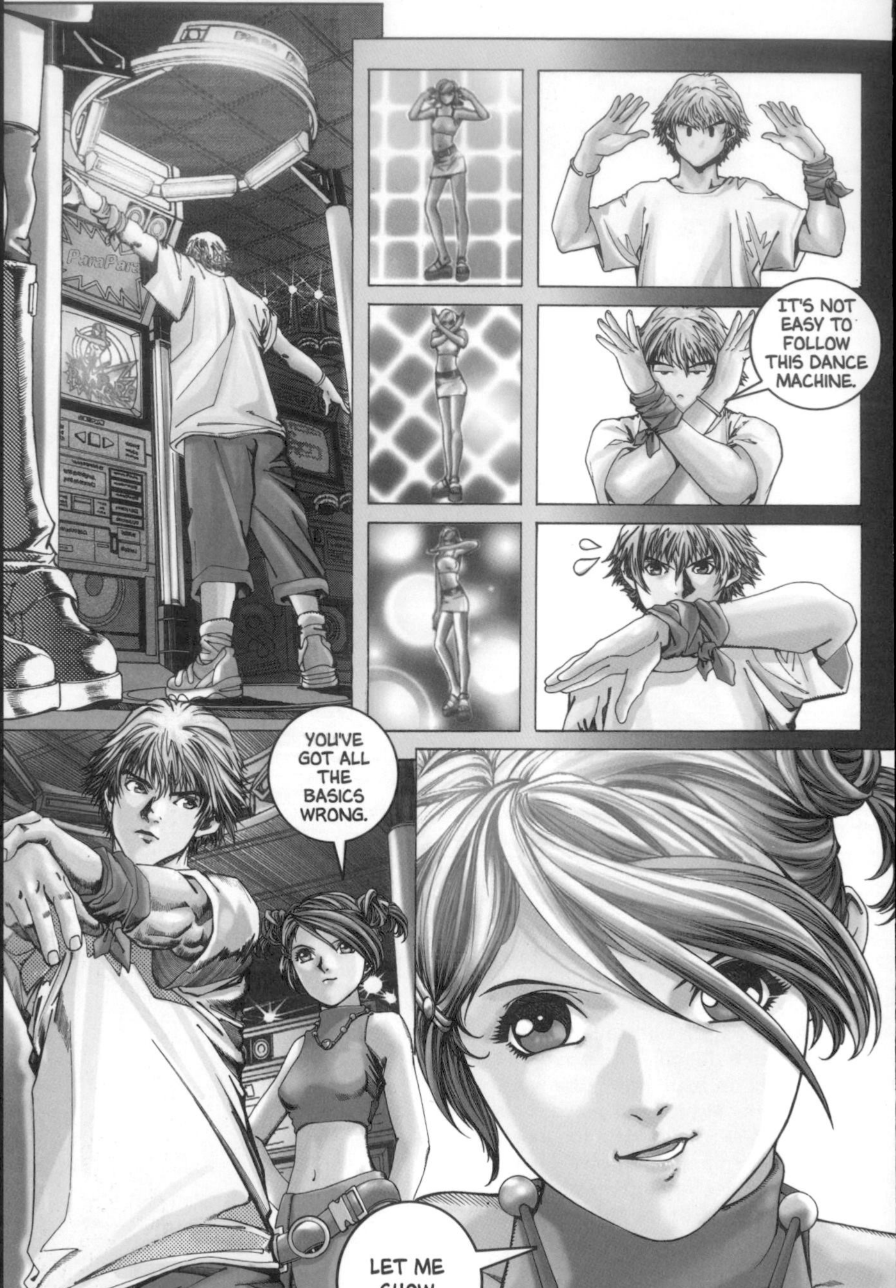
IT'S NOT EASY TO FOLLOW THIS DANCE MACHINE.
YOU'VE GOT ALL THE BASICS WRONG.
LET ME SHOW YOU.

12 HOURS AGO...

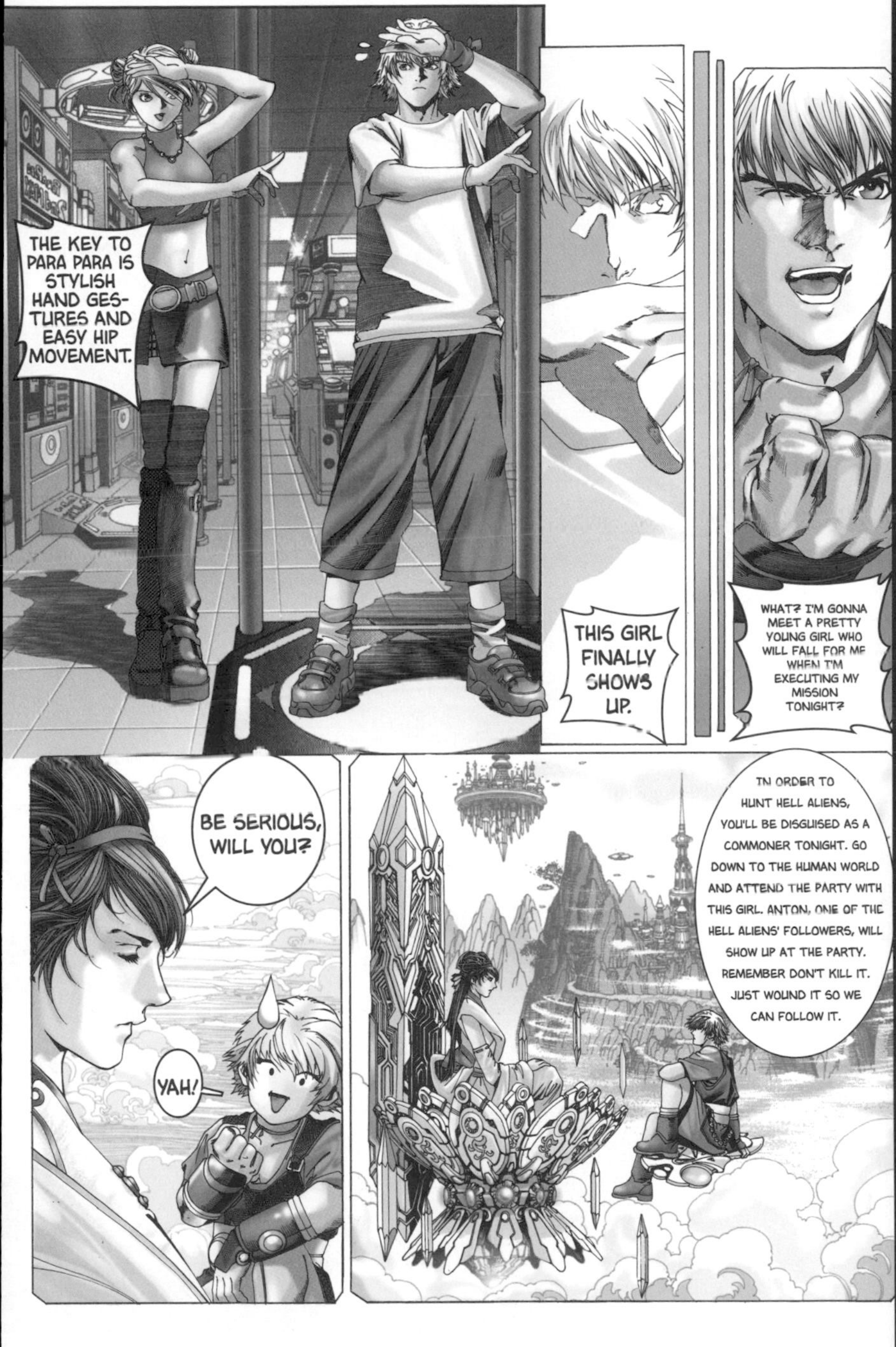

THE KEY TO PARA PARA IS STYLISH HAND GESTURES AND EASY HIP MOVEMENT.
THIS GIRL FINALLY SHOWS UP.
WHAT? I'M GONNA MEET A PRETTY YOUNG GIRL WHO WILL FALL FOR ME WHEN I'M EXECUTING MY MISSION TONIGHT?
BE SERIOUS, WILL YOU?
YAH!
IN ORDER TO HUNT HELL ALIENS, YOU'LL BE DISGUISED AS A COMMONER TONIGHT. GO DOWN TO THE HUMAN WORLD AND ATTEND THE PARTY WITH THIS GIRL. ANTON, ONE OF THE HELL ALIENS' FOLLOWERS, WILL SHOW UP AT THE PARTY. REMEMBER DON'T KILL IT. JUST WOUND IT SO WE CAN FOLLOW IT.

SAINT LEGEND SAMPLE PAGE

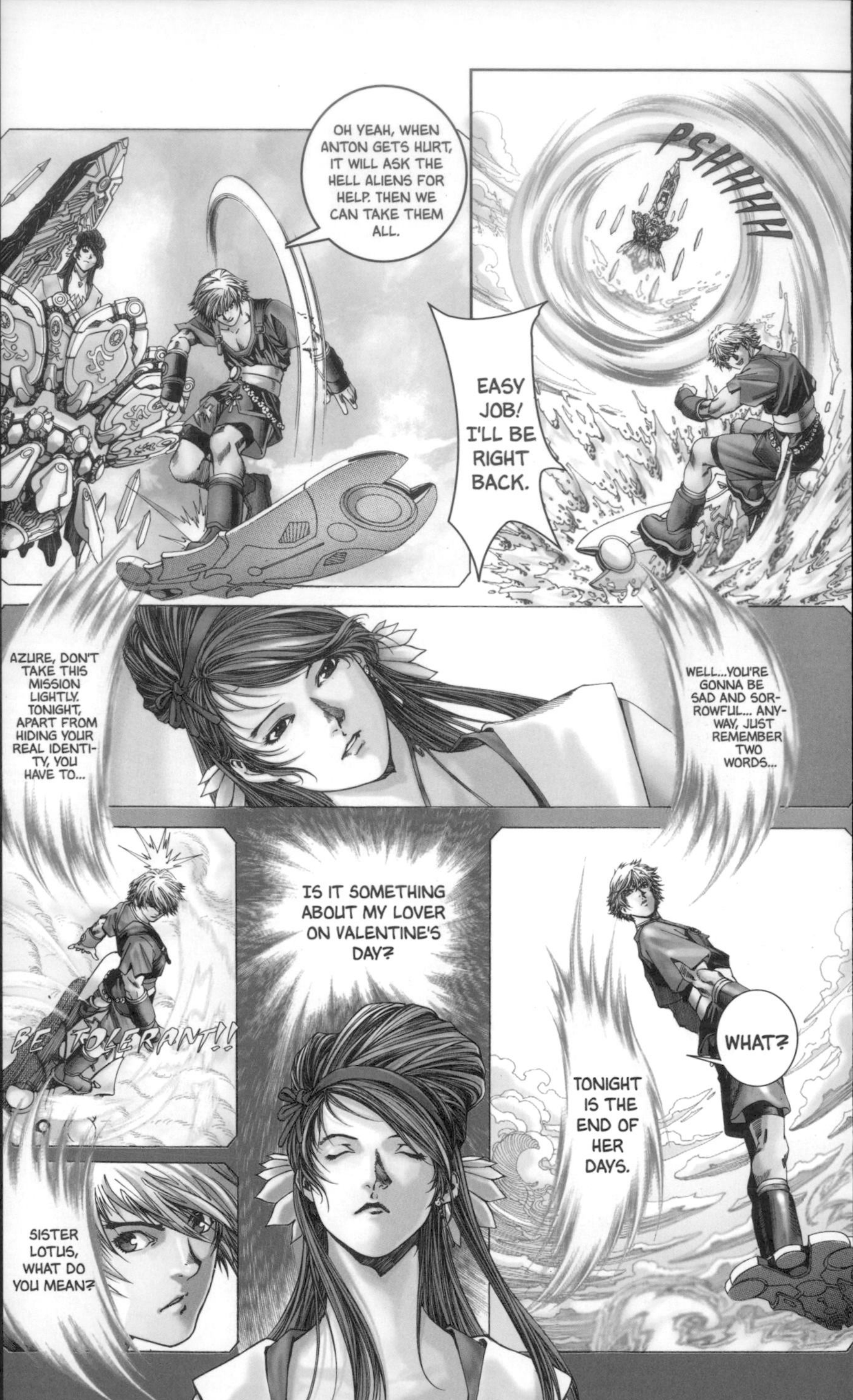
OH YEAH, WHEN ANTON GETS HURT, IT WILL ASK THE HELL ALIENS FOR HELP. THEN WE CAN TAKE THEM ALL.
PSHHHH
EASY JOB! I'LL BE RIGHT BACK.
AZURE, DON'T TAKE THIS MISSION LIGHTLY. TONIGHT, APART FROM HIDING YOUR REAL IDENTITY, YOU HAVE TO...
WELL...YOU'RE GONNA BE SAD AND SORROWFUL... ANYWAY, JUST REMEMBER TWO WORDS...
BE TOLERANT!!
IS IT SOMETHING ABOUT MY LOVER ON VALENTINE'S DAY?
WHAT?
TONIGHT IS THE END OF HER DAYS.
SISTER LOTUS, WHAT DO YOU MEAN?

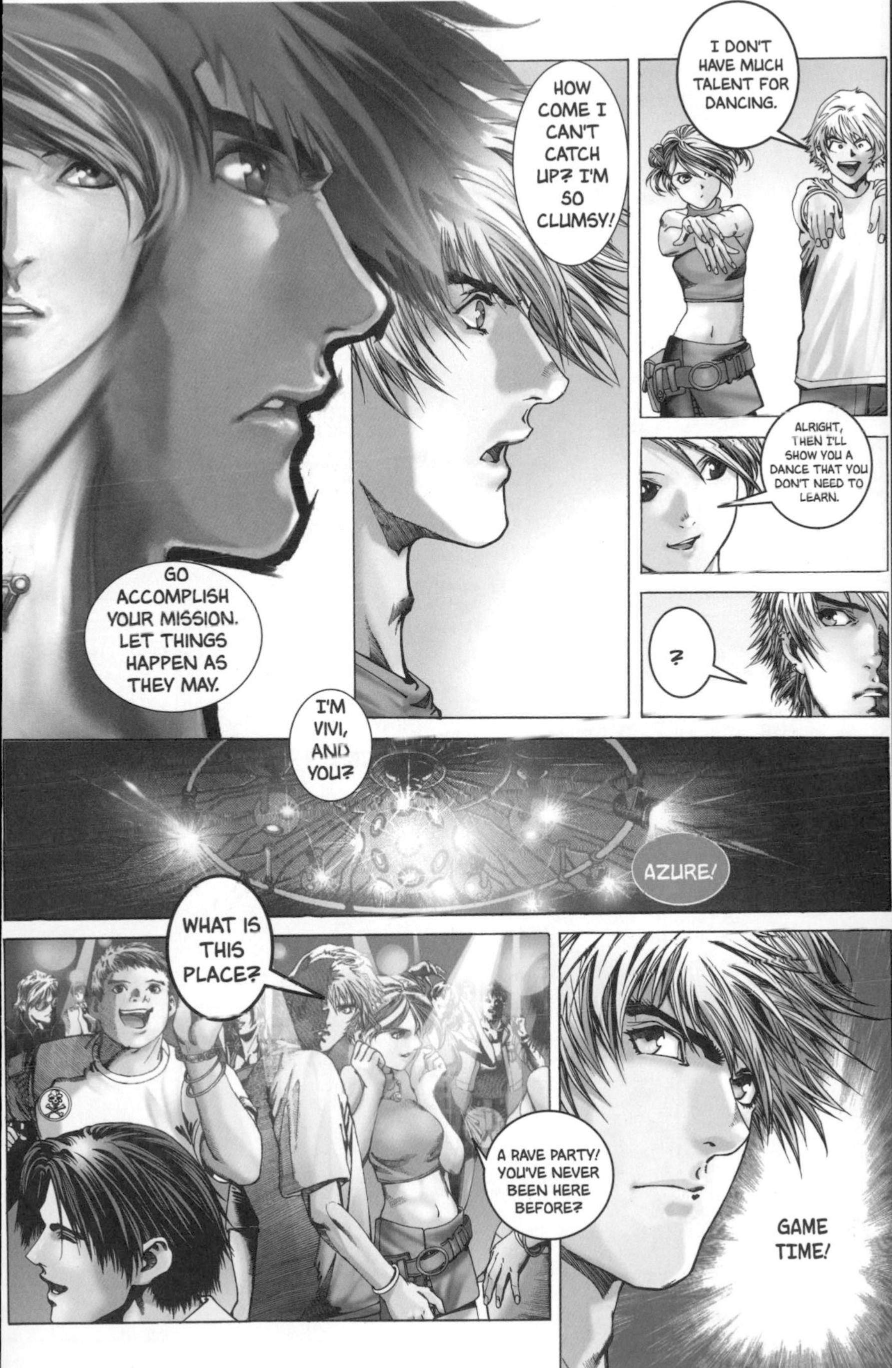
HOW COME I CAN'T CATCH UP? I'M SO CLUMSY!
GO ACCOMPLISH YOUR MISSION. LET THINGS HAPPEN AS THEY MAY.
I DON'T HAVE MUCH TALENT FOR DANCING.
ALRIGHT, THEN I'LL SHOW YOU A DANCE THAT YOU DON'T NEED TO LEARN.
?
I'M VIVI, AND YOU?
AZURE!
WHAT IS THIS PLACE?
A RAVE PARTY! YOU'VE NEVER BEEN HERE BEFORE?
GAME TIME!

SAINT LEGEND SAMPLE PAGE

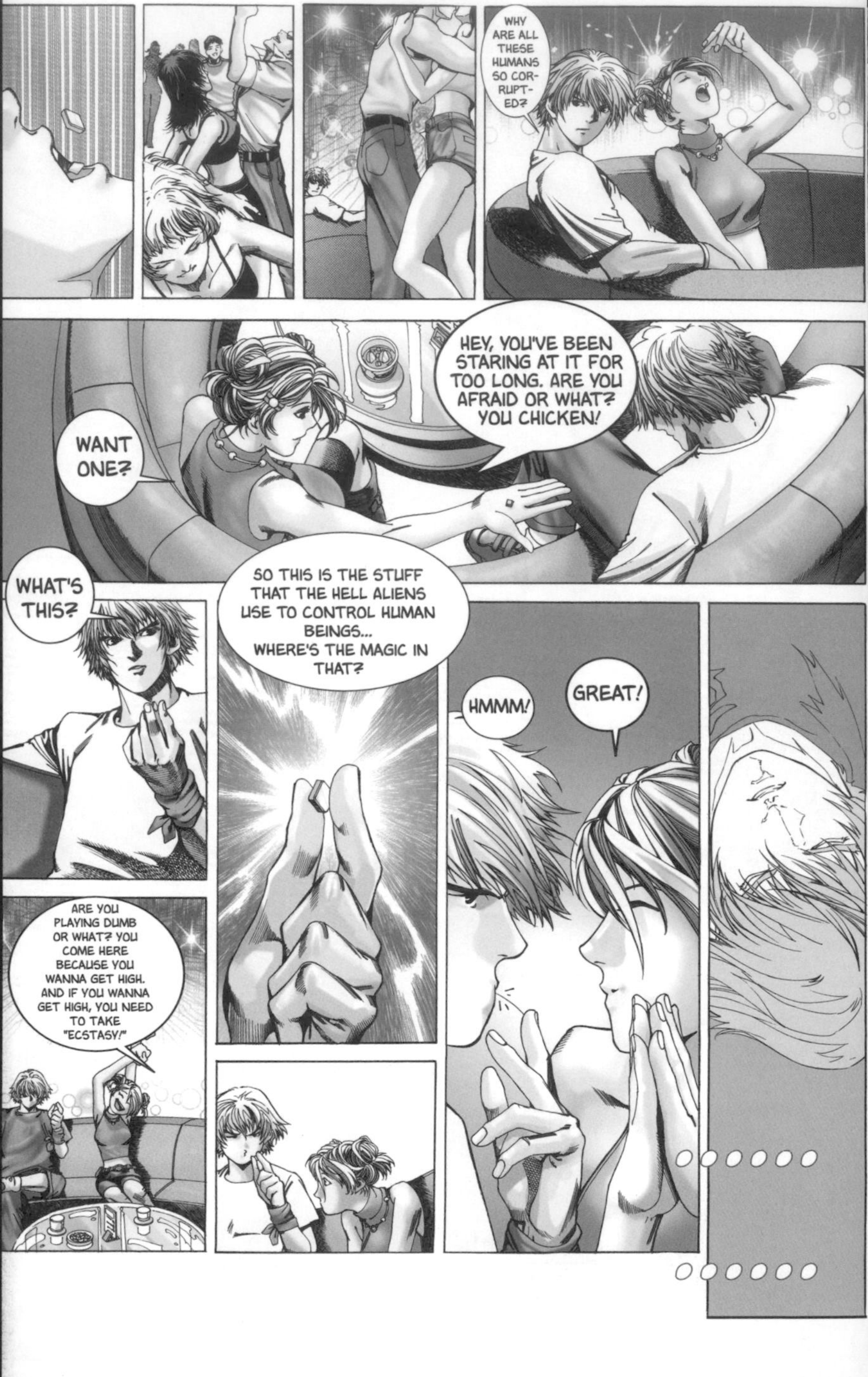
WHY ARE ALL THESE HUMANS SO CORRUPTED?
HEY, YOU'VE BEEN STARING AT IT FOR TOO LONG. ARE YOU AFRAID OR WHAT? YOU CHICKEN!
WANT ONE?
WHAT'S THIS?
ARE YOU PLAYING DUMB OR WHAT? YOU COME HERE BECAUSE YOU WANNA GET HIGH. AND IF YOU WANNA GET HIGH, YOU NEED TO TAKE "ECSTASY!"
SO THIS IS THE STUFF THAT THE HELL ALIENS USE TO CONTROL HUMAN BEINGS... WHERE'S THE MAGIC IN THAT?
HMMM!
GREAT!

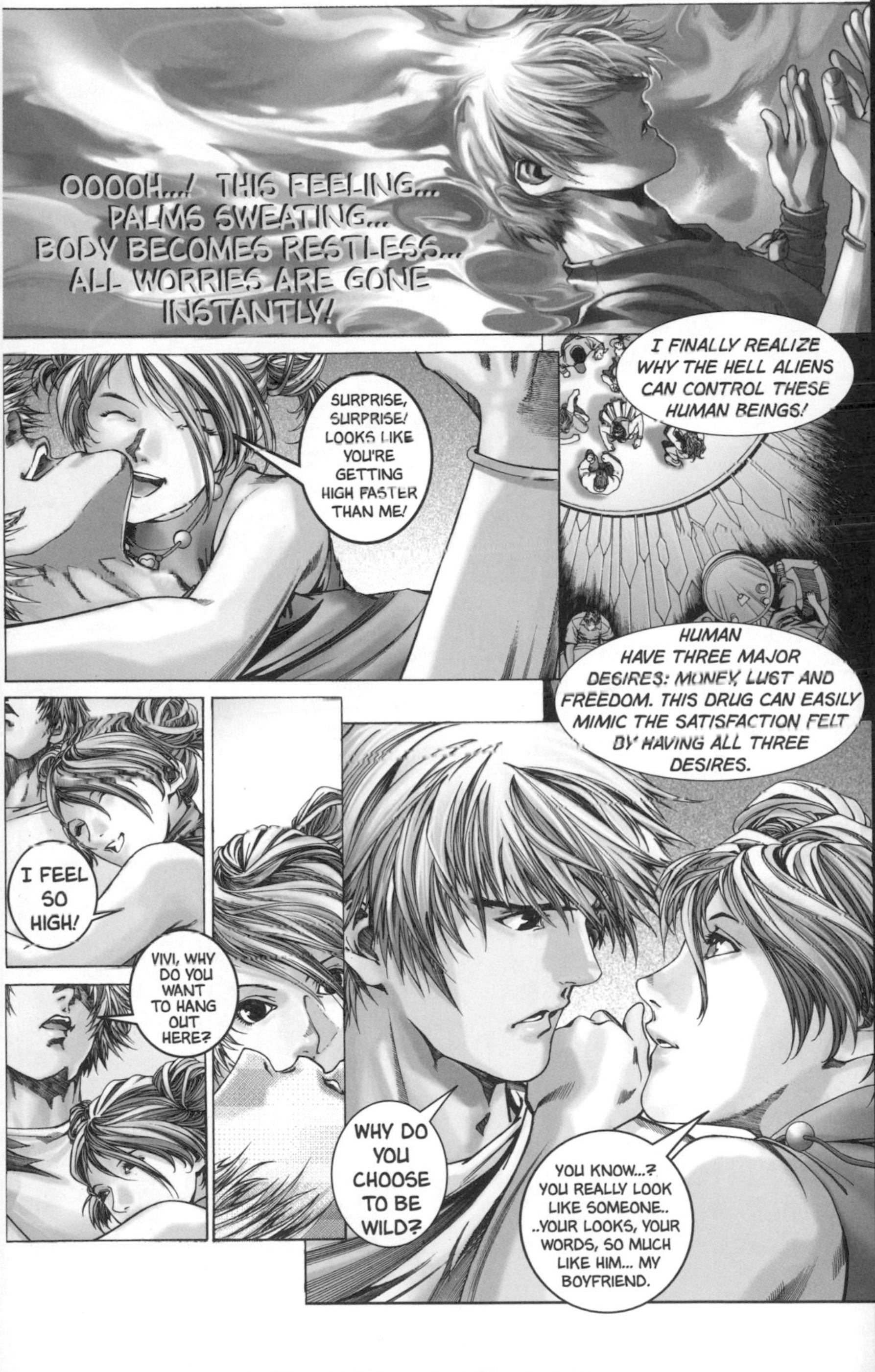
OOOOH...! THIS FEELING... PALMS SWEATING... BODY BECOMES RESTLESS... ALL WORRIES ARE GONE INSTANTLY!
SURPRISE, SURPRISE! LOOKS LIKE YOU'RE GETTING HIGH FASTER THAN ME!
I FINALLY REALIZE WHY THE HELL ALIENS CAN CONTROL THESE HUMAN BEINGS!
HUMAN HAVE THREE MAJOR DESIRES: MONEY, LUST AND FREEDOM. THIS DRUG CAN EASILY MIMIC THE SATISFACTION FELT BY HAVING ALL THREE DESIRES.
I FEEL SO HIGH!
VIVI, WHY DO YOU WANT TO HANG OUT HERE?
WHY DO YOU CHOOSE TO BE WILD?
YOU KNOW...? YOU REALLY LOOK LIKE SOMEONE.. ..YOUR LOOKS, YOUR WORDS, SO MUCH LIKE HIM... MY BOYFRIEND.

SAINT LEGEND SAMPLE PAGE

SAINT LEGEND SAMPLE PAGE

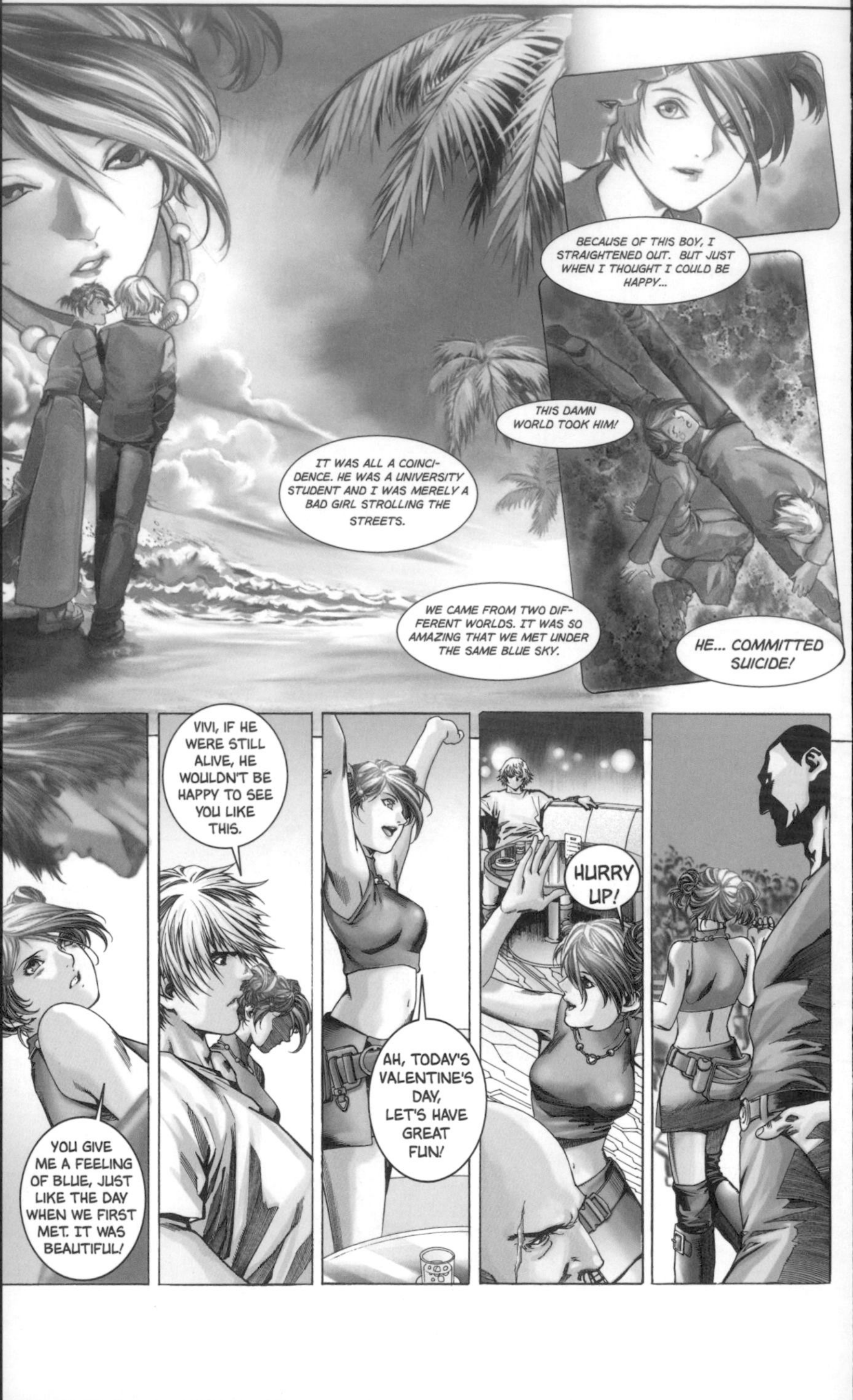
IT WAS ALL A COINCIDENCE. HE WAS A UNIVERSITY STUDENT AND I WAS MERELY A BAD GIRL STROLLING THE STREETS.
WE CAME FROM TWO DIFFERENT WORLDS. IT WAS SO AMAZING THAT WE MET UNDER THE SAME BLUE SKY.
BECAUSE OF THIS BOY, I STRAIGHTENED OUT. BUT JUST WHEN I THOUGHT I COULD BE HAPPY...
THIS DAMN WORLD TOOK HIM!
HE... COMMITTED SUICIDE!
YOU GIVE ME A FEELING OF BLUE, JUST LIKE THE DAY WHEN WE FIRST MET. IT WAS BEAUTIFUL!
VIVI, IF HE WERE STILL ALIVE, HE WOULDN'T BE HAPPY TO SEE YOU LIKE THIS.
AH, TODAY'S VALENTINE'S DAY, LET'S HAVE GREAT FUN!
HURRY UP!

SAINT LEGEND SAMPLE PAGE

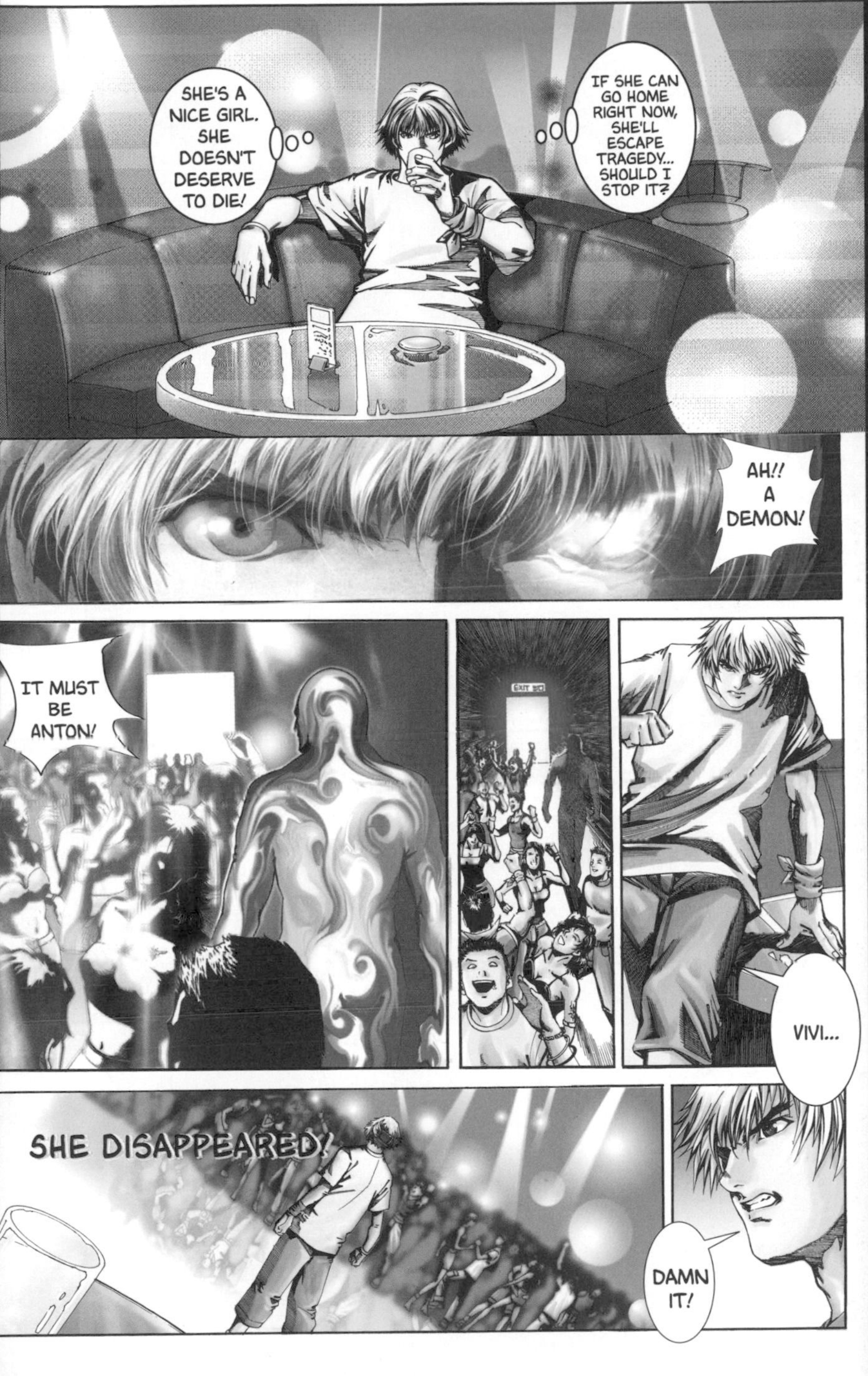
SHE'S A NICE GIRL. SHE DOESN'T DESERVE TO DIE!
IF SHE CAN GO HOME RIGHT NOW, SHE'LL ESCAPE TRAGEDY... SHOULD I STOP IT?
AH!! A DEMON!
IT MUST BE ANTON!
VIVI...
SHE DISAPPEARED!
DAMN IT!

SAINT LEGEND SAMPLE PAGE

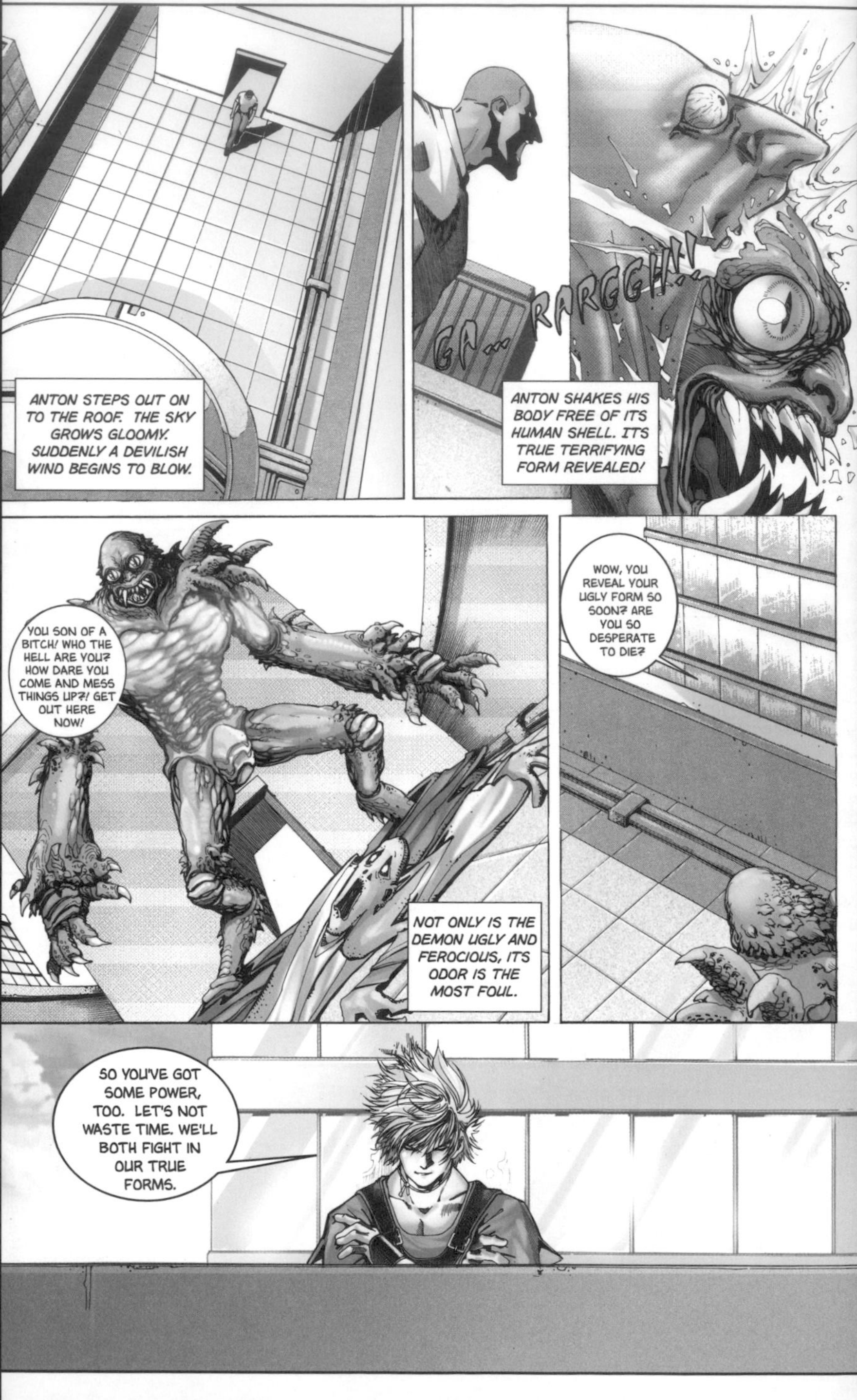
ANTON STEPS OUT ON TO THE ROOF. THE SKY GROWS GLOOMY. SUDDENLY A DEVILISH WIND BEGINS TO BLOW.
GA... RARGGH!!
ANTON SHAKES HIS BODY FREE OF ITS HUMAN SHELL. ITS TRUE TERRIFYING FORM REVEALED!
YOU SON OF A BITCH! WHO THE HELL ARE YOU? HOW DARE YOU COME AND MESS THINGS UP?! GET OUT HERE NOW!
NOT ONLY IS THE DEMON UGLY AND FEROCIOUS, ITS ODOR IS THE MOST FOUL.
WOW, YOU REVEAL YOUR UGLY FORM SO SOON? ARE YOU SO DESPERATE TO DIE?
SO YOU'VE GOT SOME POWER, TOO. LET'S NOT WASTE TIME. WE'LL BOTH FIGHT IN OUR TRUE FORMS.

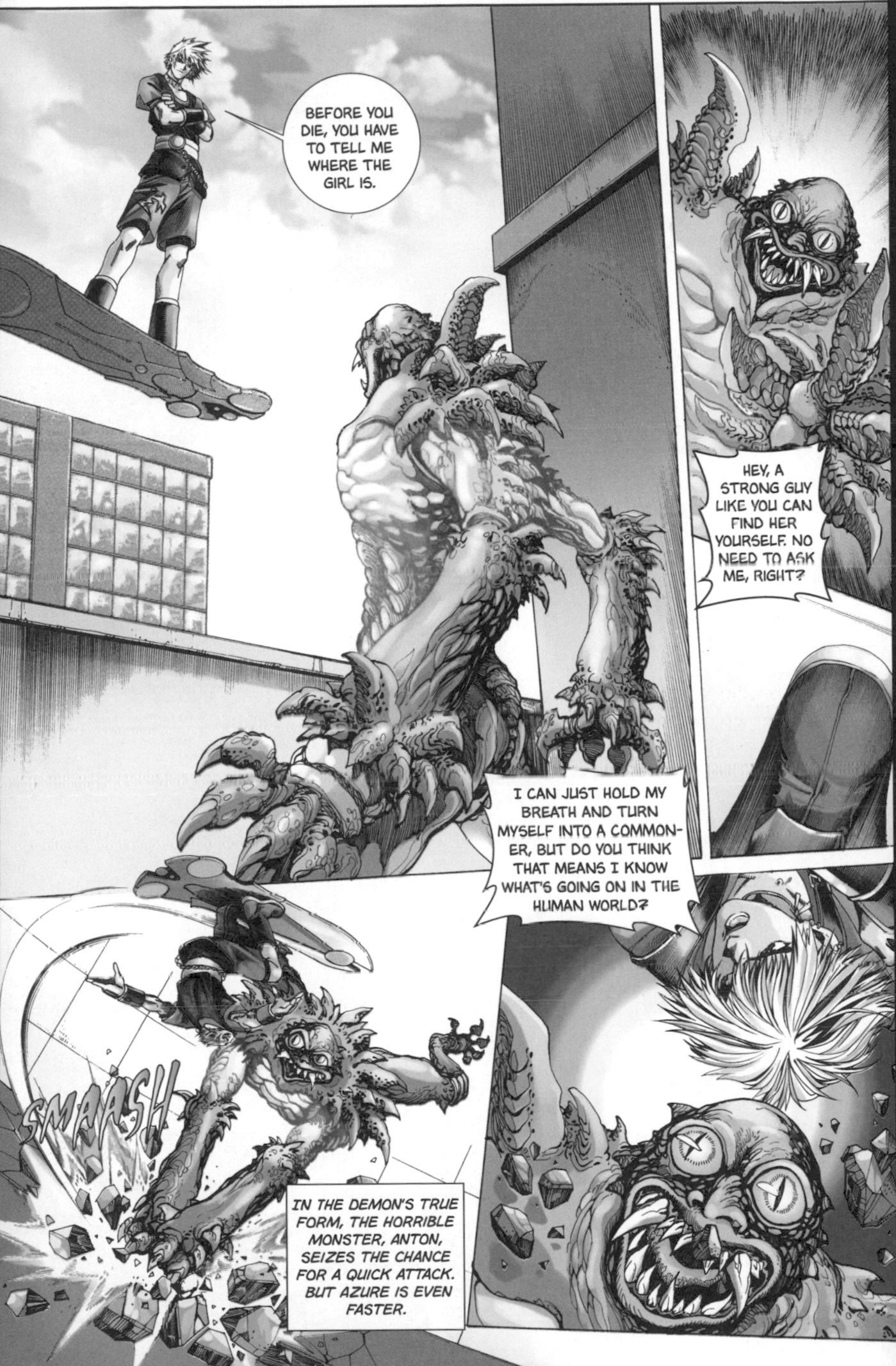
BEFORE YOU DIE, YOU HAVE TO TELL ME WHERE THE GIRL IS.
HEY, A STRONG GUY LIKE YOU CAN FIND HER YOURSELF. NO NEED TO ASK ME, RIGHT?
I CAN JUST HOLD MY BREATH AND TURN MYSELF INTO A COMMONER, BUT DO YOU THINK THAT MEANS I KNOW WHAT'S GOING ON IN THE HUMAN WORLD?
SMASH
IN THE DEMON'S TRUE FORM, THE HORRIBLE MONSTER, ANTON, SEIZES THE CHANCE FOR A QUICK ATTACK. BUT AZURE IS EVEN FASTER.

SAINT LEGEND SAMPLE PAGE

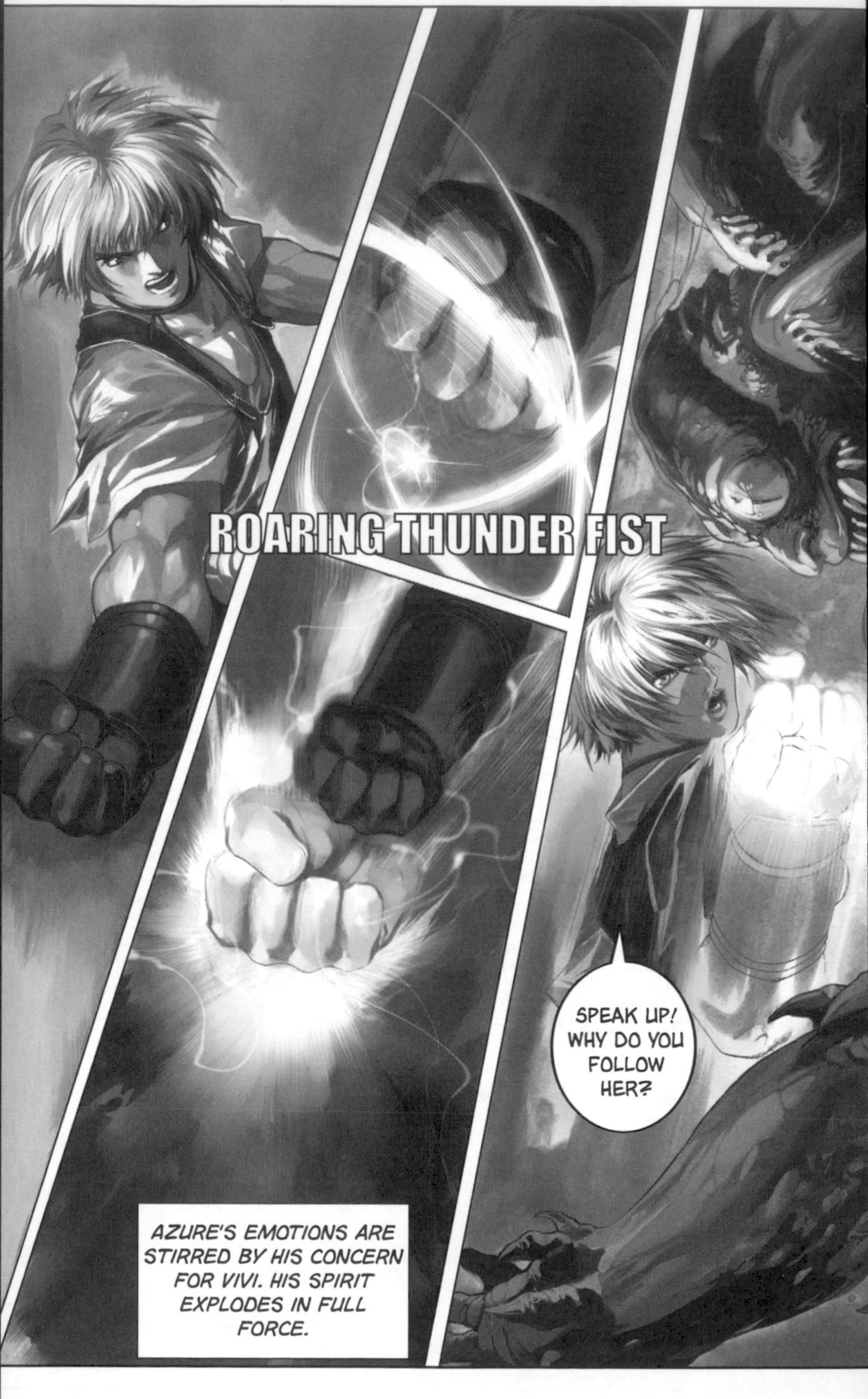
ROARING THUNDER FIST
AZURE'S EMOTIONS ARE STIRRED BY HIS CONCERN FOR VIVI. HIS SPIRIT EXPLODES IN FULL FORCE.
SPEAK UP! WHY DO YOU FOLLOW HER?

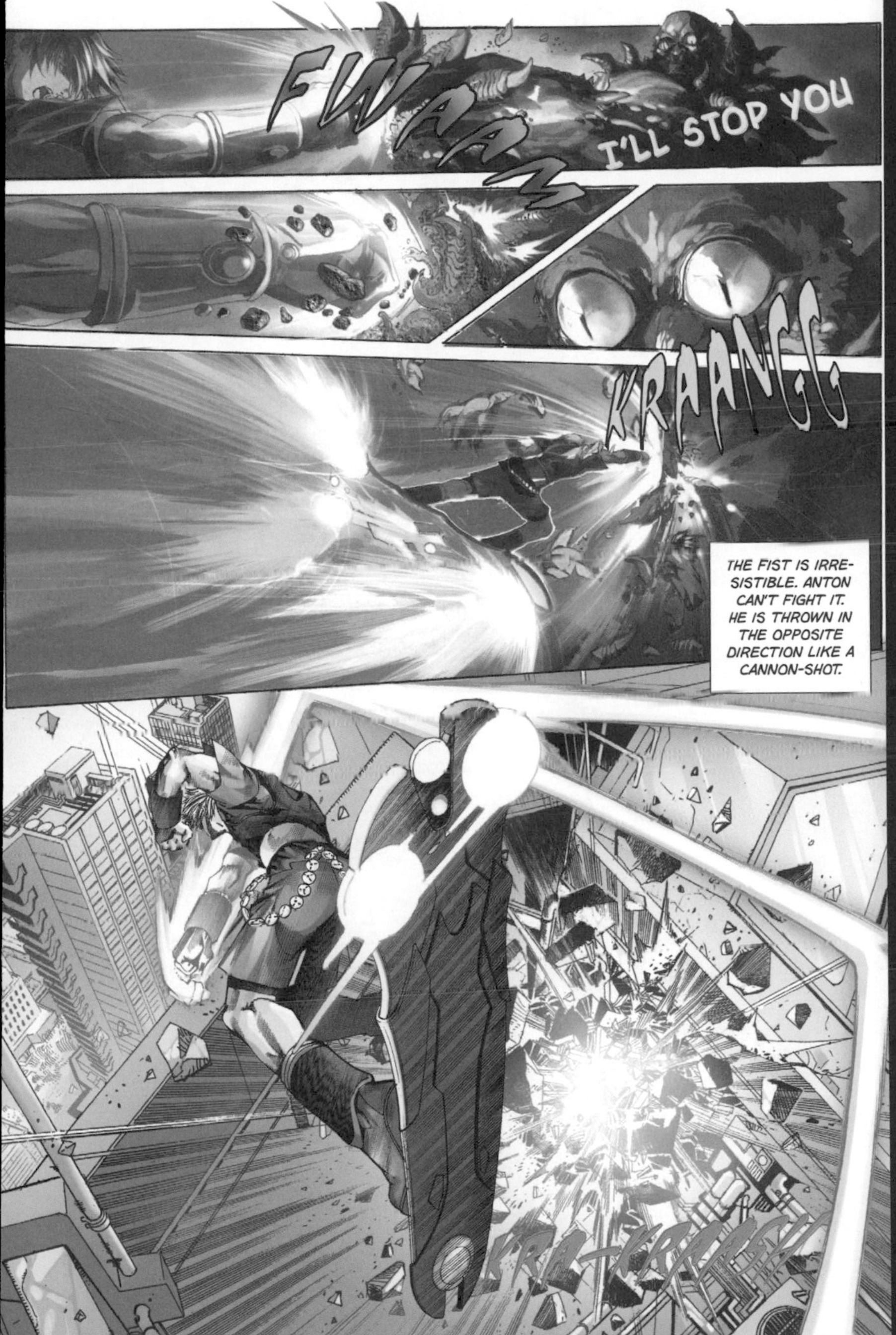
FWAAM
I'LL STOP YOU
KRAANGG
THE FIST IS IRRE-SISTIBLE. ANTON CAN'T FIGHT IT. HE IS THROWN IN THE OPPOSITE DIRECTION LIKE A CANNON-SHOT.
KRA-KRAASH

SAINT LEGEND SAMPLE PAGE

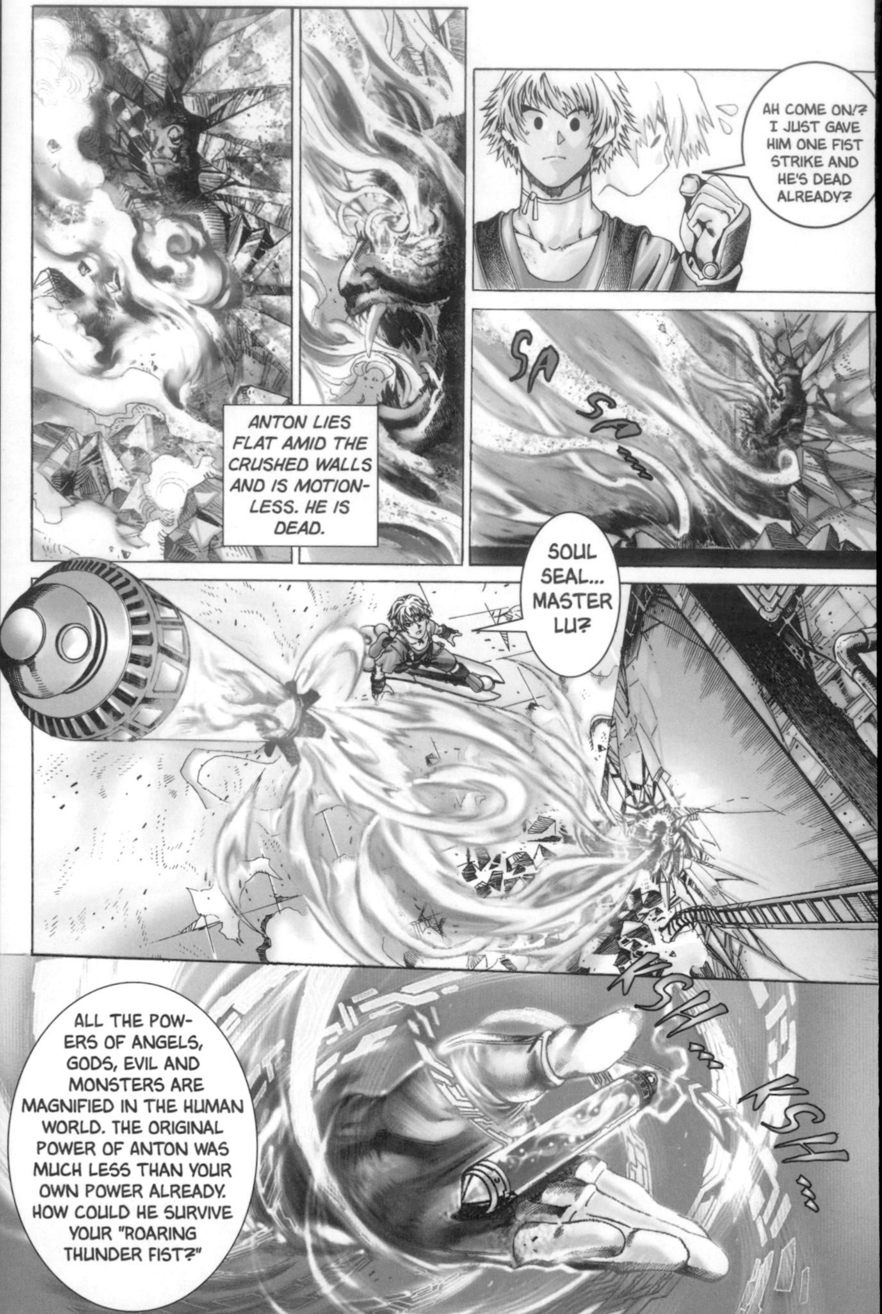
ANTON LIES FLAT AMID THE CRUSHED WALLS AND IS MOTION-LESS. HE IS DEAD.
AH COME ON!? I JUST GAVE HIM ONE FIST STRIKE AND HE'S DEAD ALREADY?
SA SA...
SOUL SEAL... MASTER LU?
KSH... KSH...
ALL THE POW-ERS OF ANGELS, GODS, EVIL AND MONSTERS ARE MAGNIFIED IN THE HUMAN WORLD. THE ORIGINAL POWER OF ANTON WAS MUCH LESS THAN YOUR OWN POWER ALREADY. HOW COULD HE SURVIVE YOUR "ROARING THUNDER FIST?"

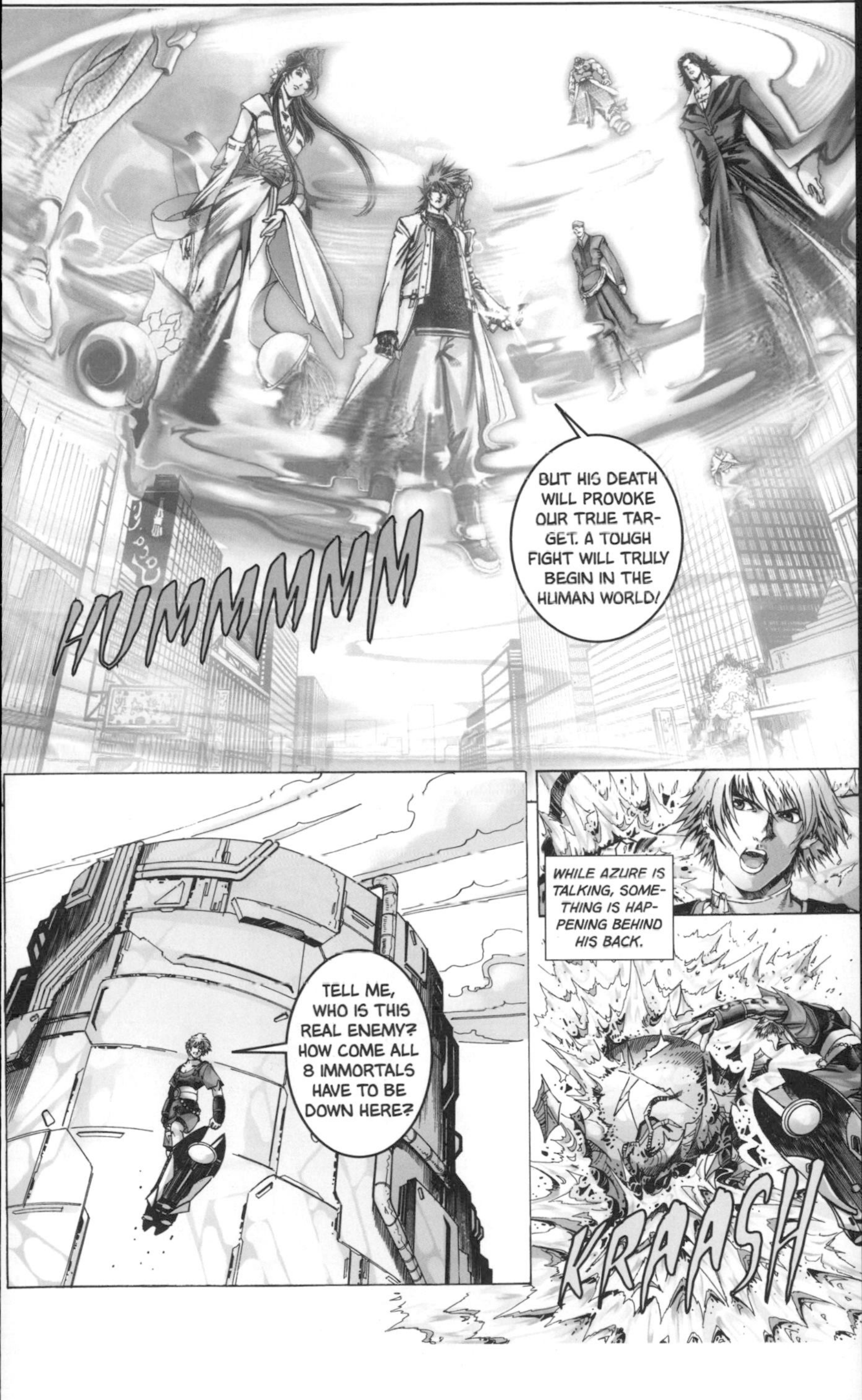
BUT HIS DEATH WILL PROVOKE OUR TRUE TAR-GET. A TOUGH FIGHT WILL TRULY BEGIN IN THE HUMAN WORLD!
HUMMMMM
TELL ME, WHO IS THIS REAL ENEMY? HOW COME ALL 8 IMMORTALS HAVE TO BE DOWN HERE?
WHILE AZURE IS TALKING, SOME-THING IS HAP-PENING BEHIND HIS BACK.
KRAASH

SAINT LEGEND SAMPLE PAGE

SAINT LEGEND SAMPLE PAGE

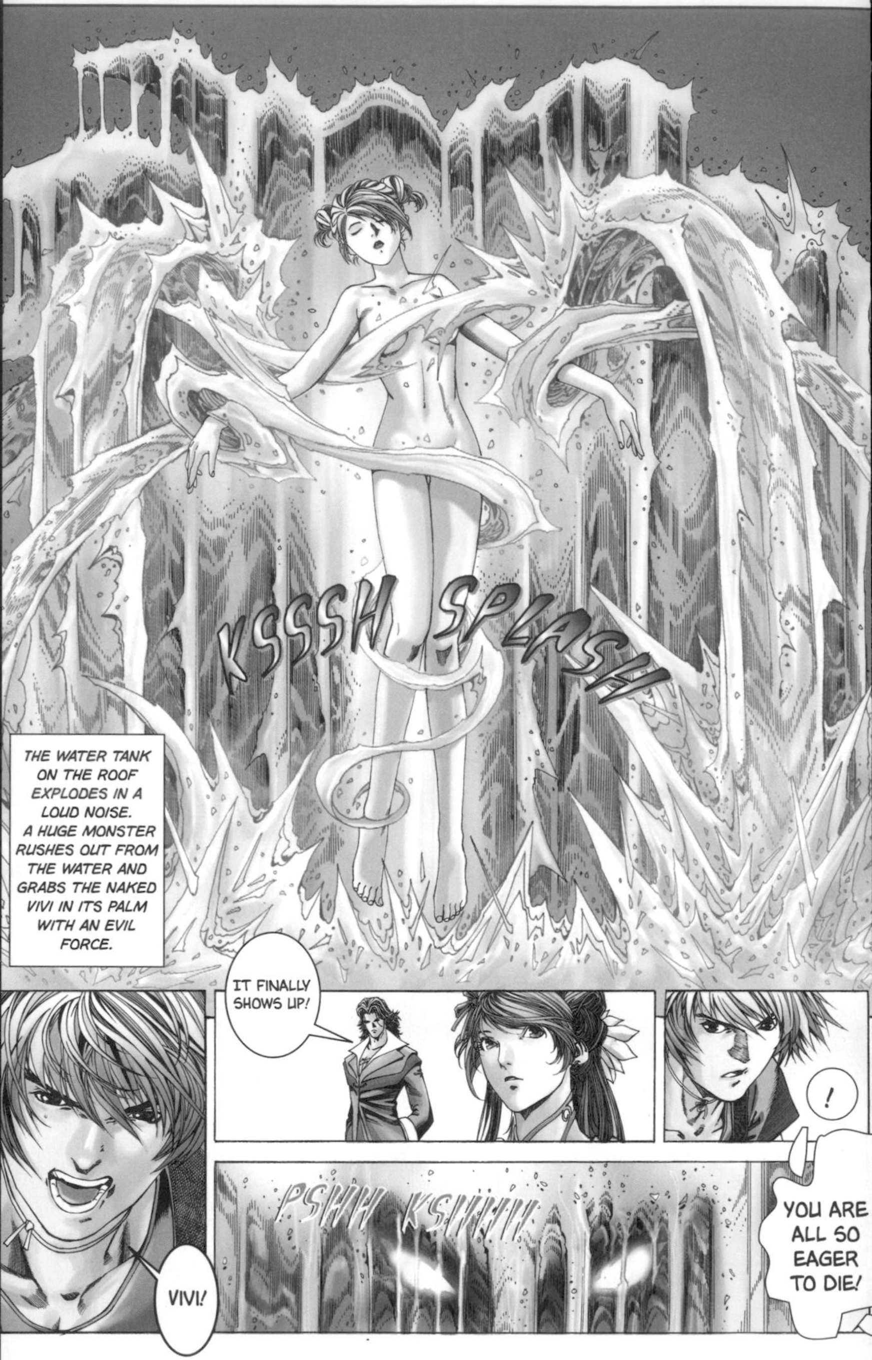
KSSSH SPLASH
THE WATER TANK ON THE ROOF EXPLODES IN A LOUD NOISE. A HUGE MONSTER RUSHES OUT FROM THE WATER AND GRABS THE NAKED VIVI IN ITS PALM WITH AN EVIL FORCE.
IT FINALLY SHOWS UP!
!
VIVI!
PSHH KSHHH
YOU ARE ALL SO EAGER TO DIE!

SAINT LEGEND SAMPLE PAGE

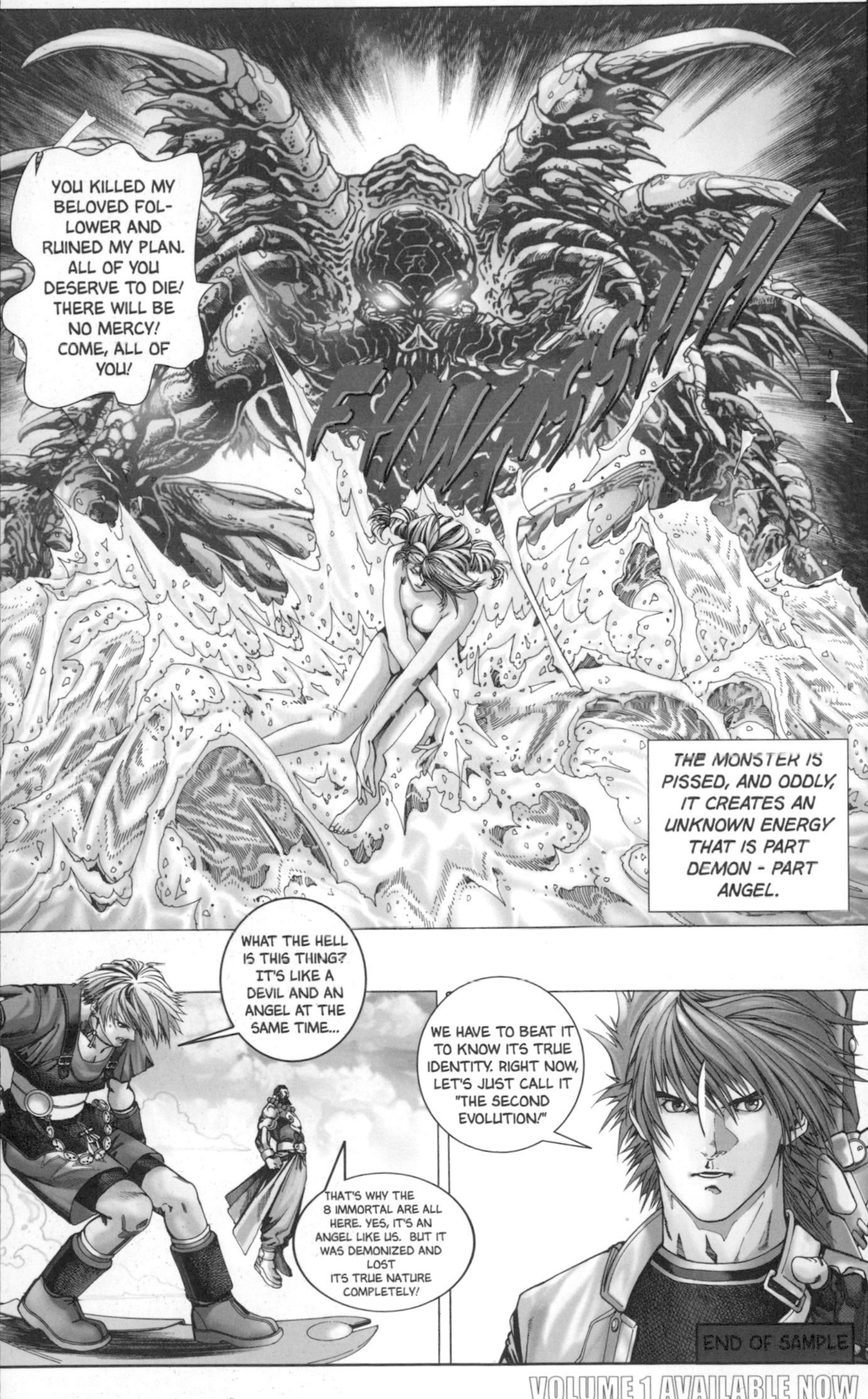

YOU KILLED MY BELOVED FOL-LOWER AND RUINED MY PLAN. ALL OF YOU DESERVE TO DIE! THERE WILL BE NO MERCY! COME, ALL OF YOU!
THE MONSTER IS PISSED, AND ODDLY, IT CREATES AN UNKNOWN ENERGY THAT IS PART DEMON - PART ANGEL.
WHAT THE HELL IS THIS THING? IT'S LIKE A DEVIL AND AN ANGEL AT THE SAME TIME...
WE HAVE TO BEAT IT TO KNOW ITS TRUE IDENTITY. RIGHT NOW, LET'S JUST CALL IT "THE SECOND EVOLUTION!"
THAT'S WHY THE 8 IMMORTAL ARE ALL HERE. YES, IT'S AN ANGEL LIKE US. BUT IT WAS DEMONIZED AND LOST ITS TRUE NATURE COMPLETELY!
END OF SAMPLE

VOLUME 1 AVAILABLE NOW

HAVE YOU VISITED THE COMICSONE WEBSITE LATELY?